T0339780

WHITE HOUSE
SPECIAL HANDBOOK

WHITE HOUSE SPECIAL HANDBOOK

HOW TO RULE THE WORLD IN THE 21ST CENTURY

Mikhail Kryzhanovsky

Algora Publishing
New York

© 2007 by Algora Publishing.
All Rights Reserved
www.algora.com

No portion of this book (beyond what is permitted by
Sections 107 or 108 of the United States Copyright Act of 1976)
may be reproduced by any process, stored in a retrieval system,
or transmitted in any form, or by any means, without the
express written permission of the publisher.
ISBN-13: 978-0-87586-515-7 (trade paper)
ISBN-13: 978-0-87586-516-4 (hard cover)
ISBN-13: 978-0-87586-517-1 (ebook)

Library of Congress Cataloging-in-Publication Data —

Kryzhanovskii, M. (Mikhail), 1958-
    White House special handbook, or, How to rule America and the world in the 21st
century / Mikhail Kryzhanovsky.
        p. cm.
        ISBN 978-0-87586-515-7 (trade paper: alk. paper) — ISBN 978-0-87586-516-4
(hard cover: alk. paper) — ISBN 978-0-87586-517-1 (ebook) 1. Elections—United States.
2. Politics, Practical—United States. 3. Intelligence service—United States. 4. United
States—Politics and government. 5. United States—Foreign relations. I. Title. II. Title:
How to rule America and the world in the 21st century.
    JK1976.K79 2007
    351.73—dc22

                                    2007011451

Front Cover: Members of the British non-governmental organization Oxfam lampoon
leaders of the G8 countries (from left to right: Gerhard Schroeder of Germany, Jean
Chretien of Canada, Jacques Chirac of France, Tony Blair of Great Britain, Junichiro
Koizumi of Japan, Silvio Berlusconi of Italy, and George Bush of the USA) during an event
held on the sidelines of the World Trade Organization meeting in Cancun. Oxfam is
trying to illustrate the G8's failure to listen to voices urging them to rewrite the rules of
international trade.
    Image: © Juan Carlos Ulate/Reuters/Corbis
    Photographer: Juan Carlos Ulate
    Date Photographed: September 14, 2003
    Location Information: Cancun, Mexico

Printed in the United States

Let every nation know, whether it wishes us well or ill, that we shall pay any price, bear any burden, meet any hardship, support any friend, oppose any foe, in order to assure the survival and the success of liberty...

And so, my fellow Americans, ask not what your country can do for you — ask what you can do for your country. My fellow citizens of the world, ask not what America will do for you, but what together we can do for the freedom of man.

— President John F. Kennedy

Inaugural Address, January 20, 1961

TABLE OF CONTENTS

PART 5. LEARNING FROM THE PAST

PART 6. WHERE DOES THE CIA FIT IN

INTRODUCTION

When I left Russia and made my way to the United States in 1995, after (as we thought at the time) the Cold War had ended, the folks in Washington gave me better than the usual immigrant's welcome. In fact, given my expertise and 30 years experience in covert operations and techniques of influence, they asked me to prepare a briefing and a set of instructions for the White House.

This in effect turned me into US President de facto. Naturally, the operation was authorized by the first Russian CIA Director — John Deutch, who wanted to see me, a professional Russian intelligence officer, in the Oval Office, even if only under the table (read about John Deutch in the chapter on "Managing Spies at the Top").

Since 1996 an astute observer may see that my guidance has been taken very much to heart at the White House, as Bill Clinton and now George W. Bush act in strict accordance to this handbook. In fact, using the models, patterns, and rules crystallized in these pages the American public can now stand a chance of making sense of today's bizarre domestic and international news and elections, as well as deciphering what may have been going on in past scandals and other tectonic shifts whose explanations have remained unsatisfactory and unconvincing.

Ten years have passed since I first delivered these pointers to Washington, and it's high time to share them with the public, with presidents, prime ministers, senators, legislators, ministers, governors and mayors, ambassadors and consuls, generals and soldiers, professors and students, spies and police officers, reporters and analysts, and those battling it out in the corporate minefield. And, finally, with those wish to be elected the US President. No matter where you live and what you do, the "White House Special Handbook" will help you make sense of the news and get ahead in the vulpine world of the 21st century. Good luck.

"Everybody wants to be the boss." So they say. But many of the candidates who have fought to become President of the United States do not seem to have been very thoughtful people. Before we even check whether you are eligible and electable, let's see if you really want the job. If you are still interested after the next few chapters, we can come back to the strategies for winning that coveted position.

PART I. POLITICAL MANAGEMENT AT THE TOP

Chapter 1. Controlling the White House

> "The Presidency is not a very good place to make new friends."
> — President John F. Kennedy

> "The executive Power shall be vested in a President of the United States of America. He shall hold his office during the term of four years. " — The US Constitution, Article II, Section I.

> "I do solemnly swear that I will faithfully execute the office of the President of the United States, and will, to the best of my ability, preserve, protect, and defend the Constitution of the United States. So help me God." — Presidential Oath of Office.

The White House costs us $ 1 billion a year.

The US President is paid $400,000 a year. He is the only person in the White House and in Washington, DC who deserves every penny of his salary.

With the election you are transformed into the most powerful person in the world, leader of America, Head of State, Head of the Executive Branch, Commander-in-Chief of the Armed Forces and Chief Diplomat. It's a tough job. It's an unimaginable responsibility. Let us look step by step at the problems, crises, mistakes that can derail you, and the skills and qualities that lead to success and a professional presidential style.

If you were a Governor or a Senator before, stop acting like Governor or Senator and become President. Unfortunately, most Presidents can't get rid of their previous working and personal style, act slow and bring chaos to the White House, especially during their first term (which could be the last). I'm sure you'll be different. Relax, be pleasant, and never, even for a second, think about yourself as a historic figure. From now on you live in a goldfish bowl — stared at, studied and investigated.

Iron-Clad Rules for the President

You are a national image (a national ideal based on pseudo-facts). You are supposed to be a symbol of national unity, national continuity and the symbol of federal government. You have to be a religious person and affirm religious values and set a moral example.

Leadership is the first quality Americans look for in you — they want a President who is steadfast in his convictions. You are done with elections, but you are not done with your image.

Inauguration speech: give a short speech and a strong message.

Next in importance will be the annual State of the Union Address and a message on the budget. Actually, every speech is important because it's an issue of political strategy.

The power to control the federal budget is your top prerogative.

Presidential Calendar

Time is your #1 value — learn how to run it properly through your White House staff. Divide your life in the White House into two 4-year-long terms and then divide your term into cycles. All you have to do during your first term is to take care of the second one — that's your agenda. The second term's agenda is to set your place in the word's history.

First year — You have enough public support to start big initiatives, not measly reforms!

Presidents have a "honeymoon," some period after the inauguration, up to 3 months, when the opposition party refrains from attacks and Congress is inclined to support you too. This is a nice time for unrealistic public expectations, so set a national agenda right away and declare strong initiatives on tax and budget issues.

Attention: once the first 100 days are gone (productive opening period), the media hounds will start baying. Once 180 days are past — Congress starts biting!

President Kennedy once said: "I made two mistakes during my first year. One was Cuba. The other one was letting it be known that I read as much as I do."

Second year — Develop your initiatives. It's a time when inevitable public disappointment comes after high expectations. Your proposals inevitably antagonize certain interest groups and your popularity declines, because some groups develop into consistent winners and others — into consistent losers. You have to help your party with mid-term elections when the entire House and one-third of the Senate is up for re-election — it's the best indicator of the nation's approval or disapproval of your presidency. (But if you are not popular at the time, don't show up in public often and don't "help" certain candidates. George W. Bush ignored this rule and Republicans lost the House of Representatives in 2006.) If you fail to do what you plan in the first two years, better get it done fast!

Third year — Go, go, go, go public preparing your re-election. Presidents often lose voters during this period.

Fourth year — All-politics year. Try to achieve some important international agreement (a treaty) for the historic record. Win re-election.

Divide each year into 2 cycles:
1st cycle — late autumn and early winter prepare State of the Union Address to Congress, new legislation and budget recommendations.
2nd cycle — in late winter and spring promote these proposals and prepare for annual "Big Eight" summit.

Then, thirteen appropriations bills must be passed each year to keep the federal government operating:
1. Agriculture, rural development and related agencies.
2. Commerce, Justice and the judiciary, State and related agencies.
3. Defense.
4. District of Columbia.
5. Energy and water development.
6. Foreign assistance and related programs. •
7. Interior and related agencies.
8. Labor, Health and Human Services, and Education.
9. Legislative branch for Congress's own operations.
10. Military construction.
11. Transportation and related agencies.
12. Treasury, Postal Service and general government agencies.
13. Veterans Affairs, Housing and Urban Development, and independent agencies

In the nine months leading up to the October 1 start of the federal government fiscal year, you and Congress must meet several deadlines to ensure that the money needed to operate the government will be available when the fiscal year begins:

- The first Monday in February, you have to submit budget requests.
- April 15 is the target date for the House and Senate to agree on a budget resolution setting guidelines for spending and taxes.
- On May 15, House Appropriations Committee and subcommittees begin acting on spending bills.
- During the summer and early fall, House-State conferences resolve differences between their versions of the appropriations bills.
- October 1 is the drop-dead date for you to sign appropriations bills into law.

There are also several terribly important activities that somehow were left out of the Constitution's description of the President's functions. As Head of State you represent the American people on ceremonial occasions. You have to:

- light the national Christmas tree
- preside over the Easter egg roll on the White House lawn
- hold receptions to honor Americans who have won international prizes, such as the Nobel Prize
- greet astronauts returning after their missions
- give out the Presidential Medal of Freedom
- give recognition to charities like American Cancer society
- attend funerals of foreign Heads of State (you can send the Vice President, Secretary of State or one of the former US Presidents in some cases)
- honor the war dead by laying wreaths at the Tomb of the Unknown Soldier on Memorial Day and Veterans Day
- issue proclamations each year celebrating national holidays such as Thanksgiving Day and Independence Day

You can use ceremonial occasions to campaign for your reelection, make policy proposals, create an atmosphere of confidence and promote patriotism and national pride. Presidents who neglect ceremonial duties may find they have more time to develop policy and actually run the government, but they are sacrificing a tool of leadership that can be used not only to inspire the nation to greater accomplishments, but also to improve their own popularity. You can also manipulate your political calendar for electoral advantage. It's OK if your popularity declines after the first year in the Office. Most important is year number 3, which starts the reelection campaign.

TIME IS SHORT

Divide your week into days.

Monday and Tuesday — decide plans and priorities for the week (with senior White House staff, Secretaries and Congress leaders). Limit those who can see you every morning to the top three — Chief of Staff, National Security Advisor and your scheduler.

Wednesday, Thursday, Friday — guide execution and make decisions. Don't forget about your weekly radio address.

Divide your day into hours and minutes.

The general rule is 30% of your weekly hours go to senior White House staff, 10% — to Cabinet, 5% — to Congress members, 5% — to foreign leaders.

No matter what, even if it's a war time, sleep one hour during the day to give your brain a break, and finish your day at 6 P.M. After 6 P.M. do not read any documents, do not take any phone calls, do not talk to anybody but family members and close friends. Most presidents are manipulated by their aides, overwork themselves and fail to reach the age to which they were expected to live at the time of their election.

And eat whatever you want, but you must know that the more calories you have to digest, the slower you think.

Have a strategy for the last day of your presidency — maybe you'd like to pardon some convicted criminals, either to soften your image, make some more useful friends — or to make life more difficult for your rivals who follow. Bill Clinton famously pardoned well over 50 personal friends, campaign funders, and close relatives, as well as assorted bank robbers.

Who are you going to be? Make a choice:

- utopist (ideas manipulator)
- manager (Government and Congress manipulator)
- challenger (reformer)

Any problem turns into a political one if it threatens your power.

- Use your legal right to press the nation and illegal ones to press the world to eliminate problems.
- Once you're in politics, you are a hostage of your status and you must sacrifice privacy in return for power.
- Never play alone — you are power as part of a group.

All your decisions are risk taking ones (any decision brings a problem). You may ask advice before you make a decision, but don't listen to anybody afterwards. You are not paid for the quantity of your work but for leadership and ultimate decision making. (If your adviser approaches you with a fresh idea, ask him why isn't everyone else using it.)

Correct political mistakes before they become political scandals, but avoid any rush — think three times and check ten times before you sign anything (an emergency is a loss of control).

No easy matter will come to you as President — if they are easy they should be settled at lower levels. Don't trust those who work too much and who push you too often (people who try to influence you go to your advisers, because they know you listen to the people close to you).

Never blame previous Presidents for the problems they left for you — that's a sign of weakness. Get rid of a White House tradition to deal with problems only if they "knock at the door." (On the other hand, remember that "life comes at you fast." It may sound good to draft a six-page "Plan for America's Future" as Bill Clinton did; of course nothing came of it. Just take care of your two terms.)

THE MEDIA

There are two power centers in the United States — TV and Washington, DC. Just as the press needs the White House to carry out its functions as the collector and interpreter of news and information, so the White House needs the press to spread its message. Your popularity depends on the amount of good and bad news about your administration's policy dispensed by the media. No straight answers! If you rule the media, you rule America.

PRESS CONFERENCES AND THE PRESS SECRETARY

A press conference is the US President's conference to proffer news items to the press, and not the press's conference with the President. Behave like a king and they will take you for a king. Don't let reporters provoke you into making any promise or statement unprepared; talk about the "bad" issues before they ask you to; never say "I don't know" but say: "The problem is under study" instead. "Cool off" reporters by re-asking the question in terms that allow you to answer it more easily.

Evade a question by pleading inability to reply on grounds of national security. Change the tone and direction of the questioning by calling on a reporter with a reputation for asking "soft" questions. (Better yet, to show off your achievements answer a question that wasn't asked.)

Use press conferences to influence public opinion and to understand public opinion judging by the questions.

Don't schedule any press conferences during an international crisis — as a rule, they inflame the situation. But you really need press conferences when your polls go down.

Your Press Secretary has to be exceptionally articulate, smart and loyal, because he is your image and echo. He is in charge of the news management and that includes:

(a) daily briefings to announce the President's initiatives and positions, appointments or pending legislation. In such a way the White House, not the media, sets the news agenda for the day (the "story of the day"). Reporters have to buy it because they need pictures. Your Press Secretary may also provide special "backgrounder" briefings for reporters to explain certain initiatives (these briefings may go "on the record," meaning that the remarks may be quoted and the source identified, "on background," in which the source can't be identified, "on deep background" when attribution of any sort is prohibited, and "off record," in which information given to reporters may not be included in their stories and is mainly provided for their guidance. Briefing sources may range from the President personally to Cabinet members, the White House staff and policy experts.

(b) stonewalling — "No comment."

(c) any bad news should be released on late Friday nights when media organizations are minimally staffed and news is likely to draw less public attention over the weekend.

(d) staged events:
- exclusive interviews to selective reporters from major news organizations, those who are known to be sympathetic toward the administration
- private interviews to Washington-based foreign correspondents from countries that are scheduled to be visited. In such a way you set the stage for your visit and define your objectives and expectations on your own terms.

(e) private contacts with media (the best way to build media support).

(f) keeping a "black list" of reporters who don't report favorably on the President and his policy.

Because of the Press Secretary's closeness to members of the news media, he is able to pick up public opinion trends and issues. The Office of Communications, which monitors the print and electronic media for stories of interest to the White House, has to bring you a one-page report every day.

Using Your Visibility

You can get as much attention as you want. You are the most public figure in the world and everything you are doing and talking about inside and outside the White House has to be recorded. Every time you leave the White House you have to choose the right place or event, or accept the right invitation and deliver the message which is most important now. You rule the situation if you rule the flow of information, and if you can't control events use your power to control the flow of information and give the first interpretation of events.

You are the White House boss but not the Washington, DC boss — you need the back up of public opinion for the next four years at least; but you must centralize policy making in the White House no matter what!

Your priorities are:

- Economic policy: government taxing and spending, regulation and promotion of business, monetary supply, agriculture support.
- Social policy: income security, housing, health care, education
- Civil rights and liberties policy: discrimination prevention; voting rights and basic liberties
- Natural resources & environmental policy: clear air and water, wildlife protection, national parks, public lands, water resources
- Foreign & national security: new weapons systems, troop levels, military alliances, intelligence activities, foreign aid, foreign trade, treaties, relations with foreign governments, immigration

HIRING

The appointment power is an extremely important tool enabling you to gain control of your administration and direct national policy.

Numbers first: 1,125 Presidential appointees require Senate confirmation, including 185 Ambassadors, 94 District Attorneys, 94 US Marshals. (The Senate, though, may use its confirmation power as a political bargaining trick and "put on hold" your nominee until you agree to do them a favor — actually, they keep him a political hostage).

Office of Presidential Personnel makes decisions or recommends President's actions on 5842 jobs. Ten forms must be executed by the candidate, including a White House personal data statement, a waiver permitting the review of past tax returns, FBI questionnaire, a financial disclosure statement for the Office of Government Ethics so that identify possible conflicts of interests.

Hiring Mistakes

(a) Avoid criminals, drug addicts, alcoholics, homosexuals. All come with a risk of future embarrassments.

(b) Avoid widespread mistake of hiring staff and the Cabinet judging by communication abilities and not by professional skills; remember — efficiency is low if staff consists of old or young people only.

(c) Do not hire your wife, please; or anyone else who cannot be fired.

(d) Look through previous administrations' lists, talk to chairs of Congress committees, college professors (law, economics, national security), big business (friends, partners, donors). Pressure from your congressional supporters will influence most of your appointments.

(e) Do not hire independent persons, no matter how experienced they are.

(f) Follow the quotas (one black Secretary and one Latino).

(g) Interview key positions candidates in person (Chief of Staff and his Deputies, all Assistants, Secretaries and Deputy Secretaries, federal agencies chiefs, US Ambassadors) and use the following criteria:

- commitment to your philosophy and program
- integrity and personal qualifications
- experience and skills
- no personal agenda
- toughness needed to fight the Washington establishment (Congress + media + interest groups)

(h) Give key positions to your campaign donors and team members who showed to you personal loyalty. No key positions go to another political party members. It's advisable that you give a Secretary of Defense position to somebody who is expert in weapons systems and defense budgeting.

(i) Find jobs for some defeated Congress members. Please.

(j) Don't hesitate to hire a personal assistant on any problem .

(k) Talk straight and demand loyalty.

It's good to take newly appointed Cabinet members and senior White House staff to Camp David for some informal meeting, drinks and the first open discussion on your future policy.

THE WHITE HOUSE STAFF

A leader needs managers, but managers need a leader. The White House staff serves to:

- protect your political interests
- act as principal political advisers
- distill information and provide a perspective from which the President can make an informed decision
- direct the implementation of your priorities by the bureaucracy
- process important political and economic information and process ideas coming from Congress, events and crisis situations, executive branch agencies, public opinion, party, interest groups, media and most important — from President and staff (ideas always have to be politically attractive)
- operate effectively inside the White House triangle: the President's schedule — the flow of papers — the press. The most powerful figures in the White House are senior staff because they provide information for your decisions, evaluate policy proposals by Cabinet Secretaries, control activities of the executive branch, maintain liaison and lobby the Congress, interest groups, party leaders and media and control access (and information) to you — that's what the Chief of Staff is doing (remember — there is no # 2).

Here they are:

Chief of Staff to the President

Assistant to the President & Deputy Chief of Staff

Assistants to the President:
> National Security
> Senior Adviser
> National Economic Council
> Domestic Policy Council
> Press Secretary
> Communications
> Counsel to the President
> Homeland Security

Presidential Personnel
> Legislative Affairs
> Intergovernmental Affairs
> Staff Secretary
> Political Affairs
> Cabinet Secretary
> Public Liaison
> Director of Presidential Scheduling
> Director of Speechwriting

Chief of Staff to the First Lady

Director of Advance Management, Administration & Oval Office Operations

Executive Agencies
> Director, Office of Administration
> Chair, Council of Economic Advisers
> Director, Office of Management and Budget

Chief of Staff

The Chief of Staff reviews most of the documents that go to you, gives his advice after intense information processing and consultations with other agencies and then — he's telling others what President wants. A lot of people, including Congressmen and Senators, will try to reach you through him. He has to give good instructions to the Press Secretary on the White House message about current headlines and the President's plans and actions (the Press Secretary works the same way with VP and First Lady press teams). He is responsible for your time and has to plan at least two months ahead your effective activity together with Communications, Scheduling and other policy offices' Directors plus VP and First Lady Chiefs of Staff.

Besides, he has to do "dirty jobs" for the President like firing people or act as a "lighting rod" to draw criticism away from the President.

National Security Advisor

> "I made a very deliberate decision not to ask President Ronald Reagan, so I could insulate him...and provide future deniability." — National Security Adviser John Poindexter on Iran-Contra affair, 1987.

The National Security Advisor controls all the documents concerning national security coming from Defense, State Departments and national security agencies, and coordinates these offices. His position is not subject to Senate confirmation, which, according to a long-standing Washington tradition, means that he can't be compelled to testify before the Congress.

He decides what papers the President should see and, what's more, he gives his comments on any document. (National security is 100% the President's business, so keep this figure at some distance and don't let him think of himself as your Number Two — foreign leaders will try to work through him to get to you or to influence you.) He has to oversee the functioning of the National Security Council (NSC), which is your foreign policy making tool and a "government inside government." This is something very special and convenient about the NSC — it's responsible only to you and there's not much Congress control over its budget. Of course, the National Security Advisor is involved in every meeting between you and any foreign leader and is responsible for the schedule.

The most powerful of executive offices after the National Security Council is the Office of Management and Budget (it's authorized to make cuts in federal agencies' budgets, to advise you on national fiscal and economic policies, supervise execution of the government budget, evaluate the performance of federal programs).

How the White House Staff Works

Staffers (and Secretaries) prefer stability and don't like it if you're "rocking the boat" — that's why they often play reform-stoppers. They don't like to work hard and prefer to send you on "very important visits" abroad as often as possible. They try to load you up with an extremely busy schedule and "feed" you hundreds of useless documents, create artificial problems and conflicts to show off their hyper-activity.

They try to be your decision makers and they do influence you because, unlike Secretaries, they have daily contact with you; that's why you don't see Cabinet members as your principal aides. They try to set you up by interpreting your decisions and orders in their own way, as every Adviser is the "American President himself." They know you won't accept "complicated," "expensive," "risky" projects and they try to sell you "simple," "cheap" and "popular" ones only.

Watch your senior staff and how they present ideas. If somebody wants to push his idea or a project, he will give you three options, making two of them unattractive. Naturally you pick the one he presented as least harmful.

They have inside rules of their own:

- Fight for access (influence) to President or to people with direct access (aiming to get a better position if President is re-elected).
- Isolate government from the President.
- Influence = relationship with the President.
- Get a table in the West Wing. They are nobody if they are stuck in the White House basement and see the President by appointment only.
- Before they send a document to the President they have to look at it a hundred times and ask themselves if it's too immoral or too radical.
- They never say "no" aloud to anybody.
- They remain anonymous and have to put up with conflicts.
- They never bring bad news to the President — let it be somebody else.
- They never say "That's impossible," no matter what the President is asking them to do.
- They disappear (and find an excuse later) if the President is in a bad mood.
- They never ague with the President if there's somebody else present.
- They learn how the President likes to do business (talking, giving orders, writing the documents and taking notes, managing official and non-official meetings) and his habits (food, drinks, cigarettes, favorite sport, movies, show business stars, writers, politicians; attitude to women) and try to copy him — the President has to feel comfortable with the people around him.
- Every appearance in public with the President is an investment in their career after the White House.
- Fight anybody who's trying to horn in on their jobs.
- Avoid taking on risky tasks controlled by the President in person (if necessary, try to "delegate" it to somebody else!).
- Try to avoid being associated with any failures.
- Don't say anything President doesn't want to hear.
- Use "Smith's Principle": If it can be understood, it's not finished yet.
- Write memorandums not to inform the reader, but to protect the writer.
- No matter what subject is under discussion, employ the language of sports and war: say "breakthrough" instead of "progress," never speak of compromise, consider "adopting a fallback position."
- Minimize the number of rivals.
- Gain independence according to how much the President needs them.
- Before asking the President for some personal favor, make him believe he's going to get some (political) profit out of it.
- Tell the President what he can do and help him try to do it, and never tell him what he shouldn't do.
- Persons lower than Chief of Staff should avoid giving any personal gifts to the President.
- There is an open power struggle between national security staff members and domestic policy staff and between those who develop new policies and initiatives versus budget staff.

Don't Blow It

Some staff members are very talented but get in over their heads.

"The Democrats are still holding firm." [Republican senators Alfonse D'Amato and Bob Dole had demanded hearings on the Whitewater scandal, but Democrat Banking Committee Chairman Don Riegle was holding them off.] "But I can't promise that they'll be with us in a month." — George

Stephanopoulos, one very smart and very wrong staffer who served President Clinton.

"Whatever I said was exactly wrong. Tears stung the corners of her [Hillary Clinton's] eyes, and it was out of control. All of that fury, for a moment, was directed at me... at the Republicans for trying to destroy health care by destroying her, at the press for its small-minded, obsessive scrupulousness when issues affecting real people were at stake, at her husband for getting her into this stupid land deal with his shady friends in the first place and then expecting her to clean it up; at her best friend, Vince, for killing himself; at herself for letting the situation spiral.

" 'You never believed in us. In New Hampshire, it was just me and Susan [Thomases] and Harold [Ickes] who believed in us. If we hadn't fought, we would never have won. You gave up on us...We were out there alone, and I'm feeling very lonely right now. Nobody is fighting for me...

"'I don't want to hear anything more,' Hillary snapped back in control. 'I want us to fight. I want a campaign now.' Looking back at me, she took one last shot: 'If you don't believe in us, you should just leave.' Then she walked out the door.

" 'You gave up on us.' How she could say that? Nobody's fought harder for them. I'm the most loyal staffer they've ever had. I went out there every day. On Gennifer [Flowers]. And the draft.

"And Whitewater. Sacrificed my credibility. I went before the whole country like a crazy person, even said he never had sex with Gennifer. People would laugh at what I would say. Then to get attacked — not for being wrong but for being disloyal, for abandoning them. F--- her. I'm arguing for what's best — for her, for him, for all of us and everything we're fighting for. F--- her. "

— George Stephanopoulos, Director for Communications, Clinton Administration, fired in 1996, *All Too Human.*

How to Manage the Staff

First, adopt a dominant management style:

1. Pyramidal, structured as hierarchy with you at the top, followed by the Chief of Staff and other key assistants — I strongly recommend this one — it insures a clear chain of command and provides precise channels of information going up and directives going down. It permits specialization at the lower levels and control at the top. Besides, those higher up in the system are able to provide you with more accurate information in a timely manner, while filtering out and eliminating unnecessary information. (The problem is — nobody wants to bring you important bad news).

2. Circular, when you are surrounded by advisers, all of whom have approximately equal access to the Oval Office. That usually means too much access and chaos, and overloading you with information — 99% of which should not appear on your table (per JFK).

All your assistants are political assistants and everyone will try to play a policy-maker. But a good thing is, they were not elected and are responsible to you only. Thus you can:

- Reform your staff freely as there's not even a word about it in the US Constitution.
- Interchange key figures if domestic crisis is approaching.
- If you don't agree with the staff on important issues, go to polls for back-up. (The best employee is the one you can blackmail. Besides, a very good "pusher" for your people is their deep understanding that they have to work together to help the President stay in office next term — if the President leaves, everybody leaves).
- Use "the carrot and the stick."
- Use "pulling by pushing" — give an important job without publicity to those who become too popular.
- Do as little reading as you can — you have staff for that.
- Do as little writing as you can — same reason.
- Involve yourself personally in your staff and Cabinet jobs as little as you can — same reason.
- Never make minor decisions — same reason.
- Don't read any intelligence or other report on more than one sheet of paper.

The Cabinet

There are alternative views on this.

> "I am the hardest working man in this country. I prefer to supervise the whole operation of government than entrust the public business to subordinates. I have conducted the government without their aid. Indeed, I have become so familiar with their duties and workings of the government, not only upon general principles but on most of its minutes details, that I find but little difficulty in doing this. It is only occasionally that a great measure or a new question arises upon which I need aid and advice of my Cabinet." — President James Polk.

What is a "bureaucrat"? Some say it's a Democrat who holds a job a Republican wants.

President Kennedy said once that "[dealing with bureaucracy] is like trying to nail jelly to the wall." It takes at least half a year for a presidential directive to be put into action through the Cabinet.

If the bureaucrats are wearing you down, you have the right to fire any Secretary. However, Cabinet members must be approved by Senate, therefore you have to negotiate with the Senate leaders and party leaders throughout the country. As a result, some positions may go to people you don't know well and can't trust.

Then, if you want to re-organize the Cabinet you have to confront the Congress, because Congress tries to protect the interests of its constituents, who are often the clients of the existing bureaucratic agencies. So if you plan changes you have to appoint people who share your strategy.

You may also need to offer a position to a group that you need to support in the coming election, or whose help you need; or to help pass legislation (these people will be more loyal to their political benefactors than to you).

Secretaries obviously have disadvantages compared to the staffers as they don't have easy access to the Oval Office (again, that depends on you). Some of them had little or no contact with you before being appointed. Actually, their task is to win the backing of key interest groups and that's why you, practically speaking, don't need Cabinet meetings (if there's no crisis). If a Cabinet member feels independent (usually, that's the Secretary of State), don't fire him — substitute him by the National Security Advisor or send him abroad on a regular basis (we'll talk more under Foreign Policy).

Secretary of Defense

The Secretary of Defense is also a very special and unique position for many reasons. This department is regarded a non-political one, defending the United States no matter what (never let him decide, though, what and where US interests are). Military leaders have a lot of friends in Congress who press the administration to accept military demands. Besides, it's not easy to manage the Pentagon, as you depend on the military for evaluations of the national military capacities; they decide also what kinds of weapons to buy and build. Half of the federal budget goes to Pentagon, making it a major department and that's the most frustrating aspect of your management.

You have to find a compromise between you, Congress, public opinion, interest groups and defense contractors' lobbyists.

The defense budget affects diplomacy and international relations, because governments worldwide scrutinize it for clues about US global intentions. For example, increases in defense spending, particularly for items such as naval vessels and aircraft, may signal a White House intention to pursue more aggressive foreign policies, and cuts in defense spending may indicate an effort to scale back on defense commitments.

The Cabinet members work hard during a crisis only. They prefer to save their plans and suggestions for private conversations with you, because that is what you need them for and they are competing with other Secretaries for your time, support and for funds. It's not easy for the President to make government agencies work effectively — first, you have no time, second — they have no competition. Anyway, you must have insiders in all departments, especially in the Justice Department (FBI), CIA and Secret Service. Fire anybody who's trying to dig dirt on you.

The Cabinet's Hidden Structure

There is a tradition according to which the Cabinet is divided into the inner circle (State, Defense, Treasury, Justice) and outer, less important one (Interior,

Agriculture, Commerce, Labor, Health and Human Services, Housing, Transportation, Energy, Education, Veterans Affairs, Homeland Security). While inner Cabinet members are selected more on the basis of personal friendship and loyalty, outer Cabinet members are selected more on the basis of geographical, ethnic or political representation and adopt an advocacy position for their Departments.

The inner Cabinet is divided into two groups:

- national security group (State and Defense Departments).
- legal-economic group (Justice and Treasury Departments). The Attorney General usually serves as the president's attorney and this special responsibility leads to close personal contact with the President. The Secretary of Treasury is very important in domestic monetary and fiscal policies and international trade and currency.

The outer Cabinet is a "domestic" group. Don't waste your time meeting them — you have enough staffers for that. Sometimes "outer" Secretaries try to build their political base of support within their own bureaucracies. Don't hesitate to fire and replace any of them if they start to criticize you and behave politically independent, counting on bureaucratic and interest groups' support.

There's one (negative for you) thing in common between all Secretaries — self-interest pushes them to protect and expand their departments and then they act more like representatives of their departments to the President then the presidential envoys they were appointed to be ("divided loyalty").

Then Secretaries of State and Defense usually form a coalition against your National Security Advisor. You must be a smart mediator as Commander-in-Chief. These two have weekly meetings, and each of them has a weekly meeting with the DNI (Director of National Intelligence), so you must know from independent sources what they are talking about in case they "forget" to tell you the details. (The Defense Secretary meets weekly with the Joint Chiefs, too.)

Cabinet Secretaries are not angels. The Cabinet is often corrupted by agribusiness (Dept. of Agriculture), the brokerage and financial world (Dept. of Treasury), corporations (Dept. of Commerce and Labor), power and fuel giants (Dept. of Energy), big business law-breakers (Dept. of Justice), weapons producers (Dept. of Defense), real estate and resource concessionaires (Dept. of Interior).

Department of State
- sets treaties with other countries
- advises the President about foreign concerns
- sends delegates to other counties
- helps US citizens in foreign countries
- gives US passports to travel to other countries

Department of Defense

- advises the President on the country's defense
- decides what kinds of weapons to buy and build
- directs the armed forces
- protects the country's borders
- provides military intelligence and look over American interests in other countries

Department of Justice

- advises the President on federal laws
- runs the federal prisons
- enforces federal laws
- investigates federal crimes

Department of Treasury

- advises the President on the US money policies
- collects federal taxes through Internal Revenue Service
- pays the country's bills
- prints and coins money

Department of Commerce

- advises the President on foreign trade
- advises the President on United States business
- makes international treaties
- keeps statistics and gives out loans to small businesses
- takes census of the United States
- tracks the weather
- grants patents

Department of Agriculture

- works with America's farmers (set up price support programs and lends money to rural businesses)
- controls the labeling of food products
- oversees inspection of processing plants and manages national forests

Department of Interior

- manages federal land (500 million acres) and protects wildlife
- directs ways to protect US land and water
- works with Native Americans

Department of Energy

- advises the President on the country's energy needs
- manages oil and coal resources
- controls the use of nuclear energy
- studies ways to use all kinds of energy
- advises people on ways to save energy (conservation policies)

Department of Labor

- enforces labor laws
- pays out benefits to people who lose their jobs

- sets down rules for worker safety

Department of Health and Human Services
- directs public health programs (Social Security)
- checks out safety of food
- approves drugs for medical use

Department of Education
- sets up work training programs
- sets education rules for children with special needs
- funds education programs
- monitors compliance with civil rights laws

Department of Housing and Urban development
- funds urban housing projects for poor
- enforces fair housing laws
- helps to start housing programs

Department of Transportation
- funds the building of federal roads
- sets transportation safety rules
- helps fund state roads projects

Department of Veterans Affairs:
- directs veterans benefit programs
- funds doctor's care for veterans
- assists with home loans for veterans

Department of Homeland Security
- prevents terrorist attacks within the United States
- reduces America's vulnerability to terrorism
- minimizes the damage from potential attacks and natural disasters

LINE OF SUCCESSION TO THE PRESIDENCY OF THE UNITED STATES

Vice President

Speaker of the House of Representatives

Senate President pro tempore

Secretary of Defense

Secretary of State

Secretary of Treasury

Attorney General

Secretary of Homeland Security

Secretary of Interior

Secretary of Agriculture

Secretary of Commerce

Secretary of Labor

Secretary of Health and Human Services

Secretary of Housing and urban Development

Secretary of Transportation

Secretary of Energy

Secretary of Education

STRATEGIC PLANNING

That's the biggest problem for all administrations. Strategic planning is the process of making present decisions based on very well-calculated future conse-quences. The basic strategic objective is a decision as to where to concentrate the government efforts — this is the essence of strategic planning.

An example of the importance of good strategic planning is the Health Care Reform plan that Hillary Clinton put forward when she was First Lady. It ended up in a 100% predictable failure. But the goal was not to get the plan passed — it was to attract attention and stake out a position. Mrs. Clinton knew very well that her "communist" idea to nationalize health-care in the United States was utopian and not be pushed through Congress in 1992; but she was already plan-ning her Senate race for 2000 and her 2008 Presidential campaign. She had noth-ing behind her to win the Oval Office so she designed a plan, had it researched and counted the possible votes. Then she "blew up" a huge PR campaign on the highest political level (which is the President himself). Now voters are waiting for her to come and pick them up in November 2008.

The worst example of strategic planning is the war in Iraq. (See "Securing world Domination" and "Strategy and Tactics in War.")

It is crucial to choose a professional crew and place people in positions where their brains will work effectively and produce quality.

Planning Formula
- design strategy
- amplify and clarify strategy into policy
- organize a team
- guide execution
- make final strategic decision

Regular Planning Model
- subject, concept, idea definition of objectives
- design of innovative options and debate
- exploration of concepts, claims and possibilities
- development of program outlines
- establishment of expected performance criteria and indications
- information gathering
- integration of ideological elements

- assignment of executive responsibility
- scheduling
- analysis and experiment
- experiment evaluation, examination of likely consequences
- comparison of expected and actual performance levels
- determination of costs
- prognosis
- strategic decision

Express Planning

- information interpretation
- project designing
- choice of a project
- decision

DECISION MAKING

The rules of Presidential decision making are simple:

- Decision making is a multiple choice process.
- Any decision involves political risk.
- If you can't make a decision, you need more information.
- Be optimistic, but remain realistic.
- Give yourself a deadline.
- No brainstorming chaos.

There are two kinds of decisions, irreversible and reversible. Better know which kind you are facing.

(a) Identify the problem

(b) Analyze the problem — what are the facts?

(c) Evaluate options — what are the pros and cons? what can go wrong?

(d) Identify choices — which alternative is the best?

(e) Implement plans — what action needs to be taken?

PSYCHOLOGICAL MODELING OF A PRESIDENT (STRATEGIC INTELLIGENCE METHOD)

Intelligence services worldwide watch political leaders during public appearances, trying to calculate their physical and mental health judging by their look and behavior. In the US they also evaluate the executives and staffers who surround the President at official meetings to calculate what's going on in the White House.

They look at:

- a very detailed biography
- personal needs, interests, philosophy
- political views
- intelligence, will-power, character, abilities

- behavior in crisis situations
- compromising facts and possible methods of influence
- personal, political and big business VIP connections
- financial situation
- administration and team
- political opposition and the President
- Congress and the President

Chapter 2. Domestic Policy

You can't separate domestic and foreign policies because they are married to the same ugly guy — the budget deficit. But we still have to break them down into bite-size pieces to analyze what is going on.

Dealing with Big Business

> J. P. Morgan: "If we have done anything wrong, send your man [the Attorney General] to my man and they can fix it up." President Theodore Roosevelt: "That can't be done." (1902).
> "We bought the son-of-a-bitch and he didn't stay bought!" — (H.C. Frick, U.S. Steel, about President Theodore Roosevelt, 1904).

Iron-Clad Rules

A. Big organized money moves big political machines, big political machines move big lobbies, big lobbies move the President.

B. The President is an investment.

C. A group that rules the economy rules the White House.

D. A "new political course" comes not with a new President, but with a change of big business' global financial interests.

E. Protect big investments — help to promote American business worldwide; don't interfere.

F. If the government doesn't meet the needs of big business, it forms a new one of its own (something like a President's Council). This usually happens when the

President can't provide financial stability and super-profits. Besides, big business has much more important foreign connections than the government.

G. Big business is:

(a) money

(b) control of many social levers

H. Any political action gets an economic (big business) reaction.

I. In terms of partisan politics, Republicans are considered to be more sympathetic to big business interests while traditionally Democrats get electoral and financial support from organized labor.

J. Forget about antitrust policy — business has become more global and efforts to enforce antitrust policies have proven deficient and are threats to national security.

THE ECONOMY

Economic strategy is as important as national security.

- Appoint bright, educated and experienced people to the Cabinet and the Federal Reserve Board, who advise you on important economic decisions.
- Press foreign governments on trade and currency issues.
- Watch the markets 24/7.
- Balance the budget (half goes to national defense — if there's no war there are no jobs in America, because 35% of US business works for Pentagon. The fact that all such spending is money down the drain, rather than building productive capacity etc., is a different matter. Let the next President worry about that.

In general, the key word in domestic policy is accomplishment — budget balanced, taxes cut, jobs created. Use your budget power to the full extent because people usually hold you, not Congress, accountable for economic downturns. Whether you win or lose your second term in the Oval Office largely depends on your budget actions.

Budget Deficit

A large budget deficit is a headache and has extremely negative effects on the economy:

1. It limits the government's flexibility to fight a possible recession; that requires tax cuts and deficit spending, which would exacerbate the debt problem. Since tax revenues fall during a recession and unemployment insurance and welfare payments rise, the budget would be under further strain precisely when deficit spending would be needed to pull the economy up.
2. It reduces the amount of funds available for achieving the nation's social and defense goals, because interest must be paid on the national debt.
3. It can threaten the economy by "crowding out" corporate and private borrowers from the credit market. Because the government must bor-

row heavily to finance its deficit, it competes with business and individuals to borrow funds. The increased competition forces interest rates higher, causing loans (including mortgages) to become more expensive. As a result, business can afford to purchase less plant and equipment to expand and modernize their operations and fewer consumers can afford to finance purchases of expensive items, such as houses and cars. The resulting reduction in demand threatens economic growth.

4. The US budget deficit has become so large that domestic savings no longer can provide enough capital to service the debt. Consequently, the government must borrow from foreign sources to make up the difference. This makes us dependent on foreign investors and raises the possibility of a "stabilization crisis," which can occur if foreign investors lose confidence in the dollar and liquidate their US investments. Such a crisis could cause the dollar to plummet and interest and inflation to rapidly accelerate.

Managing the Economy

- Regulate spending, taxation, monetary policy and foreign trade (it has to be under strict political control) — you have the right to propose legislation and veto any legislation you think incorrect. Keep in mind that Americans always insist on reducing government spending on foreign aid and space exploration, and they naturally hate any rise in taxes.
- State and local governments, both through national associations like the US Conference of Mayors and Congress Members, always press the government to get more federal funds even at the expense of inflationary budget deficits.
- Keep unemployment low and prices stable — these two factors are politically dangerous and failure here can bring a free-fall in approval ratings.
- Take credit for economic growth, price stability and low unemployment even if you have nothing to do with it.
- Still have problems? Try international initiatives.

There are four inevitable factors that will limit your control over the economy:

1) You must share power with Congress — you can't levy taxes or appropriate money all by yourself;

2) The theoretical nature of the science of economics — no single economic theory has ever explained the behavior of the economy in the future;

3) The imprecision of economic information. Economic statistics and indicators do not measure the immediate conditions of the economy, but rather the conditions that prevailed between one and three months ago, depending on the particular economic statistics. Consequently, if you take action on the basis of incoming economic information you may be reacting to a problem that no longer exists or that is much worse than believed.

4) There are forces outside the reach of the federal government, like international factors (oil prices and foreign trade policies), state and local governments economic decisions and mistakes, big business decisions that affect employment, inflation, the trade deficit and public opinion — which is always against cutting social programs.

Domestic policy rests on three legs: education, health and environment. Sorry, Americans will never support reduced funding for education, Social Security and Medicare (Medicaid) cuts and weakened environmental-protection laws. But I strongly advise you — don't bother trying to emulate Europe and the British Commonwealth by providing health care for all — the privately insured middle class (your voting majority) won't stand for it. If you don't believe me, go to the polls.

Now, are you a challenger in politics? If "yes," strengthen your political positions in Washington, DC first, then start some reforms. Before you start a reform you have to win the information war with your opponents and get public support. A reform is always a venture; the process may start taking on momentum and you won't be able to stop it. You had better continue old reforms using a new tactic because new reforms bring new problems, new enemies and new mistakes, and big economic mistakes bring you an economic crisis.

Crisis means that your government as a system is exhausted and it's unable to rule the nation and resources effectively in an extreme situation, including economic, natural catastrophes and war. A crisis has three stages — before the crisis, when the first signs appear; crisis development until culmination; catastrophe followed by impeachment.

A crisis could be "programmed" at the very beginning of your term (mistakes in political and economic courses, inexperienced personnel, faulty planning) or it can appear later (too many mistakes, change of political environment, shifts in the economic or international situation). Crisis management includes pre-crisis management and handling of the situation. You must be ready not only for a government crisis but also for sudden military attack, mass riots and natural disasters.

Speaking of which, given that George W. Bush had already secured his second term in office and didn't need the voters, what was the ultimate objective in his administration's handling of the Katrina disaster? In the long run, when we know who wins out of the situation in New Orleans, we'll have some idea.

International trade is an important part of the President's job and is a component of permanent political control. Our "friends" (NATO members, Saudi Arabia and Japan) favor a dollar (that is neither overvalued nor undervalued) and a healthy US economy with relatively full employment and low inflation rate.

If the dollar is weak, the value of much of their international currency reserves declines and their goods are less competitive in the US market. If the dollar is too strong, their investment capital migrates to the US and the high competitiveness of their products in the US market threatens to provoke calls for trade restrictions. If unemployment in the US rises, the major market for their goods declines. If interest rates are higher in the US than in Europe or Japan, investment capital moves to our country. Consequently, foreign governments press the United States to keep the exchange value of the dollar from fluctuating widely and to hold interest rates steady.

Domestic Propaganda (Psychological War) and Mind Control

To effectively manage propaganda you must understand that most political views are acquired through political socialization and the most important influences in this process are the following.

1. Family. If both parents identify with one party, there's strong likelihood that the children will begin their political life with the same party preference.

2. Education. School is a transmitter of patriotism. University is a transmitter of liberalism.

3. Religion. Roman Catholic respondents tend to be more liberal on economic issues than Protestants. Jewish are the most liberal and vote mostly Democratic. Many Northern white Protestants vote Republican, whereas northern white Roman Catholics vote Democratic.

4. Economic status. Poor people vote Democratic. Rich vote Republican.

5. Political events. The war in Iraq divided the nation one-two-three.

6. Influence of opinion leaders. Those are people who have, as part of their job, the task of swaying people's views (politicians and media). Their interest lies in defining the political agenda in such a way that discussions about policy options will take place on their terms.

7. Media. Interesting thing — there isn't supposed to be any strongly partisan or ideological bias in TV coverage, but the visual and mental images conveyed by TV have a powerful impact.

8. Race. African Americans tend to be more liberal than white on social welfare issues, civil liberties and even foreign policy. They strongly support democrats.

9. Political culture (the set of beliefs and values regarding the political system that are widely shared by the citizens of a nation). Here the most important for us are the degrees of political trust and political tolerance which are measured through a specific series of survey questions, best if done through the Internet.

Propaganda Technology

You need 24/7 effective propaganda to get non-stop public support of your policy — your war for public support doesn't stop the day you enter the White

House — it may stop the day you leave the White House. If your polls go below 40%, the United States effectively has no President.

Use the following propaganda ploys. Provide:

- only general (abstract) information on big problem
- information dosage (the less people know — the easier you convince them)
- misinformation (full or partial) presented as news, sensations, rumors
- disorientation — one bit of information contradicts another one
- provocation — information "pushes" people (before you start war)
- information over-dosage — too much information (and people lose interest)
- exaggeration of enemy's negative sides and promotion of scary data
- distraction of nation's attention from news that is bad (for you) by publishing sensations and (political) scandals
- stereotype manipulation ("nuclear threat," "international terror," etc.)
- "shuffle" — all news and facts match President's political course
- "cocktail" — mix of true and false information
- "facts transportation" from abroad (you buy a foreign reporter and he's publishing positive information on your politics; then you spread the information through American media)
- Remember the principles of mass psychology: people don't believe the government — they believe the market and the stock exchange.
- People need statements, not analysis.

Keeping Voters on Your Side

All sorts of efforts must be going on throughout your term to keep the peanut gallery satisfied. Here is a letter someone in Bush's team thought would impress me and inspire me to "invest" in their campaign.

> From: President George W. Bush
> Subject: The Difference is Clear.
> Date: Mon, 24 Jul 2006
> PRESIDENT GEORGE W. BUSH
>
> Dear Mykhaylo:
> ... Nothing threatens our hard-won reforms and economic prosperity more than a Democrat victory this November.
> That is why your support as a Sustaining Member of the Republican National Committee is vital to our Party's success in the 2006 mid-term elections...
> Working together, we can continue to keep our nation moving forward to greater peace, prosperity and security...
> > Sincerely,
> > George W. Bush

Mind Control

Every day in 2004 we watched the Homeland Security Department "terror alert colors" and very often the threat was "high" or "very high." With all my 30 years espionage experience I couldn't understand why they were telling the nation about the threat and producing the multicolor picture on TV. Why? What can ordinary Americans do about that? What happened next made the situation absolutely clear for me and posed one more question for the nation: right after President Bush was re-elected the colors disappeared — why? Again, what happened? Is there no more "terror threat" to America? There is. But there's mind control, too.

Mind control, which I call mind manipulation or MM, is used to program the "right political behavior" of the nation or "indifferent behavior," if necessary, without people's knowing or understanding the procedure. We are talking here about total illegal social control.

Principles of Mind Manipulation

(1) It's not enough if every single citizen, and the nation as a whole, thinks and behaves your way — it's much better if they *want* to behave your way and feel comfortable, and are absolutely sure it's their own choice and, finally, they become your active supporters.

(2) If you want to control the nation and program peoples' thoughts, you have to control knowledge (information, culture and communication).

(3) The political imagination (belief) of the nation has to move in the right direction and has to be accepted as the most comfortable and most acceptable way of political activity: nobody is thinking, nobody is criticizing the President, nobody is making comparisons and drawing conclusions. Everybody believes the American President and hates his enemies.

(4) Don't waste time fighting foreign ideology, take care of ordinary Americans.

(5) There is no difference between commercial and political advertising, and MM.

Technology of Mind Manipulation

(1) Create a steadfast American collective will-power: "We want to live forever in the America we live in now" — through the media.

(2) Don't ask people to change their views and beliefs — they have only to change the object of their aggression — "Now we understand who is to be blamed for the problems! (the previous President, political opponents). "Now we understand where the problem lies!"(economic cycles, etc.).

(3) Get people accustomed to accept facts but believe only in the "right" commentaries — any common sense has to be "switched off." This way you create "mass artificial schizophrenia" — people lose the ability (and desire) to connect statements and facts (notions) and just believe.

Besides, by extreme exaggeration of the enemy's negative qualities you can install step by step the national schizophrenic fear and people have to accept you, the US President, as a savior. Plus, no matter what, repeat your major statements until people start accepting them without thinking.

(4) Divide the nation into "good Americans"(patriots) and "bad Americans"(the "minority).

Then make it clear that it's much better and more comfortable to be "good" than "bad." "We aren't watching good Americans who support the President. The surveillance is for bad Americans and we make their lives and careers uncomfortable. We have to do that because enemies of America may be using them." This method is called artificial social selection and its ultimate goal is a total regulation and standardization of the nation.

(5) For successful MM, use the combined efforts of popular American writers, TV and radio anchors, talented publicists and columnists, business and show business celebrities, politicians. Thus, step by step you create the "industry of correct political behavior and correct American thinking."

(6) Use a combination: statement + image. It reduces the effort needed to understand your message and makes people comfortable with you.

(7) Shift all popular TV shows to prime time — Americans don't have to think about politics after they come home.

EMERGENCY POWERS OF THE PRESIDENT (SETTING ASIDE DEMOCRACY)

I. Powers over individuals.

- Confine any individuals seen to be threats to national security.
- Restrict travel of Americans to other nations or travel of some foreigners to the USA.
- Restrict movement of citizens within the United States.
- Require persons, because of their backgrounds, associations with certain groups, or ownership of particular articles (such as weapons), to register with government officials.
- Restrict certain persons from working in industries names as critical to national security.
- Remove federal employees regarded as threats to national security.
- Declare martial law.
- Assign armed forces to conflicts in foreign nations.

II. Powers over property.
- Order stockpiling of strategic materials (such as uranium).
- Impose restrictions on exports (such as hi-tech products).
- Allocate materials in ways necessary to aid national defense.
- Require industries to give priority to government contracts and seize industries failing to comply with such orders.
- Fix wages and prices.

III. Powers over communication.

- Withhold information from Congress and the public deemed potentially sensitive to national security.
- Monitor and censor communications between United States and other nations.
- Require foreign representatives to register with US government.
- The President also has the authority to declare states of emergency in areas of the country hit by hurricanes, floods, earthquakes or other natural disasters, and to use this to enhance his power or public image.

Chapter 3. Managing the US Congress

"To my mind Judas Iscariot was nothing but a low, mean, premature Congressman."

"It could probably be shown by facts and figures that there is no distinctly native American class except Congress." — Mark Twain

"If everybody here connected with politics had to leave town because of chasing women and drinking, you'd have no government." — Senator Barry Goldwater.

One night President Cleveland was awakened by his wife: "Wake up! There are burglars in the house!" "No, my dear," said Cleveland sleepily, "in the Senate maybe, not in the House."

"Israel controls the US Senate. The Senate is subservient, much too much; we should be more concerned about US interests rather than doing the bidding of Israel. The great majority of the Senate of the US — somewhere around 80% — is completely in support of Israel; anything Israel wants, Israel gets. This has been demonstrated again, and this has made [foreign policy] difficult for our government." — Senator W. Fulbright, April 15, 1973).

The White House, not Congress, represents the nation. You are the leader and you set the legislative agenda. They can't start business until you give them State of the Union Address and a budget message. That's your program — and theirs. Start your first term with a big legislative victory. The US Constitution says nothing on how you manage the Congress so feel free to use the advice in these pages.

Introduction: How a Bill Becomes a Law

A Senator or Representative introduces a bill in Congress by sending it to the clerk of the House or the Senate, who assigns it a number and title. This procedure is termed the first reading. The clerk then returns the bill to appropriate committee of the Senate or the House. If the Committee opposes the bill, it will table or "kill" it. Otherwise, the Committee holds hearings to listen to opinions and facts offered by members and other interested people. The Committee then debates the bill and possibly offers amendments. A vote is taken, and if favorable, the bill is sent back to the clerk of the House or Senate. The clerk reads the bill to the house — the second reading. Members may then debate the bill and suggest amendments.

After debate and possibly amendment, the bill is given a third reading, simply of the title and put to a voice or roll-call vote. If passed, the bill goes to the other house, where it may be defeated or passed, with or without amendments, If defeated, the bill "dies." If passed with amendments, a conference committee made up of members of both houses works out the differences and arrives at a compromise.

After passage of the final version by both houses, the bill is sent to the President. If the President signs it, the bill becomes a law. The President may, however, veto the bill, refuse to sign it and send it back to the house where it originated. The President's objections are then read and debated, and a roll-call vote is taken. If the bill receives less than a two-thirds majority, it is defeated. If it receives at least two-thirds, it is sent to the other house. If that house also passes it by at least a two-thirds majority, the veto is overridden, and the bill becomes a law.

If the President neither signs nor vetoes the bill within 10 days — not including Sundays — it automatically becomes a law even without the President's signature. However, if Congress has adjourned within those 10 days, the bill is automatically "killed"; this indirect rejection is termed a pocket veto.

Functions of Congress

If you want to rule America, you have to rule the US Senate. Remember, you are one person concentrated on your program. Congress is a big and disorganized, chaotic institution — not a single word pronounced by these people ever makes history. Respect Congress anyway — it creates the illusion that the American people influence big politics through their representatives.

The functions of Congress are supposed to be:

- lawmaking for all Americans
- serving constituents as brokers between them and federal government
- representation of diverse interests — which is often impossible, because members can't be delegates for everyone
- oversight of the bureaucracy to follow up the laws it has enacted to ensure that they are being enforced and administered in the way Congress intended
- holding committee hearings and investigations, changing the size of an agency budget and cross-examining high-level presidential nominees to head major agencies (a formality, nothing serious)
- fostering public education
- resolving conflicts in American society (see "Interest groups" game)

DIFFERENCES BETWEEN THE HOUSE AND THE SENATE

House	Senate
435 members	100 members
Members chosen from local districts	Members chosen from entire state
Two-year term	Six-year term
Originally elected by voters	Originally (until 1913) elected by state legislatures
May impeach (indict) federal officials	May convict federal officials
Debate limited	Debate extended
Floor action controlled	Unanimous consent rules
Less prestige and less individual notice	More prestige and media attention
Originates bills for raising revenues	Power to advise the President on, and consent to, presidential appointments and treaties
Local or narrow leadership	National leadership

The major difference between the House and the Senate is that the House's rules and procedures are strict, while Senate rules are more broad and open to interpretation.

There's one thing they have in common — inertia.

Note: Members of the Senate serve for six years, with only one-third of the body up for reelection every second year. Thus, every other Senate term is not affected directly by a Presidential election and this gives Senators greater freedom to oppose presidential initiatives without as much concern about short-term constituent pressures. The Senators' independence can be a problem for the president even if they are of the same party.

The Congress has five main checks over the President's power:

1. to override a veto
2. to approve appointees to federal jobs
3. to approve treaties
4. impeachment
5. to stop funding executive department programs

Seniority (the length of continuous service on the record of a member of Congress or Senate) is the single most important factor in determining:

- who becomes Speaker of the House or President pro tempore of the Senate
- who is influential in floor debates
- who has an easier time getting his legislative measures adopted on the floor of Congress

Never mind about Representatives (especially when it comes to foreign affairs and national security) — they understand very little and can do practically nothing due to their two-year term. Your problem is the Senate (though you have to be involved in Congressional elections every two years, too.) Yes, the Senate is a problem because it shares executive powers with the President (confirmation of appointments and approval of treaty ratification). And if it comes to impeachment, the final decision is the Senate's.

The House originates the most important thing in the United States — tax legislation, but the Senate can amend any bill and the trick is — they do this toward the end of the session. And the worst problem on Capitol Hill is balancing the budget.

Unwritten Rules

- A Congressional session is nothing else but a waste of federal time and money — you don't need debates because Congressional staffers can do all the technical work and they can negotiate between themselves and balance positions. Senators and Congressmen don't even have to come to Washington — they can vote from their local offices. So these people can spend their time helping thousands of constituents, most of whom never saw their Senator alive.
- The President is dependent on Congressional cooperation to carry out the executive responsibilities of the Office because Congress has to authorize government programs, establish administrative agencies to implement the problems and funds to finance them.
- It's important if President belongs to the party with a majority in the House and Senate. But if your party loses the majority in Congress, you have to work out new political strategy yourself. And you know what? Go to the polls right away and ask voters why they supported the other party. What happened?
- The President's prestige (popular support or political capital) affects Congressional response to his politics.
- For most Senators, the Senate is a platform for Presidential election campaign. Senators who openly express presidential ambitions are better able to gain media exposure and to establish careers as spokespersons for large national constituencies.
- The first act of a newly elected Representative is to maneuver for election to the Senate. Why? First, they enjoy their position, power and money for six years non-stop. Second, there are only a hundred Senators and the publicity is much, much greater. But...Representatives have a much better chance to be re-elected.
- Congress rejects two thirds of President's proposals.

- Senators are always looking for a BBD (bigger, better deal) and often shift from one committee to another (a good choice is those dealing with taxes, budget, energy, commerce).
- Bills to benefit big business move smoothly. (Congress doesn't like the poor — they don't contribute; sorry). To gain majority support for big business legislation members have a special trick — log rolling, when factions combine efforts.
- Senators don't depend on the people — they depend on the media.
- If a certain Senator is blocking the President's proposal, appointment or plan, that means he wants to get the President's attention.
- When Senators want to bury issues without resolving them, they create committees.
- The Senate is a relatively small structure and personal relations between Senators are extremely important.
- Senators have no incentive to study the details of most pieces of legislation and their decision is simplified by quickly checking how key colleagues have voted or intend to vote.
- To have power a Senator has to object: much of the Senate work is done by unanimous consent and if you object you'll be approached for sure by some influential people including other Senators, Secretaries, President's aides or the President himself. They'll try to press, blackmail or buy you — and that means you've got a piece of the power pie.
- Senators avoid responsibility and their legitimate functions and roles, especially in economic policy.
- Congress doesn't like it when any government agency grows, but these people love the military because military contracts are very lucrative for Congressional districts.
- Senior Senators teach "newcomers" to vote against any reform which is a threat to their stability.
- A Senator has real influence on legislation only if he has professional staff in charge of the projects.
- Senators are afraid to vote against a defense budget increase because then they may be accused of a lack of patriotism (the Pentagon gives jobs in their states too).
- Republicans and Democrats are not really enemies, here, though both sides are always looking for a "traitor" or "insider" in the other camp.
- You must have "insiders" in the Senate yourself, because the other party could prepare secretly and then launch officially some investigation against you or the members of your Administration.
- A legislator does exactly what his voters want him to do — stealing federal money from other states and districts, because for him the most important thing is numbers — polls in his state showing how many people approve his activity. His donors watch these numbers too and estimate their investment and the necessity to support re-election.
- Every member of Congress has a so-called "split personality" — a "Hill style" while working on Capitol Hill and a "home style" while back in the state or district with the voters.
- A Senator makes a decision only after thinking about what it means in terms of the re-election money that will come to him or to his opponents. His voting decisions depend on his party membership, constituency pressures, state and regional loyalty ideology, interest groups' influence. His stubbornness comes from the fact that he doesn't want to be seen by his constituents as a "rubber stamp" for President's decisions, especially when the bill in question benefits a Senator's state. (And the hidden problem is — you want

to move fast, especially during the first year while your personal popularity is high — but for the Congress speed is not important).

- Sooner or later every member of Congress starts playing the "pork barrel" game. It's nothing else but a diversion of federal funds to projects and places not out of national need but to enhance a member's chances of re-election in his district (military projects, federal buildings, highways construction projects). So be ready for a "Christmas present" when these fellows add pork barrel amendments to appropriations bills you are about to sign. They often wait until late in each session to pass critical spending bills, which narrows your range of possible responses because a veto may not be feasible if Congress has adjourned and the funds needed to run the federal government are contained in the legislation.

- In Congress a small percentage of bills (about 500 out of 10,000) actually become law because many bills are introduced merely to get favorable press. The strategy is especially effective if the legislation is "tied" to the headlines of the day (mass murders, natural disasters, ethnic riots etc.).

- In the Senate it's easier for a minority to block the bill than for a majority to pass it: a 60-vote majority is needed to force a final vote on the bill, while only 41 votes are needed to continue debate and delay a vote.

- The minority can hold the majority responsible as the party in power for whatever legislation does or does not emerge from the Senate. But both parties prefer to be the party in power in the Senate — all Senate legislation begins in the committees, whose membership and chairmanship are controlled by the party in power. Besides, each chairman has power in terms of controlling the committee budgets and deciding which hearings will be held and which legislation he will allow to be released to the Senate floor for a vote. He can also "lock up the bill" in committee until it dies. Perfect!

A Few Congressional Run-ins with the Law

1904   Senator Joseph Burton of Kansas is convicted of bribery.

1924   Representative John Langley of Kentucky is convicted of violating the National Prohibition Act.

1931   Representative Harry Rowbottom of Indiana is convicted of accepting bribes.

1934   Representative George Foulkes of Michigan is convicted of conspiracy to assess postmasters for political contributions.

1946   Representative James Curley of Massachusetts is convicted of mail fraud and conspiracy.

1947   Representative Andrew May of Kentucky is convicted of conspiring to defraud the government and accepting bribes.

1948   Representative J. Parnell Thomas of New Jersey is convicted of conspiring to defraud the government, payroll padding and receiving kickbacks from salaries.

1954   Senate censures Senator Joseph McCarthy of Wisconsin for having acted "contrary to senatorial ethics" and for bringing the Senate "into dishonesty and disrepute."

1956   Representative Thomas Lane of Massachusetts is convicted of federal income tax evasion.

1969   On Chappaquiddick Island in Massachusetts on July 18, a car driven by Senator Ed Kennedy plunges off Dike Bridge into the water. While the Senator manages to extricate himself from the vehicle, his young secretary Mary Jo Kopechne, a passenger, is trapped and dies in the car.

1970   Representative John Dowdy of Texas is convicted of conspiracy, perjury and bribery.

1972   Representative Cornelius Gallagher of New Jersey pleads guilty to tax evasion.

1973   Representative Frank Brasco of New York is convicted of conspiracy to receive bribes. Representative Bertram Podell of New York pleads guilty to conspiracy, bribery and perjury.

1975   Representative Andrew Hinshaw of California is convicted of bribery and embezzlement.

1976   Elizabeth Ray avers that Representative Wayne Hays of Ohio put her on the payroll solely because she was his mistress. The Washington Post reveals a Justice Department investigation into influence buying by Tongsun Park, a South Korean businessman. Representative James Hastings of New York is convicted of mail fraud.

1977   Representative Richard Tonry of Louisiana is convicted of receiving illegal campaign contributions and obstruction of justice.

1978   Representative Charles Diggs of Michigan is convicted of mail fraud and perjury.

1980   Representative Michael Myers of Pennsylvania is convicted of bribery and conspiracy as part of the FBI's ABSCAM investigation. Senator Harrison Williams of New Jersey is convicted of bribery and conspiracy in ABSCAM. Representative Raymond Lederer of Pennsylvania is convicted of conspiracy and bribery in ABSCAM. Representative John Jenrette Jr. of South Carolina is convicted of bribery and conspiracy in ABSCAM Representative Frank Thompson of New Jersey is convicted of bribery in ABSCAM. Representative John Murphy of New York is convicted of bribery in ABSCAM. Representative Richard Kelly of Florida is convicted of bribery in ABSCAM. (ABSCAM was an FBI sting operation in which a mysterious Arab sheik Abdul bribed top US officials and inveigled them into illegal investment schemes.)

1983   Representative George Hansen of Idaho is convicted of filing false financial disclosure statements.

1987   Representative Barney Frank of Massachusetts, who had disclosed that he was a homosexual, was accused of hiring a former sex partner as a personal assistant.

1988   Representative Mario Biaggi of New York is convicted of obstructing justice, tax evasion, conspiracy, extortion and accepting bribes. Representative Pat Swindall of Georgia is convicted of perjury. 1989 Representative Donald Lukens of Ohio is convicted of contributing to the delinquency of a minor. Representative Jim Bates of California accused of sexually harassing women on his staff.

1990   Senator David Durenberg of Minnesota is charged with receiving illegal reimbursements for housing expenses and for backdating his purchase of a share in a condominium. The Senate formally denounces him in July 1990 and orders him to make restitution for his financial misconduct. The "Keating Five": As the trial of Arizona financier Charles Keating proceeds, it becomes known that five US Senators (Alan Cranston of California, Dennis DeConcini of Arizona, Donald Riegle of Michigan, John Glenn of Ohio and John McCain of Arizona) used their influence to limit the regulation of Keating's savings bank. (By 1987 McCain received about $112,000 in political contributions.) The Senate Ethics Committee issues a report reprimanding Senator Cranston for accepting more than $850,000 in contributions to voter-registration groups that he sponsored in return for intervening on Keating's behalf with bank regulators. The other four Senators are mildly reprimanded for their conduct.

1991   Representative Nick Mavroules of Massachusetts pleads guilty to bribery and tax evasion.

1993   Representative Larry Smith of Florida is convicted of income tax evasion and campaign-reporting violations. Representative Albert Bustamante of Texas is convicted of racketeering and accepting an illegal gratuity.

1994   Representative Carrol Hubbard of Kentucky pleads guilty to filing a false financial-disclosure statement.

1995   Representative Mel Reynolds of Illinois is convicted of having sex with a minor and obstructing justice.

2006   Representative Mark Foley of Florida resigns because of sex letters he e-mailed to a 16-year-old boy.

How to Control Congress

The President can propose legislation, but Congress is not required to pass any of the administration's bills. But you know already that Senators and Representatives need re-election more than anything else. So you can go with indirect influence through appeals to the public; this is a confrontation and direct challenge to Congressional authority. You can also enlist the support of interest groups or direct influence through favors and personal involvement in the legislative process. (Get public support for a proposal before it's discussed with the Congress.) And don't hesitate to start a national debate — you have enough media attention for that.

You also have an independent tool, presidential power in the form of an executive order. You can give favors directly to members of Congress or to influential people in their constituency, or the favor may be of benefit to the constituency itself:

- appointments with the President and other high-ranking officials
- federal grants to recipients in the constituency, government contracts with local companies, the deposit of federal funds in banks, grants to local government and educational institutions
- support of projects (military installations, research and administrative facilities, public works such as buildings, dams and navigational improvements to rivers and harbors, etc.)
- recommendations for the US district court judges, attorneys, marshals, etc.
- campaign assistance (cash contributions from the party's national committee, invitations to bill-signing ceremonies, White House parties or to accompany President on trips
- You can also use bargaining and arm-twisting (pressure and threats to lose the projects).

Tools

1. The Congressional Relations Office. Used for:

- intense lobbying to form Congressional coalitions if the opposition controls one or both houses
- intelligence gathering (of policy preferences — centralized headcounts reveal the voting intentions on a particular bill and constituency concerns of individual members)
- representation
- creating "inner coalitions"
- coordination of executive branch legislative activity (monitoring and tracking bills, controlling departments' staff appointments, collaborating with departments' liaison offices)

Attention! Senators and Congressmen have to trust your people, who must keep their mouths shut or there will be no business. Anyway, watch these people — Senators can call one of your assistants and if they hear "no," they will try to reach somebody else until they get: "Yes, the President will see you." Don't let this happen — if it's "no," it has to be everybody's "no." And there has to be no difference between personal views of your adviser and your official views.

2. Congressional Relations personnel of various executive Departments are a conduit. Talk to the Secretaries and explain to them that they have to give the Director of Congressional Relations their best people.

3. The White House interest groups liaison staff (Office of Public Liaison).

4. Veto. Threatened with a veto, Senators often seek compromise.

Congress has its ways to undermine your vetoes or threats of vetoes. Because you can't veto parts of a bill, they load up major legislation with amendments on a completely different subject ("riders") that they know the President must accept. (Presidents who vetoed the most bills: Franklin Roosevelt - 635, Harry Truman - 250, Dwight Eisenhower - 181, Ronald Reagan - 78, Gerald Ford - 66).

5. Executive agreement. It permits the President to enter into open or secret agreements with a foreign government without any advice or consent of the Senate. There are two categories of executive agreements:

- Presidential agreements made solely on the basis of the constitutional authority of the President and under his sole power to faithfully execute the laws (or under his diplomatic or Commander-in-Chief powers). President needs to report secret agreement to the Foreign Relations Committees of the two houses no later than 60 days after such agreement has entered into force. Congress has no authority to disapprove it.
- Congressional-executive agreements, which cover all international agreements entered into under the combined authority of the President and Congress.

Finally, this is what you can do with a bill:

- sign the bill (the bill becomes a law)
- do nothing (the bill becomes a law in ten days)
- veto the bill (the bill does not become a law)
- pocket veto the bill (hold the bill until Congress is no longer in session, and the bill does not become a law)

THE "IRON TRIANGLE," A SUB-GOVERNMENT MAFIA

The "Iron Triangle," an anti-presidential control system, is a strong alliance among three groups — federal agencies, interest groups and Congressional committees and subcommittees, where each member has a mutually beneficial relationship with the other two and all members work together to pursue common goals. (This strong connection between federal agencies and the Congress members is especially dangerous for the President in a political sense — it's too hard to influence them). Agency careerists, interest groups lobbyists and members of Congress and their staffers with close personal mafia-like relationships discuss policy issues (proposed legislation, budget, personal concerns) and then agree on preferred outcomes on the basis of the mafia principle of exchanging favors. Bureaucrats want unlimited funding and legislation granting them maximum authority and discretion. In return, members of Congress want preferential treatment for their constituencies, technical assistance for their staff, and often help in drafting legislation. Interest groups' lobbyists want members of Congress to pass and fund programs that benefit groups and to help group members be appointed to and confirmed for key government jobs. In return, Congress wants financial and political help for their campaigns. Interest groups want a strong say in federal agencies' decisions, including the writing of regulations, ideally through a formal advisory system that would give the interest group either formal or informal veto power over such decisions. In return, federal agencies want the political support of interest groups, including positive congressional testimony and lobbying for additional funds for the agency.

Interest Groups

There are 80,000 lobbyists in Washington, DC (maybe more, by the time this Handbook lands on your desk).

The National Rifle Association has a full-time Washington, DC staff of 300 lobbyists.

Congress can't live without interest groups, interest groups can't live without Congress. They are glued together and you must know the hidden mechanism of their relations if you want to manage the US Congress properly. An interest group is any organized group whose members share common objectives. These groups actively attempt to influence government policy makers, mostly Senators and Representatives, through direct and indirect strategies, including the marshalling of public opinion, lobbying and electioneering.

Lobbyists, like professional spies, are always looking for intelligence information on everybody in Washington, DC from personal contacts, government memos, press releases, public information programs, technical bulletins and regulations. For them the most important thing is to obtain information before it's officially released — it allows their customers, i.e. corporations, to develop PR campaigns to offset possible adverse reaction to their goals. Let's have a closer look at their strategies.

I. Direct Strategies

Lobbying

The main activity of lobbying is private meetings, in which lobbyists make known to Congressmen the lobbyists' client interests, and possibly offer inducements for cooperating. Lobbyists furnish needed information Congressmen could not hope to obtain on their own. It's to the lobbyist's advantage to provide accurate information so that the policy maker will rely on him in the future.

Lobbying includes: testifying before congressional committees for or against proposed legislation; testifying before executive rule-making agencies, such as the Federal Trade Commission, for or against proposed rules; assisting legislators or bureaucrats in drafting legislation of prospective regulations (lobbyists often can furnish legal advice on the specific details of legislation); inviting legislators to social occasions such as cocktail parties or boating expeditions; providing political information to legislators (lobbyists often have better information than the party leadership about how other legislators are going to vote). In this case, the political information they furnish may be a key to legislative success).

The "Ratings" Game

The over-all behavior of legislators can be influenced through their rating systems.

Each year the interest group selects those votes on legislation that it feels are most important to the organization's goals. Legislators are given a score based on the percentage of times that he or she voted with the interest group (from 0 to 100%)

Campaign Assistance

A strong side of interest groups is that they are able to provide workers for political campaigns, including precinct workers to get out the vote, volunteers to put up posters and pass out literature. In states where membership in certain interest groups is large, candidates look for the groups' endorsement in the campaign.

Endorsements are important because an interest groups usually publicizes its choices in its membership publication and because the candidate can use the endorsement in his campaign literature. Making no endorsement can be perceived as disapproval of the candidate.

II. Indirect Strategies

By working through third parties — which may be constituents, the general public or other groups, the interest groups can try to influence government policy. Indirect techniques mask the interest group's own activities and make the effort appear to be spontaneous. Furthermore, legislators are usually more impressed by contacts from the constituents than from an interest group's lobbyist.

Generating Public Pressure

Interest groups try to produce a "groundswell" of public pressure to influence the government. Such efforts may include advertisements in national magazines and newspapers, mass mailings, television publicity and demonstrations. They may commission polls to find out what the public sentiments are and then publicize the results. The goal of this activity is to convince policy makers that public opinion wholly supports the group's position. Some corporations and interest groups use such a method as climate control — it calls for public relations efforts that are aimed at improving the public image of the industry or group and not necessarily related to any specific political issue. Contributions by corporations and groups in support of public TV and commercials extolling the virtues of corporate research are examples of climate control. By building a reservoir of favorable public opinion, groups believe it's less likely that their legislative goals will be met with opposition by the public.

Constituents as Lobbyists

A very effective method is to use constituents to lobby for the group's goals. In the "shotgun" approach, the interest group tries to mobilize large numbers of constituents to write or phone Congressmen or the President. This method is only effective on Capitol Hill when there is an extraordinary number of responses, because legislators know that the voters did not initiate the communication on their own. A more influential variation of this technique uses only important constituents (mostly local big business).

Building Alliances

Interest group forms alliance with other group concerned about the same legislation. The advantages of an alliance are that it looks as if larger public interests are at stake, and it hides the specific interests of the individual groups involved. It's also a device for keeping like-minded groups from duplicating one another's lobbying efforts.

One of the strongest iron triangles is a so-called "military-industrial complex" — its members include the Department of Defense, weapons contractors and related firms and congressional armed services committees. Some popular interest groups include: American Bar Association, American Farm Bureau Federation, American Welfare Association, Fund for Constitutional Government, National Association of Community Action Agencies, National Rifle Association, National Organization of Women.

Chapter 4. Foreign Policy

A king has to do three jobs: persuade the rich to help the poor; persuade the best woman to marry him; and persuade other kings to fight each other instead of fighting him.

Successful foreign policy needs electoral and financial support. This comes naturally when you demonstrate the permanent presence of external threats like the proliferation of weapons of mass destruction (WMD) or international terrorism, to keep the nation alert and in line.

Foreign policy serves to help you with domestic problems which often "push" you to make hard international decisions. It's not about democracy in Iraq — it's about your reelection.

You have to decide if you want to design and execute foreign policy all by yourself, even not telling Secretary of State about your confidential talks, negotiations or special operations. There's one more strong point: you also have considerable advantages over Congress in foreign policy making. Know why?

First, as head of foreign policy bureaucracy, the diplomatic corps, the intelligence agencies and the military, you control information that is vital to the foreign policy making; second you, unlike Congress, can work with speed and secrecy and this is essential if you have to handle international crisis which threatens national security. Third, since it is your responsibility to communicate with foreign governments through treaty negotiations and diplomatic channels, you can most easily formulate policy that is consistent with negotiating positions and official statements. Fourth, as the executor of foreign policy, Commander in Chief of the armed forces and appointer of diplomatic personnel, you are in the best position to judge the capacity of the government to carry out a given foreign policy initiative.

Fifth, you are elected by a national constituency and you can focus on international problems that affect the entire nation.

Getting a Good Start

Make it clear to foreign leaders right away whether you are or you are not going to follow the previous President's foreign policy (after consultations with big business). If you are not going to follow it, design a doctrine of your own (it's a strategy that is the recognized approach or policy of the US government).

National security is your top priority and is the "king's job" because actually you have no domestic political obstacles to your foreign policy (unless it's a question of war), so you are a chief decision maker there. (The CIA Director has to be excluded from this process — you don't need him. Besides, the CIA even today, no matter how hard I tried to educate the Agency, remains the worst of the worst and is not to be reformed — it has to be abolished. We have to transfer political intelligence functions to Pentagon. National security is designed to protect the United States and the vital interests, i.e., investments, of big business and to promote American values in a world of rivals, and the CIA, through all 60 years of its history, has proved to be absolutely unsuitable for the job.)

Any country has to be involved in the sphere of our strategic interests if it has a strategic geographic position, significant sources of raw materials, a well-developed transportation system, or could be used as a military base.

The strategic policy of any country rotates around the USA, and if not — that means a certain President is waiting for greater incentives to come on board.

Against target countries, don't hesitate to use the strategies of pre-emptive war, post-war (post-crisis) reconstruction, and nation building (which means erasing national identity and supplanting it by liberal values).

With China's growth and Russia's rebirth, the Cold War is back with a vengeance, so we are back to secret deals based on spheres of influence — but that's a temporary strategy.

Allow no independence for the State Department (and its Secretary) — it's nothing but a "mail box" for your decisions. It has no mission and its duty is to monitor the world (people call it the "Department of Bad News"). Make it clear to the Secretary of State that he/she is not to respond to events and not to influence any politician abroad — the State Department has to follow White House instructions only: don't make unnecessary enemies and don't push any initiatives until you are further instructed! Don't send pointless cables to the White

House Situation Room. Every time you brief the press — ask my White House staff what to say. Meet foreign leaders to make my message clear — nothing, absolutely nothing else!

Besides, the State Department cannot be taken seriously as it has no natural domestic constituency like, say, Department of Defense, which can call on defense contractors for support. It has negative constituents instead — people who oppose US foreign policy. Congress has no respect for it and looks upon it as an advocate of unpopular and costly foreign involvement. The best thing to do is to leave ceremonial functions to the Secretary of State, sending the person overseas mostly to VIP funerals.

(President George W. Bush is doing absolutely the right thing by sending his Secretary of State Condoleezza Rice on endless and countless visits abroad. If Dr. Rice had read these pages, she would have understood that the President keeps her far away from the White House because he does not need her and is angry — most probably because of her own presidential ambitions. He'd rather see his brother inheriting the Oval Office.)

After Madeleine Albright, Clinton's Secretary of State, elected international criminal Kofi Annan to be UN Secretary General, a President has no choice but to stay far away from the State Dept. If you still hesitate, read this pearl of foreign policy making: "Kofi Annan... he seemed born for leadership. Annan ... clearly the most qualified person. No one, from any continent was more knowledgeable or better prepared" (M. Albright, *Madam Secretary*, 2003).

A few words about your National Security Council staff. You take a risk by using them for secret operations because in such cases you don't have congressional and public support. If the operation is exposed, you face huge political problems. So before you start, do some strategic planning on future consequences and design counter-measures.

RELYING ON OTHERS TO ACHIEVE YOUR GOALS

You can't always do what you want without help — you are dependent on other world leaders, Congressional positions and international public opinion. Ask the Senate to help you sometimes — believe me, they'll be happy and proud to do so.

You could save a lot of federal money if you liquidate the NSC policy planning staff — they sell you "hot air" and they call it a "long-term perspective." But yes, you need the help of the "US Intelligence Community" (National Security Agency, Defense Intelligence Agency, Department of Energy, Department of

Treasury), — excluding the CIA and the Department of State Bureau of Intelligence and Research, another vendor of "hot air."

Some of the techniques are to:

- Create super-profitable conditions for big business by political penetration worldwide. Big money men start investing abroad when they find a safe environment — law and order. The more they invest the more political power they get.
- Use big investors to ruin other national economies and governments by withdrawing finances when the economic situation is worsening. As soon as the country opens its financial markets, it increases its dependence on global economic processes that it cannot control; and a financial crisis can easily be staged. Conversely, other countries' access to the US markets is a powerful economic and political tool.
- Make the US markets the most attractive for investors by provoking unstable situations in other countries and regions.
- Send troops or work through military intelligence (not the CIA) to wherever you perceive a threat to the US investments.
- Use pressure everywhere — strategic nuclear missiles are still the most powerful blackmail tool. Remember, if you are dealing with Russia or China, they will look not only for agreement, but for advantages.
- Use "personal diplomacy" — phone calls to foreign leaders (every planned phone call has to go through the National Security Advisor and be well prepared, like a serious negotiation). Most important are phone calls to our allies — NATO members. Don't forget to wish happy birthday to the leaders in person!

Don't hesitate to use summits as a tool, because:

1. If you meet a foreign leader in person, you can reduce tensions and clarify national interests.
2. Personal relationship may lead to improved relations between nations.
3. Summits allow you to focus national attention on specific issues.
4. Presidents engaging in personal diplomacy are much more capable than career diplomatic bureaucrats of understanding the domestic policy consequences of diplomatic actions.
5. Summit negotiations can yield quick results, since discussions are between leaders with the power of decision rather than between representatives who must receive instructions, make reports and wait for new proposals.
6. Diplomatic impasses may be overcome at summits by shifts in policy that only top leaders are empowered to make.
7. If presidents desire an international forum for their diplomatic policies, a summit meeting can provide one.
8. Successful summits can enhance the image of the President and the United States.

And bear these in mind:

- If you're ready to fight for national interests, forget about human rights — you can always blame infractions on the other side.
- Isolation is the greatest enemy to information.
- There's no sense in applying sanctions if big business isn't interested.
- Economic and hence, political progress for any country affects the USA through economic competition that threatens the market and jobs.
- Any initiative is risky if it's about unstable region, but you lose popularity fast if you are perceived as indecisive or weak in foreign policy.
- Any trip abroad has to convey a strong message.
- Direct military intrusion indicates weakness in your foreign policy. If it's inescapable, involve as many allies as you can.
- Don't touch our military bases abroad!
- Big debts open markets. No matter what, open national markets world-wide for American big business and remember — the markets, not Presidents, rule the world.
- Tie your allies to international economic projects and make them pay most of the expenses.
- Never talk about money in public — talk about democracy, human rights, liberal values and disarmament — people like it.
- Move forward — transform Americans' national and patriotic feelings into nationalistic ones (follow the French model) to get total support of your policy (see "Mind Control").
- Don't pay too much attention to the CIA — all they have to do is to support you with appropriate information to justify your strategic political decisions — and nothing else.
- Ignore the UN — Secretary General has no real power, but you can take advantage of such a thing as the UN peace-keeping if it corresponds with your interests — the US economic costs could be minimized. Besides, UN peacekeeping can promote a spirit of international accountability in solving a certain regional problem. Don't forget to explain your strategy to the Congress — they don't like the UN either. On the other hand, you have to manage an international crisis, if it threatens our national interests (start with strategic planning, check national security system for the adequate response, use propaganda to get domestic and international support, consult with big business and allies, start crisis negotiations if possible, use diplomacy (see below) and force or threat of force).
- To reach global leadership you must have enough resources, national support and a well-calculated strategy (see also "Strategic planning"). As you already know, the US budget is financed by foreign lending. When the dollar goes down in foreign exchange markets, it's supported by foreign central banks and you're OK as long as Japan, Saudi Arabia and Germany have an interest in propping up the American economy and do not raise the price for financing America's debt. The worst situation would be to lose support both at home and abroad.

The unipolar moment is already over, but it was fun while it lasted. The US was in a unique position of total world domination for a brief period, following the geopolitical shifts of the 20th century. From a pre-World War I multi-polar world to the bi-polar Cold War era, we now see the emergence of a different multi-polar scenario, with Europe, Russia and China as significant political, economic and military powers and the USA as a superpower. That will also be a brief hiatus, as any day now, or maybe yesterday, China will be recognized as top dog.

Securing World Domination

Securing the top position requires —

- economic domination
- military power — pre-emptive war or blackmail by war (seeking domination requires an inevitable increase in the military budget)
- a cultural and media invasion
- special operations to influence or neutralize leaders with negative attitude

To keep America on top, we would have to prevent cooperation and coalitions between China and Africa; Shi'ia and Sunni Muslims; Russia, Germany, and France; and Venezuela, Cuba and the other Latin American toddlers (oops, too late). Their trade agreements and alliances will change the geopolitical situation.

The US seems to have been responding to events rather than anticipating them, which means that until now it has had no global international plan. Watch where the "vectors of force" are directed and you'll break their strategic plans.

Don't listen to experts — crude oil world resources will be finished by the middle of the century. Get total control over the world oil market by force (Iraq and Iran) and take care of the weapons market — knock out Russia and restrain China (restrict their military research activity — Chinese nuclear and other WMD had better be our top priority in the next 20 years).

In most important world regions keep the balance by supporting the country which follows the leader.

In Europe — support Britain to balance Germany. You rule Europe if you rule the Persian Gulf. You rule the world if you rule Europe, and that's why you have to keep NATO by all means to block the military independence of Europe (Germany). And watch Russia — it's still highly militarized and holds Europe a hostage. In East Asia — support Japan, Russia and Taiwan to balance China. In South Asia support Pakistan to balance India. In Latin America — support Argentina to balance Brazil.

The US has to create and support the most attractive (stable and profitable) image for foreign investors against the background of some other countries and regimes. A credible world disorder strategy would seem appropriate for that (and once you get Iraq's oil and Iran's natural gas, establish a sufficiently stable environment there for American big business).

Foreign Policy Secret— The "Democracy Trick"

It's all about natural resources and raw materials.

General scheme:
    (a) Choose the target country.
    (b) Start war or push the local opposition to launch a coup.
    (c) Bring in "liberal values."
    (d) Help to move oil and gas into private hands.
    (e) Help to create an "open economy" and "open market."
    (f) Become the only (the biggest) customer and stockholder.

US National Security Strategy

The United States National Security Council (2007):
    Chair - President George W. Bush

Regular attendees:
    Vice President Richard Cheney
    Secretary of State Condoleezza Rice
    Secretary of Treasury Henry M. Paulson, Jr.
    Secretary of Defence Robert Gates
    Stephen Hadley, Assistant to the President for National Security Affairs
    Michael McConnell, Director of National Intelligence - Intelligence Advisor
    General Peter Pace, Chairman of the Joint Chiefs of Staff - Military Advisor

The first thing you'll notice about our 21st century national security strategy document is that it seems to have been prepared in a rush, is full of errors, and is misleading not only to the authors and the nation but to our allies and friends, too. On the whole it is a regular bureaucratic mess. Here are some excerpts, with my analysis.

> The United States possesses unprecedented strength and influence in the world. We have finite political, economic and military resources to meet our global priorities.

Wrong: we have no political leadership, no political capital (public support), no political ideas to move America forward into the 21st century. We don't have "unprecedented influence," political or otherwise, in the world. Zero.

> The US national security strategy will be based on a distinctly American internationalism that reflects the union of our values and our national interests.

Wrong: American internationalism does not exist. Nobody shares our national interests.

> Our strategic priority — combating global terror. Thousands of trained terrorists remain at large with cells in North America, South America, Europe, Africa, the Middle East and across Asia. Our priority will be first to disrupt and destroy terrorist organizations of global reach and attack their leadership; command, control and communications; material support, and finances. This will have a disabling effect upon the terrorists' ability to plan and operate. The war on terrorism is not a clash of civilizations. It does, however, reveal the clash inside the civilization, the battle for the future of

the Muslim world. This is a struggle of ideas and this is an area where the United States must excel.

Wrong: "Thousands of terrorists" simply do not exist. The world of active terror is small. Yes, there are a lot of people who talk, send letters and threaten governments. But those who are ready for action are very few. You can't attack the terrorist organizations' leadership because the CIA is dead and they have no idea how to recruit and manage informants among Muslims. And — if the war on terrorism is a "struggle of ideas," what are 150,000 American soldiers are doing in Iraq?

> 1. [Global terrorism] will be fought over an extended period of time.

Wrong. I have a small question for the Secretary of Treasury — have you ever read the National Security Strategy you signed? If you have, tell me; and then tell me how you calculate the money needed to fight terrorism far into the indefinite future?

> 2. The United States has long maintained the option of preemptive actions to counter a sufficient threat to our national security. The greater the threat, the greater the risk of inaction — and the more compelling the case for taking anticipatory action to defend ourselves, even if uncertainty remains as to time and place of the enemy's attack. To forestall or prevent such hostile acts by our adversaries, the United States will, if necessary, act preemptively. To support preemptive options we will:
>
> - build better, more integrated intelligence capabilities to provide timely, accurate information on threats whenever they may emerge.
>
> - continue to transform our military forces to ensure our ability to conduct rapid and precise operations to achieve decisive victory.

Wrong: The NSC supports preemptive military strikes, but without adequate intelligence we could end up in total international isolation and our strikes will go nowhere. You can't "build better, more integrated intelligence" because the CIA does not actually exist.

> 3. To achieve these [national security] goals the United States will transform America's national security institutions to meet the challenges and opportunities of the twenty first century.

Wrong: This is extraordinary. Listen, you can't transform intelligence bureaucrats into anything else. You just can't.

> 4. Intelligence — and how we use it — is our first line of defense against terrorists. Initiatives in this area will include:
>
> - strengthening the authority of the Director of Central Intelligence (Director of National Intelligence, since April 2005) to lead the development and actions of the nation's foreign intelligence capabilities

- establishing a new framework for intelligence warning that provides seamless and integrated warning across the spectrum of threats facing the nation and our allies

- continuing to develop new methods of collecting information to sustain our intelligence advantage

- investing in future capabilities while working to protect them through a more vigorous effort to prevent the compromise of intelligence capabilities

- collecting intelligence against the terrorist danger across the government with all-source analysis

5. Our response [to a threat of WMD] must take full advantage of increased emphasis on intelligence collection and analysis.

Wrong: You can't "develop new methods of collecting information" because they do not exist at all. You don't have "all-source analysis" because you don't have all-source analysts.

6. Centered on a new Department of Homeland Security and including a new unified military command and a fundamental reordering of the FBI, our comprehensive plan to secure the homeland encompasses every level of government and the cooperation of the public and private sector.

Wrong: I can tell you what the problem is. The September 11 attack, whoever did it, how, and why, was a severe challenge and, unfortunately, the President responded to it by a purely bureaucratic counter-challenge which was to centralize the national security agencies. The problem is — you have no experts, your people have no idea of a professional approach to the job and you have united one "nothing" with another "nothing." The idea of total domestic control is attractive to a President who wants to dominate the world, but he has to build up a professional basis for it.

7. We are attentive to the possible renewal of old patterns of great power competition. Several potential great powers are now in the midst of internal transition — most importantly Russia, India and China. In all these cases, recent developments have encouraged our hope that a truly global consensus about basic principles is slowly taking shape. With Russia we are already building a new strategic relationship based on a central reality of the twenty-first century: the United States and Russia are no longer strategic adversaries. We [United States and India] have a common interest in the free flow of commerce, including through the vital sea lines of the Indian Ocean. We share an interest in fighting terrorism and in creating a strategically stable Asia. We start with a view [too late!] of India as a growing world power with which we have common strategic interest. We welcome the emergence of a strong, peaceful and prosperous China. Yet...in pursuing advanced military capabilities that can threaten its neighbors in Asia-Pacific region, China is following an outdated path that, in the end, will hamper its own pursuit of national greatness.

Wrong: I don't feel comfortable explaining the ABCs of foreign policy to the National Security Council, but it seems I have no choice.

First, Russia and China don't have to "renew old patterns of great power competition" because for the last 40 years they never changed their superpower status. The Soviet Union collapsed, but Russia kept its nuclear weapons.

Second, there will be no global consensus between the United States, Russia and China because they all were, are and will be global powers. All are active worldwide, economically at least, and their economies depend on that.

Third, the United States and Russia were not, are not and will not be building a strategic relationship. This is what I would call a strategic lie on both sides.

Fourth, it's good that you "start with a view of India as a growing world power with which we have a common strategic interest," but you are a little bit late — the Russians have been doing the tango with India at least for forty years already.

Fifth, and not least, we do not welcome a "strong and prosperous China."

Presidential Foreign Policy Doctrines

Monroe Doctrine: European powers must keep their hands off the Western Hemisphere.

Theodore Roosevelt Doctrine: The United States will police chronic wrong-doing or impotence.

Truman Doctrine: To support free people resisting subjugation from internal or outside groups.

Eisenhower Doctrine: To intervene in the Middle East against Communist attacks.

Nixon Doctrine: To help allies while fostering their reduced reliance on troops.

Carter Doctrine: To keep the Persian Gulf free of foreign control.

Reagan Doctrine: To support anti-Communist insurgencies anywhere.

Managing through Diplomacy

Diplomacy serves to maintain smooth relations between states and resolve disputes. The goal of American diplomacy is to further our interests worldwide, safeguard our independence and security and to seek maximum national advantage without using force and preferably without causing resentment.

Actually, diplomacy is just a set of negotiating techniques by which we carry out the foreign policy. The United States has diplomatic relations with 155 countries, where Ambassadors are the personal representatives of the President as well as representatives of the Department of State. Each Ambassador heads a "country team" which includes a deputy chief of mission, heads of political, economic, consular and administrative sections; defense, agricultural and foreign commercial service attaches; a public affairs office; and, as needed, representatives of other agencies. As I've recommended above, the State Department should be removed from foreign policy making and re-positioned as a service station or a "mail box" for your decisions. It's a tough job, but don't you worry — you have a perfect tool which is called diplomatic appointment (a career diplomat is always a career bureaucrat).

Of course, the State Department wants to promote its own career senior foreign service officers to the ambassadors' positions. They say they have experience, but you don't need them once you've got this handbook for your people. Besides, their careers are not dependent on you but on a self-run promotion system, and because many regard foreign policy as an endeavor that should not be subject to partisan politics, foreign service officers have a greater reputation for resisting your policies than your people — political appointees. Trust me, the Senate will be on your side if you start a large-scale substitution.

One more thing. For specific diplomatic missions you can use your personal emissaries who are not subject to Senate confirmation. It allows you to transfer your proposals directly into negotiations without having to go through the State Department, and to have absolutely independent source of information. Usually, when presidents of states more or less equal in strength negotiate, they feel free to do whatever they feel is right. With the American President the situation must be different — your partners may disagree with you but they can't ignore any of your statements.

For four years you have to balance and bargain inside a triangle which includes big business, Congress and foreign leaders. Why big business? Because it will help you with economic problems caused by trends in the world economy.

That's not the end of your problems — you have to balance between something else. Modern diplomacy is a very complicated business — there's actually little privacy and secrecy left because our beloved media penetrates everywhere. Your plans and initiatives are being published worldwide right before you meet your partner and then what? What are you going to do? Change your whole strategy? Your partner will draw conclusions and won't say a word out of respect for the US President. Good thing you can manipulate the media to some extent and have a chance to form a favorable international opinion. More important, you can speak to other leaders through the media rather than through private negotiations — everywhere worldwide they read every word of the White House statements. And if you think there are two of you in the Oval Office — you and your negotiating partner — that's a mistake. There are four: you, your partner, the media and public opinion.

Congress is a smaller problem for your diplomacy. Here you have advantages in treaty making: first, you decide what treaties to negotiate, second you choose negotiators, third, you develop the negotiating strategy, fourth, you submit completed draft treaties for the Senate approval. And you, not the Senate (as Americans think), have the final power of ratification — once the Senate has approved the treaty, it does not become a law until you ratify it. If you decide to ratify a treaty the Senate has approved, an exchange of ratifications occur between the signatories. Then the treaty is promulgated (officially proclaimed to be a law) by you. At any time you can stop the treaty-making process, and after a treaty is ratified, you have the authority to terminate it without Senate consent. Once the US negotiators have agreed upon the terms of a treaty with a foreign government, you must decide whether to submit the draft to the Senate for consideration. If it appears that the Senate opposition to a treaty will make approval unlikely, you may decide to withdraw the treaty to avoid a visible political defeat.

If you decide to submit a treaty to the Senate for consideration, the Constitution requires that a two-thirds majority of Senators vote in favor of the treaty for it to be approved. The problem is, the Senate may attach amendments to a treaty that require you to re-negotiate its terms with other signatories before the Senate grants its approval, but you may decide not to re-negotiate.

Yes, the Senate has to approve the treaty, but you can avoid the battle on Capitol Hill by signing executive agreements with foreign governments (like trade agreements, defense pacts, arms control agreements). They don't require approval and give you greater flexibility in foreign policy. And you have one more important tool — an executive order that has the force of law without being approved by Congress. Most executive orders pertain to government officials and agencies, but they also may implement legislative statutes or help reinforce Constitution or treaties.

Diplomatic Rules for the US Diplomat-In-Chief

- Use secret visits (send the National Security Advisor) if the international problem is complex and important — in this way you don't depend on media and public opinion. Afterwards you can talk, if it was a success.
- If presidents like to drink with each other, they are ready to deal with each other.
- Avoid negotiating major issues at the end of the day when your energy is low.
- Negotiate smart, watch your initiatives. The more you tell about your position, the less your partner will tell you about himself, and the higher price you'll

pay. Diplomacy is all about money and the essence of any negotiations is the price range.

- Any information should be exchanged as a part of a compromise and not merely given away.
- Always talk less than necessary.
- No negative emotions — strong emotions indicate weak nerves.
- You'd better postpone negotiations than allow them to break down.
- Fix all questions and don't be in a rush to answer any of them.
- The slower you talk, the more confident you are.
- Never ask straight questions.
- It's important to know what questions and when you have to ask. Start with an "invitation" question that does not need a definite answer but opens up the discussion, like: "No matter what reporters say, we'll start negotiating for arms control." Proceed with "intelligence gathering" questions, like: "Are you going to abide by our last agreement on the withdrawal of military forces or do we have other options?" Go to "expertise" questions, like: "It's 5000 soldiers, right?"

There's a difference between expertise and straight questions — straight question are like: "Will you sign the treaty?" and these have to be avoided because you'll get no straight answer right away. Finish with a closing question, like: "I think that's what we intend to sign? Next time we can start from here."

Or you can press your partner: "Let's not lose this last opportunity, eh?"

Negotiation No-Nos

- Don't be confused if your partner threatens you — that means he needs your cooperation. Don't enter into negotiation right away with high demands.
- Don't touch the toughest issues first. Don't assume — that's a sign of weakness.
- Don't hesitate to pause or take a break.
- Explain your negative attitude in a smart way: give half the information and continue, depending on your partner's reaction. If you can't accept his proposal, tell him that the experts may look into it again and come to agreement. If your partner is not a complete idiot he'll understand his proposal is unacceptable (because the experts have already done all they could). But if he is an idiot, he'll agree to "kill" his proposals by passing them to the experts.
- You start to lose momentum if you start to defend yourself.
- Never say "no" to your partner's ideas — rather, pack them up in one package with your proposals.
- Stop (postpone) negotiations the moment you start to lose or you could end up in a total failure and that could be used by opposition back home.
- If you bring ideology — try to win. If you bring national interests, try to find compromise. Be flexible — that's a sign of strength, not weakness.
- Don't make aggressive statements for the media, no matter what.
- Respect is half a victory, but you usually win when your partner is scared. Avoid open confrontation and respond to personal attacks with humor.
- Watch the military experts — they are always ready to "push" you. No arms agreement can win ratification without backing from Joint Chiefs, because Congress needs and trusts their expertise, and their disapproval is a strong tool against you in case you ignore their advice. So, think three times before you appoint Joint Chiefs.

- Take negotiations on the trade deficit very seriously — they often take you nowhere and have zero results as your partner wants you to change your attitude to him completely as well as your international economic policy, while you expect the same favor from him. You can influence one partner but you can't very easily influence the international system.
- After you come back home do some positive advertising through the media — in such a way you influence other presidents and future negotiations. If the negotiations resulted in a treaty, "sell" it to the Senate for approval.

NEGOTIATIONS PROCEDURE

1. Preparation

- Write a plan.
- Define your objectives.
- Identify issues that are open to compromise and those that are not.
- Conduct research for information to support your objectives and have information to undermine your partner's position; think what information is available to your partner (State and Defense Departments will help you with that; not the CIA).
- Find out how your partner negotiates with other leaders (he might have a "rabbit in a hat" for you).
- Consult with members of a previous negotiating team about his style, strong and weak points.
- Check the current balance of power. Attention: if you start multilateral negotiation you have to know what are the conflicts or allegiances between other partners. If they are divided into groups, identify who has the power to make a decision on behalf of a group.
- Use game theory if you are intending to cooperate. Game theory is a theoretical analysis of the decision-making process taken by two or more players who are in conflict. You must actually estimate any possible strategies of the players who have to make decisions without knowledge of what other players are planning. Each player's strategy, once undertaken, will affect the others. Game theory is often illustrated by the "prisoners dilemma" paradigm. It supposes that two men have been arrested on a suspicion of committing a crime together and are being held in separate cells. There is not enough evidence to prosecute unless one confesses and implicates the other. Both of them know this but cannot talk to each other. The dilemma is that the best outcome, not being convicted, is only available if they each trust the other not to implicate him. If X decides to trust Y, but Y fears X may not be trustworthy, Y may confess to get a lesser sentence; X then gets a worse one. The best solution to this dilemma is for both to cooperate, to minimize the worst that can happen, rather than trying for the outcome that is maximum. This is called the minimax strategy and it's classified as being the most probable outcome.

2. Conducting negotiations

First of all, you have to decide whether you want to speak first or to respond to your partner's proposal. There's an advantage in letting your partner make the opening proposal as it might be much more beneficial for you than you suspect. Then:

(a) Put forward a proposal (with as little emotion as possible). You have to make your initial offer-demand high and compromise from that point onward. Your partner will understand perfectly well it's too much, so make your initial demand greater than you expect to receive, and offer less than you are expected to give. (For the same reason feel free to reject the first proposal received.) While talking further, leave yourself room for maneuvering, presenting your proposals, and don't try to pin down your partner to a fixed position too soon, because he needs room to maneuver, too. Make a final offer when the atmosphere is most cooperative.

(b) Respond to proposals in a smart way (again, no emotions). Capture any similarities on both sides. Don't hesitate to make conditional counter-offers: "If you do this, we'll do that." Cut the unexpected introduction of new issues and follow strictly a concise step-by-step agenda. Probe your partner's attitudes: "What would you say if we both lower our demands?" but indicate that every concession you make is a major loss to you. Ask as many questions as you want — the more information you have, the more you control negotiation. To think over and re-design your strategy, ask for a break as many times as it's acceptable. Summarize your partner's proposals.

(c) Move towards a bargain. You must know perfectly well the response to each of your points before you open your mouth. If your aides can't help you, you have the wrong aides and you even might be a wrong president. Offer the lowest price first, as you may not need to go any further. Negotiate a "package," don't concentrate on one demand and link other, smaller demands to it. While making a final offer look at the other party and check the body language (see below), your team members must confirm by body language that this is your final offer. It's OK to press the partner by emphasizing the need to reach agreement, like: "We know our nations are waiting to see the treaty signed." (If your partner looks at his watch, it means he wants to end the talk.) If you see you are approaching a dead end, ask your partner to talk off the record, in private, but if you talk in private, you have to keep your word no matter what.

Now, sometimes negotiations (as in the Israel-Palestine case) run into serious problems and breakdowns. Strong diplomats never say "never" and never leave forever, and always are ready to come back and agree right away on new dates to continue talks, as though a breakdown is just one more pressure trick. The best thing to do is to re-establish communications as soon as possible and you have to do this through your team member who has good connections and influence with other party. Act fast, especially if the consequences of "no deal" would be worse than the last deal that was on the table. If the situation is not improving, you have nothing else but to use a mediator. I do not recommend you to take responsibility as mediator or to use a mediator for your diplomatic needs. International experience shows that these old and "experienced" people usually make the situation worse, like bringing in a lawyer — even if the situation looks better for the next couple of years. But if you have no choice and your partner, and your aides insist on using a mediator to resolve the situation you have to think it over ... and agree.

Mediation is the process in which deadlocked parties consider the suggestions of a third party, agreed upon in advance, but are not bound to accept the mediator's recommendations. The mediator works as a referee between the negotiating parties and tries to find common ground among their agendas. Once some common ground is established, the mediator can begin to look for mutually acceptable ways out of the deadlock. A mediator between presidents has to be a president himself, very influential, and well informed on the situation to be able to make effective recommendations. He has to:

(a) consider the situation from all angles

(b) help both parties to understand each other better

(c) help the parties to create new approaches

(d) suggest a solution, give alternatives

But if the two sides' demands are too far apart, no outside party can bring them together at all.

3. Closing negotiation

That's the most important part, a final mutual agreement or disagreement, a test for your foreign policy making strategy and tactics and personally for you, your power and your image. Any treaty you sign with foreign leaders, if it meets American interests, is not your personal success, but that of the nation. There are three options:

(a) the agreement with all conditions is acceptable to both parties

(b) the agreement is acceptable to one party only

(c) the agreement is unacceptable for both parties

DIPLOMATIC TRICKS

At the very first negotiation your partner will show you some diplomatic tricks, so you better be prepared for this poker-like game. Tricks in diplomacy are usually used to distract your hard working team, shift the emphasis of the negotiation in order to shape the deal on terms of your adversary or manipulate your team into closing negotiation and accept terms you don't really like. And the tricks are:

"Leap" — Your adversary is losing and starts "jumping" from one point to another.

"Pile" — Your adversary "piles up" problems, tries to provoke a chaotic discussion or stop negotiations.

"Empty chair" — A day or two before negotiations start your adversary informs you that he's not ready yet, trying to press you.

"Deaf" — Your adversary keeps asking questions instead of answering yours.

"Provocation" — Your adversary doubts your team's professional level and your ability to negotiate.

"Busy guy" — Your adversary breaks negotiation for an hour or two pretending he has to do some very important business (or that he got a very important call).

"Mirror" — It's a very interesting "programming" trick. The technology is simple: you try to "mirror" your adversary's style and behavior, adopt a similar posture, use his gestures, and follow the speed of his speech. First, he will like it subconsciously and will be more open to you. Second, you'll understand better his way of thinking.

"Sandwich" — Apply pressure (often military), negotiate, again apply pressure.

"Show" — Using certain arguments, your adversary appeals to your emotions.

"Circle" — A very sophisticated trick: your adversary tries to "push" his proposal in different variants and finally comes back to his initial variant, trying to convince you that's the best choice.

"Carrot and stick" — Threat (blackmail) plus promises (money).

"Student" — Your adversary talks too much about the details, asking a lot of minor questions, trying to make you nervous and make mistakes.

"Ball" — Encourage your adversary if he's looking for "global decisions" and he'll do a lot of minor favors.

"Rubber" — Delay, if you can't predict the result, and press your adversary by delaying the answer

"Last train" — you can press your adversary by an ultimatum right before negotiations are over, if he really is interested in some result. "Spice" the ultimatum with some important reasons and give your adversary a choice of variants.

You can also leak opposing demands to the media (be careful with this one. Do not betray diplomatic trust by talking about secret deals or demands that actually have been mentioned). You may also escalate your demands during negotiation and manipulate public opinion to line up behind your demands.

Diplomatic Double Talk

Statement	Meaning
We are disappointed.	We got nothing.
The situation disturbs us.	It's unacceptable, no matter what.
There are still differences between our approaches to the problem.	There are huge differences.
We can't accept this deal.	This means trouble.
We reserve the right to use any means to prevent further worsening of the situation.	This means war.
Discussion helped us to understand each other better.	We've wasted our time.
We don't understand your attitude.	Stop it immediately.
I'm trying to understand your position.	Understand me too, idiot!
If I've understood you correctly, you don't agree.	Do you have any other option?
We both will pay a very high price if we don't reach agreement.	Yes, that's a threat!

Body Language

It's very good to have someone in your team who is attuned to body language and can help you to "crack" your opponent. Here are some signals (codes) and their meanings:

Partner is sitting upright with hands loosely crossed in front of him.	He is ready to accept proposal and finish negotiation.
Partner is smiling unnecessaily and is speaking fast.	He's nervous.
Partner looks and turns his lower body toward the exit.	He wants to leave.
Open palm gesture.	I'm open and I'm telling the truth.
He's leaning his body forward.	He's ready to assist you to get out of the situation.
Wide open eyes and a smile.	He wants to be persuaded.
Raised eyebrows.	Negative surprise.
Chin rests on knuckles.	Agreement to listen (with interest).
Neutral facial expression.	Unformed opinion.
Gesturing a hand.	Adding emphasis.

Indirect gaze.	Uncertainty.
Crossing arms or legs.	Disapproval.
Leaning back on a chair.	Boredom.
Leaning forward.	Agreement.
His team's members exchange glances.	They are sure they've won.

PROTOCOL

I'm sure the protocol aides will help you when it's time to meet foreign lead-ers, but some extra tips on cultural differences can only help.

Europe. You are expected to clean your plate.

Middle East. You are expected to try a taste of everything on your plate. If you want to give a gift, remember that Muslims consider green to be a color of God and it's reserved for the most respectful items. They are offended by any-thing depicting dogs or pigs.

Japan. Japanese do not start negotiations until they feel a suitable relation-ship has been established. Remember that white is a color of mourning. Don't give them anything that comes in set of four, because the Japanese word for 4 sounds like the word for "death."

Great Britain. Don't flash the V-for-victory sign with your palm facing you — it's obscene.

Australia. Avoid the thumbs-up signal for the same reason.

The United States. The best thing about the White House is the food. Have a look.

Dinner Menu at the White House

On the occasion of the visit of
The Right Honorable
The Prime Minister
of the United Kingdom of Great Britain and Northern Ireland
and Mrs. Blair

Honey Mango Glazed Chicken
Spicy Vegetable Noodles
Herb Tuile

Grilled Salmon Fillet "Mignon"
Seared Portobello Mushroom

Tomato Shallot Fondue
Baby Vegetables and Balsamic Reduction

Marinated Fresh Mozzarella
Roasted Artichokes and Basil Tomatoes
Salad of Mache and Arugula
Lemon Oregano Dressing

Strawberries and Cream
Devonshire Sauce
Brandy Snaps Shortbread
Honey Nougat Chocolate Fudge

Newton Chardonnay "Unfiltered" 1995
Swanson Langiovese 1995
Mumm Napa Valley DVX 1993

(The White House, Thursday, February 5, 1998)

RUSSIA

The Russians also know how to put on quite a banquet, but in their case we will focus on other topics.

1. Government: — lie, steal, run to the USA.
2. Mafia:
    no breaks, no respect
    shoot first, then negotiate
    politically active
    total control of big business
3. KGB:
    analyze everything
    trust nobody, suspect everybody
    no rush, no friends, no questions, no bribes
    don't cheat on your wife
    don't work overtime (it's a sign of a "mole")
    don't contact criminals (if it's not a job)
    drink vodka only
4. Army: humiliate, degrade, drink vodka
5. Stereotypes: — all Americans are spies
6. National problems:
    deciding whom to blame for problems — the nation or the government?
    fussing about what is to be done (and hoping for the best)

7. Rules:
> be on time
> avoid responsibility, dentists, foreigners and non-drinkers
> steal
> don't work hard, wait for the wonder to happen (big money)
> trust the newspapers
> talk politics, but don't get involved

8. Religion: church is a business, the Bible is religion

OVERTHROWING GOVERNMENTS

Coups

Coups, like war, are one of the most violent tools of the foreign policy and they can be artificially staged in target countries by "feeding" and "pushing" the political opposition or by using VIP agents in the government. Most coups are "Bureaucratic," and entail mainly a change of leader, usually by person #2. That person might be the trigger or might be induced to practice "passive sabotage" and allow certain others to take over.

Conditions for a successful coup:
- the army is supportive or at least neutral
- the leader is out of town (vacation, visit abroad) or is ill
- a political or economic crisis.

Military Coups

Changing a civilian government to a military one, usually in developing countries. Conditions: a long-term political and economic crisis that threatens national security and the unity of the country. Military chief(s) eventually let the people elect a civilian president and form a civilian government after "re-construction" of political and economic systems. They usually leave for themselves the right to control further political process.

"Democratic" Coups

A democratic coup would be a change of the government by the most aggressive (nationalistic) political party. Conditions:

- artificial or actual government crisis
- mass anti-government propaganda
- organized "democratic" movement all over the country
- provoked mass protests and civil disobedience actions
- government buildings blockade

Revolutions

A change of government and political and economic systems by political gangsters, usually fed, pushed, incited, and possibly funded and equipped by the secret services of another country. (Even the American Revolution would not have succeeded without French military advisors and financial support.) Government buildings are blockaded, the government isolated, all communications and transportation systems captured, government media closed, new government formed. Conditions:

- political and economic crisis
- mass anti-government propaganda (in the army too)
- provoked mass protests and civil disobedience actions
- terror and urban guerillas

The Military and Diplomacy

Finally, a few words about the military support to diplomacy — it's very important in furthering our interests abroad. The components of support to diplomacy include peacemaking, peace building and preventive diplomacy. Peacemaking is a process of diplomacy, mediation, negotiation that end disputes and resolve the issues that led to conflict. Military activities that support peacemaking include military-to-military relations and security assistance operations. Other military activities, such as exercises and peacetime deployments, may enhance the diplomatic process by demonstrating the engagement of the US abroad. Military-to-military contacts and security assistance programs also serve to enhance diplomacy by influencing important groups in regions of conflict and by promoting the stable environment necessary for the success of diplomacy.

Peace building consists of post-conflict actions, primarily diplomatic, that strengthen and rebuild civil government in order to avoid a return to conflict, and reconstruct the economy — that's what the US says it is trying to do now in Iraq. Military support also includes assistance in selected areas such as the conduct of elections. Preventive diplomacy involves diplomatic actions taken in advance of a predictable crisis to prevent or limit violence. In more tense situations, military activities may support preventive diplomacy, and such support may include preventive deployments or higher levels of readiness. (The tasks of a preventive deployment force may include acting as an interpositional force to forestall violence, protecting the local delivery of humanitarian relief or assisting local authorities to protect and offer security to threatened minorities, to secure and maintain essential services (water, power) and to maintain law and order.

Keeping Tabs on Who is For You and Who is Against

By now, even readers of *USA Today* know that several branches of the US government, and corporations of all sorts, are monitoring, recording and analyzing records of who buys what, goes where, talks to whom. Massive data-profiling projects help each Party decide how they want to carve new voting districts, and enables specialists to predict which districts' votes will not be useful in a re-count. Any candidate for election to a top job in the US government needs to have savvy statisticians on hand to help focus the campaign on the right people, and to help decide what issues are important to the right people before — and after — election.

If you don't think databases are maintained at every level, how did I receive such a letter as this?

319 First Street, SE
Washington, DC 20003
PLATINUM MEMBER

Mykhaylo Kryzhanovsky
Member Since 2006

This Platinum Card has been issued to the bearer by the Republican National Committee in recognition of an extraordinary level of commitment to the Republican ideals and values.

The bearer of this card should be given special considerations by all Republican leaders as one who has provided the lifeblood of our Party over many years.

I believe your exemplary record of loyalty and patriotism proves you are a leader President Bush can count on. It is therefore my distinct privilege as Chairman of the Republican National Committee (RNC) to present you with your 2006 Republican Party Platinum Card on behalf of President Bush and every Republican leader nationwide.

Your leadership as one of our Party's elite Platinum Card holders is critical to electing principled

Republicans in this year's crucial midterm elections and implementing President Bush's agenda.

President Bush is counting on proud Americans like you to stand with him this year — and to help him make sure the policies we support and the Republican candidates who share your values do not fall to defeat by the forces of partisan politics.

I believe your exemplary record of loyalty and patriotism proves you are a leader President Bush can trust to fight with him for America's safety and security. Your proven leadership is just what President Bush and our party need right now.

Please accept this honor with my sincere thanks.

Sincerely,
Ken Mehlman
Chairman, Republican National Committee

PART 2. MANAGING SPIES AT THE TOP — SECRET SERVICES

I didn't invent anything like a "new espionage system." All this is based on my own experience and analysis, and will work well into the 21st century.

Chapter 5. Which Service is the Best

When I talk about "the best," I mean the highest intelligence level — illegal spies, intelligence operatives who are secretly deployed abroad and covertly operate there under assumed names and well-documented cover stories, masquerading as native citizens. The process of training and "installing" such officer is rather complex and includes:

(a) Special training. Foreign language, general, political and special (espionage and counter-espionage) knowledge of the target country; personal cover story — new biography, special technical devices, recruitment methods). Up to three years.

(b) Illegal probation period abroad. A trip abroad through intermediate countries with numerous changes of passports and cover stories, jobs, personal connections. Then he gets to the target country, stays there for another 1-2 years and goes back to his country for additional training and correction of cover story — actually, it's his first combat assignment. The most important part of this assignment is to check the reliability of the cover story and documents; the cover story has to be reinforced with new and old true facts, like short-term studies at universities or professional training courses.

(c) Intermediate legislation. On his way back the officer could stay in an intermediate country for another 1-2 years, make contacts with business, scientists, government employees, celebrities.

(d) Basic legislation. Officer comes to the target country, obtains genuine documents, gets a job which allows him to travel and talk to many people, recruit informants thus creating an illegal station.

The illegal is usually supplied with a variety of cover documents to make him "invisible" for counter-intelligence — some are used only to cross the borders on the way to a target country, others — to live there, other documents — only for travel to "third countries" to meet with officers of legal or illegal stations or to be used in case of urgent recall to home country (in that case the illegal is supposed to transit at least two or three countries).

His further activity depends on how professional counter-espionage service is working in the country. He could fail in his mission also because of:

- poor training and low quality documents
- neglecting security rules.
- one mistake in pronunciation can give you away
- treason (traitor-informant or a "mole" inside his own service)
- low personal security level (while working with sources)

CARDINAL RULES — WHAT IT TAKES TO BE THE BEST

- Show no mercy, no ideology, no emotions.
- Intuition is nothing but the ability to watch and analyze.
- No evidence is evidence in itself.
- Distrust is a mother of security.
- Never look as if you are sizing up the person — that's a sign that gives away cops and spies.
- Don't start first if you don't know the rules.
- The way you act is the way you think — behavior is a system of codes (information) which could be calculated by the enemy. Watch your face — that's a shop window.
- Think fast, talk slow.
- Avoid self-programming and never think bad about yourself.
- Don't smoke, drink or take drugs if it's not necessary; spare your stomach from very hot or cold food or drinks; avoid too much noise and light.
- Don't be shy to lie — the more you lie the more people respect you.
- Let people talk out and "empty their brains" — then load your information.
- People never change — everybody wants to get pleasure and avoid pain.
- "He knew too much" means "He talked too much."
- Never ask extra questions — wait. Wait and the object will get used to you and open himself — nobody can stay tense for long.
- Lonely people live longer in espionage business.
- A "no exit" situation is one you don't like or don't understand.

Avoid:

- personal enemies (they fix negative information on you)
- silent types (they notice and think too much)
- other professionals (they'll blow your identity)
- extra stress (it damages your heart and blood vessels and that kills your brain and your ability to think)

- talking too much

COMPARING TWO RIVALS

CIA	KGB
Cuts corners to save money on intelligence.	No limits.
Poor professional training and knowledge.	The KGB was famous for brilliant analysts.
"A state within a state."	Mostly patriots.
Results first. Use people and get rid of them.	Security first. Respect your sources.
Promise and forget.	Promise and do it.
Saw Russia as #1 enemy.	Saw US as #1 enemy.
Money first.	Job first.
Alcohol.	Oh, yes.
"We are the best."	No, we are the best.
Unreformable.	A fluid structure.

THE KGB

Since 1991, the KGB has been re-named the SVR (Russian Intelligence Service), but it has basically the same structure.

Structure

KGB Chief and his Deputies

Directorates:
> "R": operational planning and analysis
> "K": external counter-intelligence
> "S": illegal spies
> "T": scientific and technical intelligence, acquisition of Western strategic, military and industrial technology.
> > "RI": intelligence assessment
> > "RT": operations within the Soviet Union
> > "OT": operational technical support
> > "I": computer services
> > "P": political intelligence

Geographic Departments

Services:
> "A": disinformation, covert actions to influence foreign nations and governments

"R": radio communications with overseas stations
"A" of the 8th Chief Directorate (cryptographic services)

KGB stations abroad
    KGB Resident (Chief of the station).
    "PR" line: political, economic and military strategic intelligence
    "KR" line: counterintelligence and security
    "X" line: scientific and technological intelligence
    "N" line: illegal spies' support
    "EM" line: émigrés
    "SK" line: Soviet colony in the country
    Embassy security officer
    "OT" officer — operational technical support
    "Impulse" station — monitors radio communications of surveillance teams
    "RP" line officer: SIGINT
    "I" line officer — computers
    Cipher clerk
    Radio operator

KGB inside humor:
    "Recruit a woman if you can't get anybody else."
    "You can lose nothing and you can find nothing inside the KGB."
    "Never make friends inside the KGB."
    "Before lunch we fight hunger, after lunch we fight sleep."
    "The law stops here."

KGB slang sounds funny too: "music" (listening device), "Bible"(a book with listening device hidden inside), "gods"(officers who worked with informants inside churches and sects), "sailor" (informant — informant's KGB registration card was crossed by a red stripe), "crust" (KGB ID), "To take a skin off" (to take information from the informant), "to spin information" (to "enrich" information with false facts), "lime-tree" (false information).

There are still stereotypes about the KGB, like "the KGB knows everything" or "the KGB never arrests innocent citizens," or "KGB officers take special pills and that's why they are never drunk." Yes, KGB officers drink vodka on weekends and sometimes in the office with the usual Russian appetizers like smoked sausage or fish, caviar and pickles, but it's a rare thing to see somebody really drunk. They drink mostly to ease tension from the job and social isolation. If you don't drink alcohol with your colleagues it means disrespect and is not very good for your promotion. They take no pills and are just accustomed to regulate themselves.

The KGB business goes in cycles and it's like any other bureaucratic government agency — July and August are "dead" months (vacations) as well as November and December (planning and waiting for promotion). The crazy busy months are January, February, March and June, because the departments and divisions chiefs try to do most of the job (especially recruitment) that was planned for the whole year. If you still don't do anything it's not a problem but if you miss the recruitment targets, you are in trouble. First, it's not professional and even your friends won't understand; second, it's a problem now for somebody else, because if you haven't met the recruitment target somebody has to recruit instead of you — and in a rush.

KGB officers, due to professional demands, are physically fit, intelligent, well educated, have no mental problems and know how to talk and charm people — that's the art of recruitment. All these qualities create a big problem for married men (99% are married) because women like them.

Almost every officer has a lover, but divorce is out of question. First, it's bad for your career, second, it's a terrible headache for you and your bosses because if you divorce and want to marry again, they have to check this woman — she must have a "clean" biography: no criminals in the family, no relatives abroad, no mentally ill family members, and she has to be normal too.

In earlier years, every KGB officer was a CPSU (Communist Party of the Soviet Union) member and there were no political problems between the Party leaders and KGB chiefs. Still, there existed a super-secret Special Investigation Department in Moscow which was responsible for investigation of espionage or other criminal activity by senior Party members or government officials.

What we learn from KGB practice:

(1) KGB intelligence never tries to save money on agents, especially those recruited or planted inside foreign government bureaucracies and special services. This rule explains how KGB got the American nuclear bomb.

(2) The KGB tries to get its agents out of jail no matter what, unlike the CIA which treats such agents as "disposable."

(3) The KGB practiced forcible confinement of dissidents in psychiatric hospitals, where debilitating drugs were administered (as an alternative to straightforward arrests and to avoid the unfavorable publicity that often arose with criminal trials).

(4) Censorship of literature, media and art in general.

(5) KGB mounted professional "active-measures" operations using forged US Government documents, pictures, evidences, stories, rumors and other "official" sources and media campaigns abroad to discredit all aspects of American policy and promote conflicts between the United States and its NATO allies and other states. No doubt the other top international agencies have similar operations throughout the world.

The political effect of this type of operations can be very strong. American biological warfare was blamed for AIDS — it was "manufactured during genetic engineering experiments at Fort Detrick, Maryland." This information was "pushed" in 1986 through a retired East German, Russian-born biophysicist, professor Jacob Segal, who gave an interview to the British *Sunday Express*. He insisted that this extremely dangerous virus had been synthesized from two natural viruses, VISNA and HTLV-1. In the first six months of 1987 alone the story received major coverage in over forty third-world countries, and on German and British TV. Africa still believes the story.

Another example is a widespread story that the United States is developing "ethnic-specific weapons" that would kill "nonwhites only." Some people think SARS and Ebola are among the results, and wonder what the Bird Flu is all about.

Or how about the "baby parts" story widely published in over 50 countries in which Americans were blamed for butchering Latin American children and using their bodies for organ transplants.

And finally there is a widespread belief among American blacks that the CIA introduced them to crack cocaine to "slow down the civil rights movement." Some people wonder as well who was pushing marijuana and hallucinogenic drugs, free sex, wife-swapping, and a variety of other "trends" that tore the social fabric in the United States in the 1960s, a tear that has never been mended? Any of the top intelligence services could have a role in encouraging developments which weaken America; or which distract and deflect the energies of restless students, intellectuals, the media and others who might criticize the war.

(6) Every KGB officer is an analyst, unlike CIA employees.

(7) KGB intelligence (SVR) always pursues global goals, which are currently:

- to block NATO's expansion
- to block US hegemony
- to expand Russia's weapons market
- to continue high-tech, military and space technology espionage. (Before, the KGB was involved in the support of "national liberation wars" in the Third World, providing arms, advisers, military training and political indoctrination of leftist guerrillas.) In 1992 Russia signed an agreement on intelligence cooperation with China which is a direct threat to US national security.

There are two more important special services — FAPSI (Federal Agency for Government Communications and Information) and the Presidential Security Service. FAPSI is a target for us because its in charge of a special switchboard which includes coded telephone communications by Russian President, the prime minister and their assistants. FAPSI is also empowered to monitor and register all electronic financial and securities transactions and to monitor other electronic communications, including private Internet access.

RSHA (German Reich Security Main Office, 1939-1945)

Structure

Chief of RSHA

Departments:

I Personnel and Organization (recruiting and assignment for RSHA)

II Administration and Finance: organization and law, legislation, passports, budget, technical matters (transportation, etc.)

III SD, internal intelligence (internal security of Germany): law and legal structures, racial and ethnic matters, cultural, religious matters, industry and commerce, high society

IV GESTAPO, secret state political police with unquestionable powers to arrest opponents of the Nazi regime, including Communists, liberals, Freemasons, Protestants, Jehovah Witnesses, Jews. It was responsible for counter-espionage and counter-sabotage.

V KRIPO, the criminal police, was responsible for preventive measures, repressive measures, identification.

VI External Intelligence (outside Germany and on occupied territories)

VII Written records

I'd like to talk about Nazi special services omitting any ideology, from a professional point of view only. In 1939 all the German police forces — GESTAPO (Secret State Police), KRIPO (Criminal Police) and SD (Internal Security Service) were united into the RSHA (Reich Security Main Office) with External Intelligence Service added later. The special services concentration was a clear sign of political power concentration. Note that under President George W. Bush, son of an ex-CIA Director, the US intelligence services have been united under one "czar."

What we learn from RSHA practices:

(1) Investigated and fought against all activities which might endanger in any sense the security of Germany.

(2) Kept operations simple and effective. Take for example the "public places total control" method: agents were recruited, first of all, at every big restaurant, bar, hotel or store. They delivered information on any client whose behavior was somewhat different from the general one: he was too excited or too depressed,

too greedy or too generous, too open or too closed, too well dressed or vise versa, etc. And very often such a client deserved special attention.

(3) Aggressive total recruitment — by the end of World War II there wasn't a single guerilla detachment, resistance or espionage group on occupied Soviet and European territories that had not been in part or completely eliminated by the GESTAPO or SD — 100 per cent professional counter-terrorist and counter-espionage job based on agent infiltration

(4) The "Night and Fog" operation. By 1941 the RSHA analysts reported that the "taking hostages" practice was not effective any more as resistance on the occupied territories was even increasing after that went into effect. It was decided that resistance fighters had to be secretly arrested and secretly transported to Germany where, after investigation, they just vanished without a trace.

The US in recent years has been taking insurgents and others arrested (often on suspicion alone) in Afghanistan, Iraq, and around the world, and transferring them via secret flights to secret jails in Eastern Europe and elsewhere for "interrogation". One might have predicted that the public outcry would quickly stamp out any such abomination as the prison at Guantanamo, but as we see the "current incivilities" have already gone on longer than World War II and the camp is still there.

(5) The RSHA was abhorred for using "third degree" methods of interrogation (see "Special Influence")

CIA or "The Company" (a virtual agency)

Structure

> Director (Director of Central Intelligence)
> National Intelligence Council
> Office of Congressional Affairs
> Center for the Study of Intelligence
> Directorates:
> Directorate of Administration

> Offices:
> Communications, Facilities and Security Services, Finance and Logistics, Information Technology, Medical Services, Human Resources Management, Personnel Security, Training and Education, DCI Center for Security Evaluation, Center for Support Coordination
> Directorate of Intelligence Offices:

President's Support Division, Operations Center, DCI Crime and Narcotics Center, DCI Nonproliferation Center, Collection Requirements and Evaluation Staff, Office of Advanced Analytic Tools, Office of Transitional Issues, Council of Intelligence Operations, Office of Support Services

Geographic Offices

Offices of Advanced Projects, Development and Engineering, Research and Development, Clandestine Information Technology Office, Technical Collection, Technical Service, Community Open Source Program, Foreign Broadcast Information

National Clandestine Service (planning and carrying out covert destabilization operations, dissemination of propaganda, paramilitary operations)

Directorate of Plans

Counterintelligence Center

DCI Counterterrorist Center

National HUMINT (human intelligence) requirements center

The Central Intelligence Agency (CIA) was created by the National Security Act of 1947 to gather and analyze information from every corner of the globe and to provide the President with a covert operations capability. The CIA inherited the functions of the Office of Strategic Services (OSS).

It's supposed to:

- correlate and evaluate intelligence relating to national security and provide for its appropriate dissemination
- collect, produce and disseminate foreign intelligence and counterintelligence (which if collected within the United States must be coordinated with the FBI)
- collect, produce and disseminate intelligence on foreign aspects of narcotics production and trafficking
- conduct counterintelligence activities outside the United States and, without assuming or performing any internal security functions, conduct counterintelligence activities within the United States in coordination with the FBI
- conduct special activities approved by the President

Since 1947 the CIA has been on forward-march and has advanced inexorably.

1951

The New York *Herald Tribune* listed some outstanding CIA failures:
- failure to predict the June 1950 North Korea invasion of the South Korea
- failure to predict the "Fall of Czechoslovakia"
- failure to foresee "Tito's defection" from Moscow
- failure to predict the "Fall of Chinese Nationalists"

- failure to foresee the Israeli victory in Palestine
- failure to judge the mood of the Latin American states at the Bogota Conference in 1948

1962

Prior to the 1962 Cuban crisis, the CIA reported to President Kennedy that the USSR wouldn't risk a nuclear war. During the crisis they insisted that the USSR might risk nuclear war. In both cases their National Intelligence Estimate was grossly off-base.

1980

The Reagan transition team for the CIA (November, 1980) reported the following:

> "The fundamental problem confronting American security is the current dangerous condition of the Central Intelligence Agency and of national intelligence collection generally. The failure of American intelligence collection has been at the heart of faulty defense planning and misdirected foreign policy."

[The team pointed out the following intelligence failures.]

- The general and continuing failure to predict the actual size and scope of the Soviet military effort and military sector of the Russian GNP
- the consistent gross misstatement of Soviet global objectives
- the wholesale failure to understand or attempt to counteract Soviet disinformation and propaganda
- the general failure to explain the characteristics of Soviet conventional weapon systems and vessels — for example the new Russian guided missile cruises
- the wholesale failure to understand and predict the nature of the so-called wars of national liberation in Africa and Central and South America
- the consistent miscalculation regarding the effect of and general apology for massive technology transfer from West to the East
- the apparent internal failure of counterintelligence generally.

[The team went on to observe,]

> "The unhealthy symbiosis between the CIA and the Department of State is the chief underlying cause of the security position of the United States.
>
> "The next Director of the Central Intelligence Agency ... will be told repeatedly by virtually everyone in policy positions at the Agency that the CIA is a highly professional, non-political agency that produces 'objective' intelligence. Those assertions are arrant nonsense. In part out of mutual drive for individual and corporate self-preservation, the CIA has become an elitist organization which engenders unshakable loyalty among its staff. The National Intelligence Estimate process is itself a bureaucratic game. These failures are of such enormity, that they cannot help but suggest to any objective observer that the agency itself is compromised to an unprecedented extent and that its paralysis is attributable to causes more sinister than incompetence."

1991

The CIA appears to have failed completely to predict the Soviet empire col-lapse and the end of the Cold War as such. Robert Gates, the fifteenth CIA Direc-tor (and later George W.'s Defense Secretary), as much as said in his acceptance speech on November 12, 1991 that the CIA is a mafia: "The people at Langley were more than a team; they were a family. I hope this sense of family, with all that implies, can be strengthened in the time ahead."

2001

The US lost 3,000 lives at Pearl Harbor in 1941 because someone was in-structed not to pay attention to certain intelligence information that was avail-able. Who was managing the intelligence and deciding where to look closer and where to turn a blind eye on September 11, when another 3,000 American lives were lost?

What we learn from CIA practice

Nothing positive.

(1) The CIA's history up to today is a history of paralysis.

The greatest problem is that the US government can't preemptively handle foreign policy and national security matters because it has no adequate intel-ligence information; in fact it has no idea (neither has the CIA) what such high level political intelligence information would look like.

Yes, I'm talking here about the Senate Intelligence Committee, which has primary oversight responsibility for the CIA in Congress.

Ask the National Security Agency to start intercepting world leaders' talks and phone calls worldwide — if we are spending this much money on NSA spe-cial intelligence, we ought to be able to intercept the calls and break the coded communications.

This information would have to be the essence of the US President's Daily Briefings and this information has to be the base of National Intelligence Daily Report and National Intelligence Estimate — which is a regular failure of the CIA — many presidents ignore these reports as trash. This information would have to be the basis of National Security Council decisions. Sorry, we don't have a global US intelligence strategy or intelligence strategists and I'm not going to do the job while 16,000 "good ol' boys" drink the day away at Langley.

(2) I strongly recommend stopping the CIA's secret funding right now, fund-ing that is not made public or audited by the Congress. The CIA has its own budget but they want more, which they will waste, and some so-called "opera-

tions" are financed by secret transfers of funds from the appropriations accounts of other agencies, primarily the Defense Department.

(3) You can't reform the CIA — they are too accustomed to a comfortable existence, uncontrolled and irresponsible, because they, unlike military intelligence, do not function according to discipline, strict and understandable orders and patriotism.

The CIA has to be shut down, and its political intelligence functions and funding have to be transferred to the Defense Intelligence Agency. Platitudes like "the transition period is complex and takes time" are not convincing — military personnel should take over the Langley headquarters with not a single CIA employee (and all the inevitable "moles") within a week and start cleaning up the so-called top-secret papers and files, 90% of which is "information noise."

While the CIA is a "family" ruled by the so-called "four princes" (heads of four directorates), the Army is a brotherhood of patriots whose leader is the US President, the Commander-in-Chief. He can trust them — show me a single American (or anyone else) who trusts the CIA.

CLANDESTINE SERVICE CAREERS ARE AVAILABLE

[This ad was an invitation to international terrorists and spy agencies.]

Be a part of a mission that's larger than all of us. The CIA's National Clandestine Service is searching for qualified applicants to serve in the US and abroad. These exciting careers offer fast-paced, high impact challenges in the worldwide intelligence collection efforts on issues of US foreign policy interest and national security concern.

Applicants should possess impeccable integrity, strong interpersonal skills, excellent written and oral communication skills, and the desire to be a part of something vital that makes a difference for family, friends and country. Qualified applicants should possess a minimum of a bachelor's degree with a preferred GPA of 3.0 or higher, an interest in international affairs and national security, and be willing to relocate to the Washington, DC area. Foreign language skills are highly desirable, particularly in those critical languages listed on our website. New or refresher language training will be provided for all positions requiring language proficiency.

Foreign travel opportunities exist for all positions and some require relocation abroad for 2-3 year tours of duty. All applicants for National Clandestine Service positions must successfully undergo several personal interviews, medical and psychological exams, aptitude testing, a polygraph interview and a background investigation. Following entry on duty, candidates will undergo extensive training. US citizenship required. An equal opportunity employer and a drug-free work force. For more information and to apply.

— visit: www. cia. gov (*The Economist*, March 11-17, 2006)

MOSSAD

The Israeli MOSSAD (Institute for Intelligence and Special Tasks), formed in 1951, has responsibility for human intelligence collection, covert action and counterterrorism with the focus on Arab nations and organizations throughout the world.

MOSSAD Structure

Director

Collection Department: espionage operations

Political Action and Liaison Department: political activities and liaison with friendly foreign intelligence services and with nations with which Israel does not have normal diplomatic relations —who is responsible for Israel's image, which is extremely low on the international arena? What these people are doing over there? Drinking kosher vodka?

LAP Department: psychological warfare, propaganda and deception operations. I have the same question for this department.

Research Department: intelligence production, including daily situations reports, weekly summaries and detailed monthly reports.

15 geographic sections.

Special Operations Division: assassination, sabotage, paramilitary and psychological warfare projects

Technology Department: development of advanced technologies to support operations

What we learn from MOSSAD practice:

(1) Very effective method of non-stop 24/7 monitoring of all Arab terrorists leaders' movements all over the world. Don't you think they know where Osama Bin-Laden is? — if MOSSAD had informants among his aides before, it has them now.

(2) Unlimited practice of political murders — which means MOSSAD has no idea how to recruit and work with Arab agents (monitoring is a passive tool).

(3) MOSSAD has been super-active at the United Nations, with zero effect — 99% of the UN delegates vote against Israel on every issue.

My Israeli colleagues have some unfortunate qualities: they promote an unprecedented level of PR according to which every MOSSAD officer is a genius and each MOSSAD Director is "Mr. Intelligence." MOSSAD unfortunately soiled its reputation in the international espionage community after the case of the exceptionally unprofessional John Pollard. The following morality tale emphasizes the first rule of recruitment — do not recruit psychos.

John Pollard was born in 1954 in Texas to a Jewish family. He studied at Stanford University and being a schizophrenic and drug abuser, claimed he was a colonel in the Israeli army and a MOSSAD spy. After Stanford the US Navy hired him in 1979 as a civilian intelligence analyst at Naval Operational Surveillance and Intelligence Center, the Naval Intelligence Support Center and the Naval Investigative Center.

In 1984 they brought him into the Anti-Terrorism Alert Center where he gained access to the whole federal intelligence system and a high level of clearance known as SCI or Sensitive Compartmented Information, and a special "courier card" that opened the CIA, FBI, State Department and National Security Agency restricted archives for him.

In May 1984, through a New York businessman, he was introduced to Israeli Air Force colonel Aviem Sella. Pollard told him that he had positive proof that the USA, the only Israel's ally, friend and sponsor, was not sharing all the intelligence data it should with Israel, and Pollard was angry with the US and willing to help his historic motherland. (In truth, although Israel does not share much with the US, Israel was receiving full political, economic and military support from the US plus $3 billion a year at that time — and even more in recent years.)

The report about the "walk-in" volunteer was passed to Rafi Eitan, the LACAM (Israeli military technology espionage agency) chief, and in a month Pollard was recruited. For a year Pollard was supplying Israel with top secret documents, including satellite reconnaissance photographs which were of a special interest to LACAM. The documents were going straight to Prime Minister Shimon Peres, Foreign Minister Yitzhak Shamir and Defense Minister Yitzhak Rabin.

Finally on November 21, 1985 the FBI went after him. In a chase, he made it into the Israeli embassy in Washington, DC, but the MOSSAD officers threw him out. He may spend the rest of his life in jail. So far President George Bush and President Bill Clinton have refused the multiple Israeli requests to pardon him.

Since 2000 MOSSAD has advertised its recruitment of collection officers (a concept which is unthinkable for the KGB).

MINISTRY OF STATE SECURITY (MSS), CHINA

China's MSS aggressively targets the US high tech sector heavily concentrated in Silicon Valley. Cover for Beijing's espionage includes the 1,500 Chinese diplomats, 15,000 Chinese students who arrive here each year and 2,700 visiting delegations each year and the US correspondents of the major Chinese newspapers, including *The People's Daily* and Xinhua News Agency. (Altogether the MSS has established "branches" in 170 cities in nearly 50 countries all over the world).

Chinese intelligence targets the US high-tech sector, but what is much more important is China's strategy to bribe the President, Senators and Representatives by discreetly financing, through intermediaries, federal and state elections. In such a way China is getting favorable American treatment on trade policy, including selling nuclear weapons and technology to such countries as Iran and Libya. In 1991 the National Security Agency intercepted communications indicating that China was trying to "influence" 30 Congressional candidates (mostly Democrats) through campaign contributions. Republican House Speaker Newt Gingrich was one of those candidates. According to James F. Lilley, a former US Ambassador to China: "The FBI discovered Chinese efforts to interfere in American campaigns as early as 1991 and warned a number of Democratic members of Congress to watch for Chinese donations passed through intermediaries...It's the way they operate in Asian countries. They do it by bribing government officials; they bribe them to change policy." Senator Fred Thompson, who chaired the 1997 campaign finance hearings, said that "High-level Chinese government officials crafted a plan to increase China's influence over the US political process, and took specific steps to do so, including the allocation of substantial sums of money to influence federal and state elections."

Secret services always conduct detailed research before they "do" a certain person, and in Bill Clinton they found one who was a ripe target. China recruited Johnny Chung, a democratic fundraiser, who got $100,000 from another agent, Liu Chaoying (who worked on defense modernization for China People's Liberation Army), and gave the money to Democratic National Committee. Then, by the order of Chung's boss, general Ji Shengde, $300,000 were deposited into the Torrance businessman's account to subsidize campaign donations intended for Clinton. Another $500,000 were "donated" to an international trading firm, established by a former Clinton's aide. Then Chung escorted the wife and son of Chinese military intelligence to a political fundraiser in Los Angeles in 1996, at which Democratic officials asked for a $25,000 contribution for the opportunity to introduce his "friends" to Bill Clinton. And then Clinton overrode then-Secretary of State Warren Christopherson's decision to limit China's ability to launch American-made satellites on Chinese rockets.

Later Bernard Schwartz, the "Loral" CEO and the largest individual contributor to the DNC, appeared on the stage. What happened? I don't know what happened in 1996, but in 1998 the US federal grand jury was investigating whether "Loral" illegally gave China space expertise that significantly advanced Beijing's

ballistic missile program. Schwartz was ready to export to China airborne reconnaissance cameras, weapon delivery systems, and target acquisition and missile guidance systems. Clinton "shut up" the federal grand jury by approving the
"Loral" deal. Bravo, China!

Federal Intelligence Service (BND), Germany

Like the KGB, the German BND chose total global espionage as its basic
strategy. This means strong government support, perfect semi-classified financing. It means Germany wants to dominate not only in Europe but worldwide
— a very dangerous tendency if you think about the past. I once met a BND officer under cover as an engineer in Ukraine; we had beer and vodka and he talked
to me pretty straight about Ukraine and its post-Chernobyl radioactive future.
He informed me about a super-secret deal Ukrainian President Kravchuk signed
with Germany, allowing the transfer of German radioactive waste to Ukraine.

The BND is very sensitive to international illegal weapons, radioactive materials and the drugs trade.

General Directorate for External Security (DGSE), France

French security officials, like those of other countries, are suspicious of foreigners and have perhaps less mercy and respect for their colleagues and for
quarries from other countries. In the USA they are very aggressive in high-tech
and industrial espionage.

Secret Intelligence Service (MI6, "The Firm"), Great Britain

Thank God, our British friends don't seem to be focusing on us — but who
knows? Right now they are too busy working against Germany (industrial and
military secrets) and France (military technology). God bless them.

Chapter 6. Techniques of Special Influence

Torture

Torture is a category of methods of interrogation designed to shock, hurt and humiliate the object and get information or to make him do something (if used for blackmail). Points to remember:

- ongoing torture decreases pain sensitivity
- people with strong will power take torture as a test
- resistance to torture is often a form of hysterics after arrest
- the object could take himself as a martyr if you torture him too much
- torture could damage object's psyche and you won't be able to work with him
- people usually trust "after torture information" more than voluntary confessions.
- There are different types of torture and professionals often combine them.

Techniques of psychological torture include:

- fake execution
- complete isolation ("wall therapy")
- daylight deprivation
- forcible narcotics addiction
- making the object observe others being tortured (such as family members)
- abuse of object's national, religious feelings or political views

The effects of psychological torture are:

- anxiety, depression, fear
- psychosis
- difficulty concentrating

- communication disabilities
- insomnia
- impaired memory
- headaches
- hallucinations
- sexual disturbances
- destruction of self-image
- inability to socialize

Techniques of physical torture include:

- food, water, sleep deprivation
- damage to vital body organs (brain, lungs, kidneys, liver, private parts) plus electric shock. The brain is particularly dependent on a continuous and stable supply of oxygen and glucose
- rape
- face deformation

The effects of physical torture are:

- extreme (unbearable) pain
- hypertension
- fatigue
- cardio-pulmonary and other disorders
- brain atrophy

SPECIAL PSYCHOLOGY

1. "Brain washing" (implantation of new ideas). The process is: isolation from outside world ("information vacuum") — sleep and food limitation (very effective) — "bombing" with slogans — ideological aggression —achieving the result (brain is loaded). The object is now ready to brainwash newcomers.

2. "Behavior modification" (by placing into a group). The process is: initial contact — introduction to a group — mutual interests — mutual activity–mutual ideas — control and prevention of any negative contacts outside the group. No rush, no pressure.

3. Special psychotherapy methods: talk + drugs + blondes + alcohol (used for recruitment)

Attention: An alcoholic is more impulsive, untrustful and unreliable; he demonstrates a poverty of ideas and incapacity for attention. He usually has serious personality maladjustments. He's immature, insecure, oversensitive and anxious. Without alcohol he's unable to meet and enjoy people socially, and suffers from marked feeling of inferiority. Besides, alcoholics suffer from vitamin B1 deficiency, which leads to anatomic changes in the central nervous system and heart with symptoms like anorexia, fatigability, and sleep disturbances. Other common symptoms are irritability, poor memory, inability to concentrate, heart pain.

4. "Transfer" (the object is placed in a regular hospital and then he's transferred to a mental health clinic or jail). In jail you can use such methods an accelerated work schedule (to exhaust the object), turning him into a number to traumatize his psyche, physical punishment or a threat of punishment to keep the object tense and depressed; senseless labor to destroy his personality. Remember: the lower the intellectual level of the object, the more aggressive he is and more sensitive to incentive or punishment.

You can actually re-organize any object's behavior by combining rewards and punishments, exposing him to feared situations and teaching him an instinct of a total (political) obedience.

Imprisonment is a very strong (sometimes — ultimate) tool. My friend who spent 10 years in jail described the changes in his behavior like this:

> 1st year — aggression as self-defense method (to survive)
> 2nd year — less personal tension, attempts to adapt the mind and body to the new, isolated way of life
> 3rd, 4th, 5th — gaining some inside status
> 6th, 7th — life in jail looks like natural routine
> 10th — euphoria before gaining freedom

5. Psychotronic weapons

Forget everything you heard, read or know about psychotronic secrets — it's a mess of pseudo facts, pseudo experiments, rumors and stories told by psychos.

Forget about long-distance control of human behavior, long-distance secret transporting of bio-chemical objects into the body, creation of bio-robots, long-distance information erasure, magnetic fields and acoustic waves, control of governments and criminal groups, suppression of protests and demonstrations, mass long-distance health control, control from space, long-distance control of communications, controlling the weather.

All we really have are molecular biophysics experiments with neuropeptides, which control human emotions and memory, and can induce uncontrollable unreasoning fear, panic, depression, schizophrenia and even death; chemical experiments like fluoride in the water supply that is shown to make people more docile; and genetic engineering, all intended to control short or long-term human mental processes. Intelligence, military and police services are researching the use of everything from music in public spaces to "tasers" and heat-ray guns to pacify or paralyze crowds.

BLACKMAIL

Used to force a person to do something (or stop the action) against his will; it's used also for recruitment. Blackmail methods include:

- Leaking "dirt" on the object through media
- Creating problems in his personal life and career
- Straight blackmail (threatening to make public certain compromising facts about him)
- Placing weapons, drugs, secret documents in object's house or office, followed by search and arrest
- Accusations of rape (robbery) (use hookers for that)
- Blackmail by pressing family members. Careful, object may commit suicide after intense blackmail, especially if he is an intellectual.

INTERROGATION

Interrogation is a conversational process of information gathering. The intent of interrogation is to control an individual so that he will either willingly supply the requested information or, if someone is an unwilling participant in the process, to make the person submit to the demands for information.

Before you interrogate the object, you have to gather some intelligence on him — examine his documents, read his files (if any), interrogate his partners or co-workers. Then you must establish and develop rapport, when the object reacts to your statements. Rapport may be developed by asking background questions about his family, friends, likes, dislikes; by offering incentives like coffee, alcohol, cigarettes, meals, or offers to send a letter home; by feigning experiences similar to those of the object; by showing concern for the object through the use of voice vitality and body language; by helping the source rationalize his guilt; by flattering the object. Be convincing and sincere, and you'll control the object for sure.

After that you can start questioning using follow-up questions (they flow one from another based on the answer to previous questions), break-up questions (to "break" the object's concentration, if he's lying, by interrupting him all the time), repeated questions (to check the previous information), control questions (developed from information you believe to be true and based on information which has been recently confirmed and which is not likely to be changed. They are used to check the truthfulness of the object's responses and should be mixed in with other questions throughout the interrogation), prepared questions developed in advance of interrogation to gain precise wording or the most desirable questioning sequence (they are used primarily for interrogations which are technical in nature), leading questions (to prompt the object to answer with the response he believes you wish to hear) to verify information.

There are two types of questions that you should not use — these are compound and negative questions. Compound questions are questions which ask for at least two different pieces of information and they are, actually, two or more questions in one. They allow the object to avoid giving a complete answer. Negative questions are questions which are constructed with "no," "not," "none." They should be avoided because they may confuse the object and produce false information.

Then you can use the following tricks:

(a) "good cop / bad cop"

(b) "story under a story" (after intense interrogation the object tells a different story — which is not true, either)

(c) "bombing" with questions

(d) pressure by not interrogating

(e) "silence makes your situation worse"

(f) "admit one small episode and that's it"

(g) "I help you — you help me"

Remember, every object has a breaking point and there are some indicators that the object is near his breaking point or has already reached it. If the object leans forward and his facial expression indicates an interest in the proposal or is more hesitant in his argument, he is probably nearing the breaking point.

If you are being interrogated, your major objective is to buy time and use "effective talking," disclosing information that is correct, but outdated or worthless.

MURDER

(a) Regular — shooting, explosives or poison (cyanides, curare).

Use a sniper or a "mouse" car (loaded with explosives and parked on the object's route) if access to the object is impossible because of high security. Anyway, the murder is obvious and investigation is inevitable.

General scheme. The best thing to do is to recruit or " install"» somebody with access to the object's security system and get information on his schedule (plus health and habits), places where he likes to relax. Try to gain access to his phone. Then prepare the plan and train three groups: surveillance (with optics and radios), action (includes snipers, explosives technicians or staged accidents specialists), and security (these people neutralize bodyguards, witnesses and other people who could interrupt the action; they complete the action if the action group fails; and they can neutralize the action group later, if planned so; they "cover" the safe retreat of action group and "cut" the chase).

For some operations you can modify the ammunition to make it more deadly — hollow cuts in the tip of the bullets will cause the lead to fragment upon impact, making a huge exit hole. You reach same effect using bullets with a drop of mercury in a hollow tip and you can also coat bullets with arsenic or cyanide. Use depleted, non-radioactive uranium bullets (uranium is much heavier than lead — it can be used to make a bullet with a smaller slug and a larger portion of explosive). Teflon bullets are good because with Teflon's antifriction characteristics they pierce bullet proof vests.

(b) Complex — staged accidents (suicides, catastrophes, drowning or a fall), robbery or rape followed by murder, technical accident (fire, electricity, gas), drugs, weapons, poison, explosives misuse. Also, staged natural death (stroke, heart attack, chronic illness as a result of special technical devices like irradiation). Attention: you can conceal injection sites by choosing areas that could not be easily detected, such as fingernails or toenails. For staged accidents you can use acetone (absorption of large quantities via either the respiratory or gastrointestinal tract results in decreased respiration, stupor and death); carbon monoxide — acetylene gas, illuminating gas (coal gas), automobile gas, furnace gas; or a simple novocaine + coffee combination. In some cases nonbacterial food poisoning is suitable. It can occur following the ingestion of (1) certain species of mushrooms such as Amanita Muscaria, which contains the toxic alkaloid muscarine, and Amanita Phalloides, which contains phalloidin or other toxins, (2) immature or sprouting potatoes, the active poison of which is colanin, (3) mussels — death may occur as a result of respiratory failure, (4) grain, especially rye, which has become contaminated with the ergot fungus, Claviceps Purpurea. Ergot contains a number of active principles including ergotoxin, tyramine and ergamin (histamine), (5) fruits sprayed with salts of lead or arsenic and food stored in cadmium-lined containers.

Staged botulism is effective, too. It's an acute intoxication manifested by neuromuscular disturbances, following ingestion of food containing a toxin, elaborated by Clostridium botulinum, a common soil bacillus. The disease is always caused by the ingestion of improperly preserved food, usually a home-canned product, in which the toxin has been produced during the growth of the causative organism. The spores of Clostridium botulinum are highly resistant to heat; in water they require exposure for 5 hours at 212°F to ensure their death.

The preserved food wherein the toxin is most commonly found are string beans, corn, spinach, olives, beets, asparagus, sea food, pork products and beef. The mortality of botulism may be as high as 65 per cent. Most of the fatal cases die between the 2nd and 9th days following the ingestion of the toxin. Death usually results from respiratory paralysis or from secondary bronchopneumonia. In those who survive, the disease usually reaches its height in the first days of illness. Recovery is characteristically very slow and residual weakness of the ocular muscles may persist for many months.

Some cases demand usage of poisons, both organic — like concentrated nicotine that enters the body through skin or concentrated inhalation of horseradish, garlic or rotten meat, which causes breathing paralysis; poisons extracted from rattlesnake, cobra, stonefish, and inorganic — arsenic, thallium, cyanides. Teflon can generate a deadly methane gas; or carbon tetrachloride can be boiled or burnt so that it gives off lethal phosgene gas. Any poison could be mixed with an agent that enters the body through the skin and takes anything with it.

Against terrorists, use their own weapons — high and low explosives. High explosives include TNT (trinitrotoluene), nitroglycerine, dynamite, plastique. Nitroglycerine is a mix of nitric acid (made by mixing saltpeter, potassium nitrate and sulfuric acid, then heating them and condensing the fumes), pure sulfuric acid and glycerin. TNT (nitric acid, sulfuric acid, toluene) is far more stable. Plastique is composed of cyclotrimethylene trinitramine, isomethylene and motor oil.

Low explosives include gasoline, saltpeter, picric acid, acetone peroxide, urea nitrate.

Many ingredients like gasoline, paraffin naphtha, acetone, swimming-pool cleaner, high-nitrogen fertilizer are generally available. Saltpeter is extracted from any soil with old decayed animal or vegetable matter — pour boiling water through, filter the water through wood ash, boil solution, remove salt crystals and leave the remaining solution to evaporate until only the potassium nitrate (saltpeter) crystals are left.

Mixed with sulfur, lampblack and sawdust it becomes a black powder. Urea nitrate involves boiling a large quantity of urine down to one-tenth of its volume, mixing that with nitric acid and filtering for the urea nitrate crystals. Like saltpeter, these crystals are used in pipe bombs. Picric acid is used as explosive or as a booster for high explosives. Very easy thing to make is nitrogen tri-iodide — filter ammonia through iodine crystals and when the resulting brown sludge dries, it will explode on contact.

Fertilizer mixed with fuel oil can be used in a pipe bomb.

A 5-pound bag of flour used with a small amount of low explosive and an incendiary such as aluminum powder can create a dust explosion big enough to demolish a room.

Swimming pool cleaner is used in pipe charges. Bleach, acetone and sulfuric acid combined can form a primary explosive. The explosive substance from a commercial detonating product can be mixed with acetone and mineral oil — then a book or newspaper is soaked in the solution, and dried, to create a powerful explosive that can be detonated with a blasting cap.

Use incendiaries (firebombs) like a Molotov cocktail — a mixture of gasoline and oil in a corked bottle with a gasoline-soaked rug as a fuse. Similar is the fire bottle with mixture of gasoline and sulfuric acid.

Light bulbs can be booby trapped with explosives. Letter and parcel bombs can be made with friction-sensitive tabs.

Chapter 7. Surveillance

Actual espionage is not what you see in the movies and you have absolutely no chance of evasion if a real professional surveillance crew is following you. Why? Because they use multiple methods and mixed methods.

Physical surveillance

1. "One line" — officers follow the object forming a line behind him and passing him one by one.

2. "Two lines" — officers form two lines on both sides of the street.

3. "Circle" — officers block the area and start searching (used in case they lose the object).

4. "Fork" — one officer (a car) moves in front of the object, another one — behind, other officers (cars) move along parallel streets.

5. "Box" — used when the object enters supermarket, hotel, restaurant. One or two officers follow the object, the others wait for him at the exits.

6. "Demonstration" — officers demonstrate their presence to pressure the object and reduce his activity.

7. "Provocation" — officers attack the object, beat him, steal (secret) documents. Often used to reduce his activity if he's trying to play James Bond.

8. "Outstrip" — officers do not follow the object because they know exactly where he's going.

9. "Football" — officers pass the object to each other (car — a group — bicyclist — car...)

10. "Movie" — the crew watches the object in stages: first day — to the subway only, second day — from subway to his office, etc. This technique is often used abroad. The crew has to have a female member if they are watching a woman (she could use the ladies room for a secret meeting) and members of various ethnicities (white, black, Latino) because the object could go to a specific ethnic area.

If you're the object and you've noticed surveillance:

- Don't rush, move at the same speed.
- Relax at the nearest bar (and relax the crew).
- Don't show how professional you are by trying to disappear, otherwise they could intensify surveillance or even neutralize you (smash your car, beat you up).
- Postpone the operation you were engaged in.
- Use a "draught" if you need to see your agent no matter what. Change lanes (if you are driving), stop the car and then drive left or right.

If you don't see surveillance, that means either there's no surveillance or you've failed in counter-surveillance. Discreetly watch the agent who's coming to meet you and try to detect any possible surveillance; or you may have been "outstripped."

Frequent Surveillance Crew Mistakes

- The same crew follows the object all day long.
- The object "rules" the crew and calculates it (he moves faster — the crew moves faster).
- One crew member(s) is too noticeable (unusual dress, haircut, disabled parts of the body, too fat or too skinny, too ugly or too pretty).
- The crew starts to search possible hiding places for espionage evidence right after the object leaves (and he may be watching).
- The crew leaves traces after a secret search of the object's house (office).
- The crew does not report its mistakes or the fact that they've lost the object.
- The crew is not professional (using childish tricks like jumping out of a subway train just before the doors close).

Technical Surveillance

(a) Visual surveillance. Done through special holes in the ceilings and walls, through the windows from the opposite building (car) or by installing the camera inside the house (you can substitute something, like a clock, for the same thing but "stuffed" with a camera or recorder.) You can use informant as well to watch the object outside his house (especially if you want to do a secret search).

(b) Listening devices. The easiest thing is to listen to the object's phone (record all calls, including those dialed "by mistake"). If you work inside his apartment, make sure you equip the room where he usually talks. Attention: avoid widespread mistake when your agent keeps the listening device on his body; install a miniature device in his clothes or shoes, because the object could try a test and ask the agent to take off his clothes or invite him to the sauna or pool.

(c) If you are working abroad, listen 24/7 to local counterintelligence surveillance radiofrequencies.

(d) Reading the mail. When you control the object's mail, remember he could use multiple addresses and PO boxes. Open all the letters with no return address or PO box. Watch when you open the letter — the object could leave a tiny piece of paper, hair, etc. to check if anybody opened the letter. Analyze the text carefully — there could be a cipher or the words with double meaning (jargon), especially when you read mafia mail.

(e) Combination of above-mentioned methods

Chapter 8. How to Run Agents (Secret Sources)

You can get tons of information through technical devices but no device can influence decisions made by leaders of other countries. That's why for thousands of years to come, a reliable agent will be the top tool of any special service, and their actual names have to be kept secret forever, please. A VIP agent (a top government employee) is a very rare thing and depends hugely on luck, because he can make or influence big political decisions. If he has access to the Oval Office, he can change the President's plans and strategy, and can sabotage political, economic or military actions. When major presidential initiatives fail, time after time, one might wonder who is sabotaging whom.

The most important thing a counterintelligence agent can get is a reliable information on any possible attempt on the US President's life, or concerning a decision of a foreign government to start a war against the United States. A professional agent is actually is both an instrument (to get information) and a weapon (to influence or neutralize people).

Categories:

A. "Garbage" (60%), the "no trust " category.

Recruitment is the #1 priority for the officer and a part of his working plan and very often he has to recruit people who are not born agents. You can work with a nice guy, teach him, pay him, press him — and he still avoids any cooperation (busy, sick, on vacation, etc.). It's hard to get rid of him because, first, you have to explain to your superiors why you recruited garbage and second, there's a rule: if you want to get rid of a passive agent, recruit an active one first.

Also, agents who work under pressure (blackmail) sooner or later slide into this category.

B. Good agents (30%), middle category.

They adhere to the rules of discipline and keep the schedule (that's very important even if there's no information), deliver a lot of information that you have to verify through other sources, but don't show much initiative. Used for regular espionage: go and talk to the object, copy documents, make a recording, take pictures, listen, watch. You can trust them and check often, anyway.

C. Born agents (10%).

You are very lucky if you can recruit such people. They betray their country with pleasure and sometimes do not even ask for money because it's in their character — they are looking for adventure or are not happy with their personal or professional life and seek improvement or revenge. They take risks, have good analytical abilities, good education, make (VIP) connections easily, "crack" any object, play the "good guy" whom you can trust. Sometimes they come to you as volunteers, and if they bring valuable stuff — recruit them.

D. Women.

Women are a special category here, as elsewhere, and the rule is: if you can't recruit a real agent, you recruit a woman. It's not professional to recruit a woman for a serious operation but if you want to get to an important object, a woman can introduce you. OK, you can recruit a US Senator's secretary or a typist from the Pentagon, but it will be on your conscience if she gets caught. Such cases entail a life sentence, usually — how would you feel? Besides, women often fall in love with their objects and tell them everything. Finally, a married woman is a much bigger problem than a married man.

RECRUITMENT

Recruit a small number of well-informed people.

Do not recruit:

- psychos
- volunteers (unless it's a "mole" or other government employee who brings you top secret information right away. In a counter-intelligence set-up, a "volunteer" will try to get information about you, telling the minimum about himself.)
- persons with low educational and intellectual level
- people under 30 or over 70, unless it's a VIP. (Did someone get Jim Baker? Dick Cheney?)
- mafia members
- people who are happy with their lives and careers

The best formula when you recruit is a mix of money and ideology (brain-washing). It's not necessary to sign recruitment obligations — people take that as a blackmail tool. It's enough if the fellow brings a good piece of information and get paid (make a video, anyway).

Recruitment Pyramid

Priority recruitment candidates in the USA:

President
The White House staff
The Cabinet and federal agencies
The US Congress
Big corporations
Big scientific institutions
Local politicians
VIP world (celebrities — big media, show biz, big sports figures)

Finding Candidates for Recruitment

1. All spies who work in the USA under legal "cover" as diplomats, report-ers, scientists, businessmen, actors, artists, musicians, sportsmen have the legal right to make and develop any contacts and invite people to private parties; then they "transfer" these contacts to professional recruiters. Any embassy can invite any politician to official and private parties and "work" with him there. Besides, all those people can invite prospective candidates to their countries or to other country to develop the contact; it's much easier to recruit abroad. And remem-ber, any contact, any talk, any piece of biography is already information.

2. You can get information about candidates through other agents and through the media.

3. It's useful to install listening devices in the government buildings or listen to the phones, and collect compromising information on politicians. I recom-mend listening to the phones all over the city, if it's the capital of the country.

Working with the Agent

Do not tell the agent about problems and mistakes of the agency, about your personal problems, about other agents, about his own file and compromising in-formation you have on him. Don't show him any classified documents — you might provoke him to sell the information to somebody else. Don't trust your agents too much; they can use you to compromise their personal enemies.

Never criticize the person — be an adviser. Don't talk straight if he avoids cooperation or brings you garbage — just reduce or stop payments, or get rid of him.

You lose the agent if you don't pay him for a job well done, ask him to "produce" fake information (to show your bosses how much great espionage activity you have going on) or if you don't care about his personal security and his personal problems (health, career). And — never give poison to your agent for security reasons.

Questioning the Agent

This is of extreme importance — the right question brings you the right answer and top secret info. Give your agent a chance to tell and show you everything he's brought, no matter how chaotic the story might be or how ordinary the documents look. Don't make written notices. Don't bring written questions even if you are talking about some advanced technology — look and be professional. Don't let the agent analyze the information before he talks to you and don't let him bring it in a written form — it's usually not complete; he can lose it; or it may be stolen from him. If there are documents, he has to bring a microfilm. Ask questions — when? where? what happened? why? what's going to happen next?

After that you tell the story back to him and he adds details. At the end of the meeting give the agent another task and don't ask him to bring you "something," because he'll bring you just that "something" and nothing else.

Remember, questioning is not interrogation; do not bring another officer to the meeting because it will look like cross interrogation.

Teaching the Agent

Teach your agent to:

- follow security rules while talking to people, working with the documents and especially meeting the officer (some foreign agencies practice open contacts with many people, hoping that the meeting with the agent won't attract much attention — I don't recommend that)
- always stay calm in stressful situations
- always keep discipline and arrive on time
- use analytic abilities working with people and documents — ask yourself as many questions as you can

Checking the Agent

You can never be sure you are not working with a "double agent," even if he brings you top secret stuff. Besides, agents are human beings and they make mistakes — they forget about security, spend too much money, talk too much and ask extra questions; if arrested they may not play the hero but will tell everything. Anyway, you can check an agent,

a. by fake arrest followed by severe interrogation.

b. through provocation (tell him you know about his "double game" and watch his behavior after the meeting (it's good to have a listening device or a camera in his house).

c. by making an analysis of all the information and documents he delivers and comparing it with information from other sources.

d. through other agents.

e. through your "mole" in counter-intelligence (if you're lucky).

f. through technical devices (reading the mail, listening to the phone, secret searching his house and office, watching him through hidden cameras, trying surveillance in the street).

Liquidating the Agent

It doesn't happen often but you have to be able to recognize some special situations which might require you to terminate the agent:

1. He knows too much (talks too much) and is ready to betray you.

2. A VIP agent (politician) is under suspicion and you can't help him for political reasons (diplomatic, international scandal, etc.) — in such a case an accident could be staged. This happens when the agent is too close to the President.

3. The agent was involved in special operations (murders) and is dangerous as a witness.

4. He is trying to blackmail you.

5. You need to pressure (blackmail) other agents.

Chapter 9. The FBI and Domestic Control

Don't die a hero — that's bad planning, poor training and lack of experience; the dead man goes to a hall of shame and stupidity. Bad planning is an operational failure; once things have gone off track it is far more complicated to achieve the objective. Multi-step complex operations come from the fantasies of bureaucrats who watch too many movies. Keep it simple if you want to get it right.

Never provoke people to break the law — that's not professional.

Always look for an insider if you need to conduct a sophisticated operation (bank robbery, etc.).

Investigation Process

- Secure and examine carefully the crime scene (every person who enters the scene is a potential destroyer of physical evidence).
- Record the scene (make photos, sketches, notes with detailed written description of the scene with the location of evidences recovered).
- Collect physical evidences (blood, semen, saliva, hair, documents, drugs, weapons and explosives, poisonous substances, fingerprints, traces, soils and minerals, fiber) and package everything.
- Collect confessions and eyewitness accounts and then make a plan of investigation and correct it later.
- Research similar crimes and criminals involved.
- Make a model (profile) of the suspect.
- Analyze expertise data.
- Work with secret sources.
- Cooperate with other divisions (abroad, if needed).

Every extra day cuts your chances of success in half.

ARRESTS

In daytime arrest people discreetly — don't bring extra public irritation. There's a general rule: more arrests — less crime prevention (after being in jail, people engage in more sophisticated and secret criminal activity). After mass arrests at certain locations (buildings), repeat the action in a day or two.

Here's the procedure:

- Chasing the object, block the area into circles (follow the plan for a certain area) and try to "push" him to a certain place where your team is waiting.
- Taking the object in the street: look around for his partner(s), who could shoot you from behind.
- Be on the alert if anybody tries to talk to you in the street — it could be an attempt to divert your attention.
- Arresting a crew, shoot and disarm any people with guns first.
- Never hesitate to shoot terrorists — some of them have mental problems and won't think a second before shooting you.
- Arrest a dangerous object while he's relaxed (drugs, alcohol, sex, sleep) and don't let him kill himself, eliminate evidences or warn his partners. (Most people feel more relaxed when traveling abroad.) To take the object alive, scream, shoot over his head, use smoke and light grenades.
- Camouflage your team (as ambulance workers, construction workers, vendors, etc.).
- If there's a crowd around the object, shoot in the air and order everybody to lie down— the object has no choice.
- If the object is well armed and very dangerous (and you have intelligence information to that effect), you have to shoot him even in a very crowded area as you never know what he's going to do next — take hostages, shoot people or blow up a bomb (three wounded people is a better score than three hundred dead).

THE MAFIA

The Mafia is "working" in many countries at the following levels:

1. Lower: drugs, weapons, racketeering, money laundering and other regular criminal activity.
2. Middle: involvement in economy (big banks and corporations) and politics.
3. Upper: government infiltration.

The Mafia's Inside Rules:

- Help your brother no matter what.
- Revenge is inescapable.
- Obey orders and keep quiet, an order is a sign of trust.
- Leave no evidences (no papers).
- Don't lie, steal, or cheat.
- There's no justice but Mafia justice.
- Live and die together.

How the Mafia System Operates

The basic principle is a total secrecy of structure, methods, operations, names and banking accounts. The most powerful tool is an exchange of favors. The Mafia covers any country with a chain of connections, creating a perfect terrain for total corruption. The first row of the Mafia's best friends are corrupted police and FBI officers, second row — local and federal politicians. The Mafia cultivates mutual help, protects better than a law and that's why mafia laws are primary for the members of a family. Members get help from the family automatically and it's a very strong incentive. The Mafia launches political murders only if certain politicians seriously offend its big financial interests. Have you noticed that every presidential candidate is ready to fight crime but nobody is talking about fighting the Mafia? You can't win, but you can keep the Mafia under control. And you have to control the Mafia because it penetrates politics, and political psychology (behavior) could be substituted by a criminal psychology, and that will be the end of America.

I have met Russian mafia members both in Russia and in the United States and know them very well. I can't agree with FBI and police experts who don't see much threat from those people. First, they don't hesitate to kill, even if it's a cop. Second, they are not afraid of American prisons and even have people who stay in jail for years to "teach" the next generation of gangsters. Third, they don't mix with other ethnic groups (for security reasons). Fourth, they usually look for big illegal business opportunities, like serious money laundering or drugs, weapons and diamonds trafficking. (When it comes to drugs, it has to be wholesale only — Russians don't sell drugs on American streets.)

"Russian" (former Soviet) mafia organizations in USA

1. Kikalishvili
2. Fineberg
3. Chechnya
4. Dagestan
5. "Lubertsy"
6. Mazutkin
7. Baklanov
8. Kazan'
9. Brandvein
10. Sorkin
11. Rudyak
12. Brook
13. Ibragimov
14. Ittayev
15. Efros
16. Sogomonyan

17. Arakelyan
18. Brikyan
19. "Vilnus"
20. "Vorkuta"
21. "Solntsevo"

POLICE TRICKS

(a) "House trap": Spread information that a certain place is packed with money or drugs, and prepare an ambush.

(b) Advertise discreetly (through your sources) some semi-legal or illegal business. People who are willing to get involved in dubious operations will "fly" to you (change cities).

(c) Encourage wars between mafia families.

(d) "Car trap": Install a video camera in an expensive car and leave it in the "bad" area. A thief gets in a car and ... the trap is closed.

Have some fun, guess who this is: blue jeans, blue baseball jacket, work boots, silver chain (with a badge under T-shirt), short haircut, clean-shaved face, "walkie-talkie," Pepsi and cheap cookies, walks like a President of the United States and looks straight into your eyes like a pastor. (NYPD undercover).

HOW TO MANAGE CIVIL DISTURBANCE

The FBI and the police have to join forces in response to any serious tip about a "planned crowd," one which is being organized to assemble at the call of a leader and step forward with serious political demands, and is ready to create a civil disturbance. Civil disturbance arises when a crowd gathers to air grievances on issues and transfers its anger from the issues to the people dealing with the issues, swells uncontrollably as curious bystanders and sympathetic onlookers join forces with the activists or protectors, is incited to irrational action by skillful agitators, adopts irrational behavior and becomes a mob. And if the crowd comes to encompass two or more groups with opposing views, they become engaged in a violent confrontation.

The crowd is the engine and the basic human element of a civil disturbance action. When blocked from expressing its emotions in one direction, a crowd's hostility often is, or can be, re-directed elsewhere. In a civil disturbance environment, any crowd can be a threat to law and order because it is open to manipulation. Leadership has a profound effect on the intensity and direction of the crowd behavior. In many crowd situations, the members become frustrated by confusion and uncertainty and they want to be directed. The first person to give clear orders in an authoritative manner is likely to be followed. A skillful agitator can increase a crowd's capacity for violence and direct a crowd's aggression toward any target included in his statement (he can also use the media to reach millions of people and incite them to unlawful acts, or even a revolution, without having a direct personal contact). On the other hand, an experienced leader is also able to calm down a crowd and avoid a social explosion.

A crowd is affected by negative emotions and panic, which can occur during a civil disturbance when people think or feel danger is so close at hand that the only course of action is to flee; when they think the escape routes are limited or that only one escape route exists; think the limited routes are blocked; believe an escape route is open after it was blocked and in trying to force a way to the exit, cause those in front to be crushed, smothered, or trampled; are not able to disperse quickly after being exposed to riot agents and begin to believe their lives are at risk.

Planned Crowd Tactics — Nonviolent or Violent

Nonviolent tactics may range from name-calling to building barricades. Demonstrators may converse with police officers to distract them, to gain their sympathy, or to convince them to leave their posts. Often their leaders want to provoke the authorities to take actions that later may be exploited as acts of brutality. Sometimes women, children and elderly people are placed in the front ranks to discourage countermeasures. Demonstrators may form human blockades to impede traffic by sitting down in the street or at the entrances of the government buildings, or they may lock arms, making it hard for the police to separate and remove them. People may resist by going limp, or chain (handcuff) themselves to fences, gates and other objects or to each other to prolong the demonstration. Terrorists may try to agitate crowds as a diversion for terrorist acts.

Violent tactics includes physical attacks on people and property, setting fires, and bombings. Crowd members can use homemade or regular weapons, rocks, bricks, balloons filled with paint to use as "bombs," picket signs can be used as clubs, or pipes wrapped in newspapers; fire-crackers dipped in glue and covered with nails can be used as grenades.

A crowd may erect barricades to impede police movement, and use vehicles, trees, furniture, and fences for that. Rioters may drive vehicles to breach roadblocks, and set fire to buildings and vehicles to block the advance of police (flood an area with gasoline and ignite it). Leaders may order snipers to shoot police or demonstrators to provoke authorities to use excessive force; or the inverse: the authorities may do that, secretly, to justify heavy-handed intervention. Bombs can be exploded ahead of police to block the street. Small crowds are very mobile; they are easily dispersed, but they can quickly re-assemble elsewhere. And liquor and drug stores must be closed.

The most important thing you need to manage an upcoming civil disturbance is information about the presence and location of leaders, goals, time, location and causes of disturbances, identity of persons, groups or organizations that have threatened to cause disturbances, estimated number of people who will be involved in the action, sources, types and locations of arms and other equipment available to the rioters, and the plans to use them. Reliable information gives you the opportunity for such preventive measure as arrest and conviction of ringleaders.

Now, if a peaceful demonstration has been turned into a civil disturbance, you have to isolate the area immediately to prevent the disturbance from spreading. Move uninvolved people from the area quickly, prevent unauthorized people from entering the affected area, prevent the escape of rioters. Necessary measures for isolating an area include barriers, patrols, pass and ID systems (a quickly-erected barrier can be made by parking vehicles bumper-to-bumper and fitting a wire-covered wood or metal frames on the bumpers. Once a crowd is isolated, time is on your side.

Then you have to set up an inner and outer police perimeter. The inner perimeter contains the area and keeps the disorder from spreading. The outer perimeter prevents outsiders from entering the disturbance area. The use of two perimeters also creates a clear zone where you can stop people who breach one of the lines. In large crowds police officers stand shoulder-to-shoulder, in small crowds they stand double arm's length apart, or they link themselves together with riot batons.

You have to protect facilities, because the loss of water and electricity endangers the health of the community, the loss of government buildings disrupts government functions; radio and TV stations, if seized by demonstrators, can be a powerful tool for spreading disorder. Actually, you have four options to manage the crowd:

1. Monitoring. This includes establishing communications with crowd leaders to convey official interest and intent to the crowd, efforts to get cooperation of crowd leaders, monitoring of the crowd activity and noting developments (size, location, mood, the developing situation). If communications exist with crowd leaders, the authorities may be able to divert either the leaders or the crowd from their stated or apparent goal. Pressure can be put on the leaders to channel the crowd into an area that minimizes the damages.

2. Containment. Containment limits a crowd to a certain area and prevents the disorder from spreading. Crowds can be contained by crowd control formations, perimeter patrols, and barriers.

3. Blocking. It physically denies a crowd's advance. Crowd control formations, mainly the line formation, and barricades are used to block.

4. Dispersing. The intent of dispersal is to fragment the crowd. This option is most useful for small crowd situations in congested urban sites. The use of proclamations, a show of force, crowd control formations, and riot control agents can disperse crowds. You can make a verbal proclamation, officially establishing the illegal nature of the crowd's actions and ask (do not order!) people to disperse and leave the area peacefully. Alert, aggressive patrolling of the disturbance area is a good show of force, and it deters the gathering of crowds.

Crowd control formations — the line, the wedge, and the echelon, may be employed. The line formation is used most often because of its offensive and defensive applications. As an offensive formation, the line is used to push or drive crowds straight back, across an open area, or up a city street. As a defensive formation, the line is used to hold the crowd or to deny access to restricted streets or areas. The echelon is an offensive formation used to turn or divert groups in either open or built-up areas to move crowds away from buildings, fences, and walls. The wedge is an offensive formation that is used to penetrate and split crowds. You can also use a circle formation when all-round security is required.

Riot control agents (grenades and dispersers) or water can be used to distract, deter, or disable a violent crowd (wind direction affects how these are to be used). In most cases riot batons serve best to calm down people.

Terror

Terrorism is the unlawful use of violence against people or property to coerce or intimidate governments or societies, often to achieve political, religious or ideological objectives. The common strategy of terrorists is to commit acts of violence. Terrorist acts are of course not limited to the US; many spectacular and devastating incidents have occurred in Russia, throughout the Middle East and Europe.

There are two types of terror: "Red" terror is aimed against certain politicians; "black" refers more to mass murders. Of course, the two can be mixed.

Purposes: to scare the nation, neutralize the government and show its inability to rule the country; to make the government admit that terror organization is a real political power; to draw public (international) attention to a certain political problem, to provoke the government to use military force and start civil war;

to prove some political or religious ideology; prevent or delay important political decisions or legislation; discourage foreign investments or foreign government assistance programs; change the government through revolution or civil war.

The media is a "valuable helper" by giving terrorists international recognition. The danger is that this kind of attention tends to incite acts of violence by other terrorist groups. Terrorists use different methods and taking hostages, bombing, assassinations, ambushes and hijacking are the most popular ones.

List of major attacks attributed to terrorists on United States targets:

(I can only indicate who was charged with these attacks; it is not possible to say who inspired, supported, provoked or knowingly permitted them to act.)

1983	US Embassy, Beirut, Lebanon, 63 killed, attackers not identified.
1984	US Marine compound, Beirut, Lebanon, 241 killed, attacked by Shi'ites
1983	US Embassy Annex, Beirut, Lebanon, 16 killed, attacked by Hezbollah.
1988	PanAm flight, Lockerbie, Scotland, 270 killed, attacked by Libyan Abdel Al-Megrani
1989	World Trade Center, NYC, 5 killed, 1000 injured, attacked by Sheik Omar Abdul Rahman group.
1995	Saudi Arabian military facility with the US troops, Riyadh, Saudi Arabia, 7 killed, attacked by the Movement for Islamic Change and Tigers of the Gulf.
1996	US military housing complex, Dhahran, Saudi Arabia, 19 killed, attackers not identified.
1997	Summer Olympics, Atlanta, Georgia, 1 killed, attackers not identified.
1998	US Embassies, Kenya and Tanzania, 224 killed, attacked by Al-Qaeda.
1999	USS "Cole," Aden, Yemen, 17 killed, attacked by Al-Qaeda.
2001	Anthrax attacks: anthrax letters were mailed from Trenton, New Jersey to NBC News, CBS News, ABC News, "New York Post," NYC, "National Enquirer," Boca Raton, Florida, Senators Daschle and Leahy in Washington, DC; 5 died, attackers not identified.
2001	World Trade Center (NYC) and the Pentagon, 3019 killed, attacked by Al-Qaeda.

Terrorist groups can be divided into three categories:

a. Non-state supported groups which operate autonomously, receiving no support from any government.

b. State supported groups, which operate alone but receive support from one or more governments.

c. State directed groups, which operate as the agents of a government, receiving substantial intelligence, logistic, and operational support.

Organized terror is "organized construction":

- search and recruitment of people, including informants and supporters in government agencies, counterintelligence and police
- getting money (robberies, illegal operations with drugs and weapons, legal business, searching for donors with the same political views
- security system, including a system of "cells" (small groups). Preparing places where members can hide, relax, get medical care; keep weapons, money, special literature. System also includes fake IDs and counter-intelligence (detection of traitors, preventing collapse of the group and uncontrolled criminal activity (robberies)
- training camps (shooting, working with explosives)
- "brainwashing" sessions
- planning the actions
- making special connections with other groups and mafia

Hostages

You must always negotiate if hostages have been taken. Negotiation produces some advantages for you. These advantages are: (a) the longer situation is prolonged, the more intelligence can be gathered on the location, motivation and identity, (b) the passage of time generally reduces anxiety, allowing the hostage taker to assess the situation rationally, (c) given enough time, the hostages may find a way to escape on their own, (c) the necessary resolve to kill or hold hostages lessens with time, (d) terrorists may make mistakes. The negotiation team must have information to support negotiations (you get it from interviews with witnesses, escaped and released hostages, and captured suspects — it's very important to get the identities, personalities, motives, habits and abilities of the offenders).

Bombing

Bombing is another common tactic. The bomb is a popular weapon, because it is cheap to produce, easy to make, has variable uses, and is difficult to detect and trace after the action. In Iraq they usually use booby-trapped vehicles and car-bombs (cars filled with explosives).

Ambush

A well-planned ambush seldom fails. The terrorists have time on their side, and can choose a suitable place.

Assassination

Assassination is the oldest terrorist tactic. Targets mostly are government officials.

Fighting terror. There's no other way to fight terror but to recruit informants and construct a massive surveillance web to control the nation in every way.

Chapter 10. Identifying Spies

Moles

A "mole" is a spy inside the government, recruited or "installed" most often within the special services, by an outside government/agency. The 3 most dangerous things a "mole" can do:

1. Calculate President's plans and decisions judging by information he's asking for.

2. Manipulate information being sent to President, and thus influence global political decisions.

3. Paralyze to some extent the government (if he's CIA or FBI Director).

How to Detect a Mole

A. Use index cards (special file) — never use computers to save this information!

Prepare a file on each officer and mark there the signs of a "mole" — has or spends too much money, asks too many extra questions; uses professional skills to check for physical and technical surveillance; has discreet contacts with foreigners; discreet copying of top secret documents; attempts to get a job in most secret departments; talks with close friends and family members about the possibility of making money as a "mole"; behavior deviations — extra suspiciousness, excitement, depression, drugs or alcohol addiction. Three signs are enough to start an investigation — the "triangulation" principle.

B. Use provocation. If a prospective "mole" is looking for a contact with the enemy and is ready to betray, and you have exact information, organize such a "meeting" for him. Do not arrest the person right away — play along, as he may give you connections to other people who are ready to betray. There's one more provocation method: you supply the suspects with "highly classified information" and just watch what they do.

C. Use a "filter" or "narrowing the circle." Include all the officers you suspect in a "circle" and narrow it until one name is left as the most likely suspect.

D. Make a "model" of a "mole," judging by information you have on him.

E. Recruit an insider. Recruit a "mole" inside your enemy's intelligence service and he'll help you to find the one inside yours (it's called "grabbing the other end of a thread").

F. Don't trust anybody.

What to Do If You Detect a Mole

- Assess the damage.
- Restrict his access to classified information and start feeding him with fake data.
- Stop all operations he was involved in and create the illusion they are still in progress.
- Bring home officers and agents who work abroad and had contacts with him and those to whose files he had access.
- Start 24/7 surveillance if you've decided to play the game and look into his contacts.
- Arrest the mole discreetly (if you want to continue the game).

Effective methods to prevent treason do not exist.

Identifying Spies

If a spy is an intelligence officer working abroad under cover (as a diplomat, businessman, reporter, or representative of an aid agency), you can identify him by:

- following the careers of all diplomats who work at your enemy's embassies all over the world
- recruiting a mole inside the intelligence service (or inside the station)
- setting up your agent for recruitment by the enemy's station
- watching foreigners who try to make discreet contacts with native citizens with access to secrets
- making a model of a spy (professional behavior, attempts to detect surveillance, attempts to recruit sources or just get any classified information during normal meetings, throwing away money trying to get access to government employees, military and scientific circles)
- using secret surveillance and listening devices inside the station and practicing secret searches

If a spy is an intelligence officer working in your country under cover as a native citizen (or he is a native citizen who was recruited), you identify him by making a model (contacts with identified spies — that's often the only sign that indicates a spy, and that's why surveillance is very important in getting information from a mole).

How to Cover Your Mole

There are special methods to cover your own mole and a "switch" is the most effective — it's when you switch counterintelligence to other, innocent persons who work with the mole. You can try information "leaks" through a double agent — it looks like you are receiving top secret information through another traitor or by breaking into the electronic security systems. Or you can try an information leak through publication in big newspapers — it looks like the information is not secret and is known to many people, or there's another mole.

By the way, was John Deutch, Bill Clinton's CIA Director, a Russian mole?

John Deutch was born in Belgium to a Russian father and he was the only Russian CIA Director. His biography is very impressive. He graduated from Amherst College and earned a B.S. in chemical engineering and Ph.D. in physical chemistry from MIT, where the KGB loves to recruit future scientists. He served in the following professional positions:

1970-1977 MIT Chemistry Dept. Chairman, Dean of Science, and provost

1977-1980 The US Department of Energy

1980-1981 President's Nuclear Safety Oversight Commission

1983 President's Commission on Strategic Forces

1985-1989 The White House Science Council

1990-1993 The President's Intelligence Advisory Board

1993-1994 Under Sec'y of Defense for Acquisition and Technology, Deputy Defense Secretary

1995-1996 Director of Central Intelligence

1996 The President's Commission on Aviation Safety and Security

1998-1999 Chairman of the Commission to Assess the Organization of the Federal Government to Combat the Proliferation of Weapons of Mass Destruction

Since 2000 he's been at MIT as a professor, and is a Director for Citigroup. He was awarded Public Service Medals from the following Departments: State, Energy, Defense, Army, Navy, Air Force, Coast Guard plus Central Intelligence Distinguished Medal and the Intelligence Community Distinguished Intelligence Medal.

John Deutch was appointed Director of Central Intelligence (DCI) by President Bill Clinton and stayed in Langley for a short period of time, from May 10, 1995 to December 14, 1996. My professional opinion is: John Deutch, a former

Russian DCI, is a "mole" and he's not been arrested because President Clinton obstructed the investigation and pardoned this enemy of state in 2001. Three signs are enough to triangulate a "mole" and here they are for Mr. Deutch:

1. Two days after Deutch retired from the CIA, on December 16, 1996, technical personnel discovered at his house highly classified information stored on his unclassified computer, loaded from his agency computer. He refused to explain why he violated strict security rules.

First, a normal Director of Central Intelligence doesn't need highly classified data on his home computer because he is a bureaucrat, not an analyst.

Second, here we have a trick — the Internet-connected computer is accessible by anyone with some technical knowledge and you don't have to send anything — the Russians will read secret information right from your home computer. Simple.

2. In 1997 the CIA began a formal security investigation. It was determined that his computer was often connected to the Internet with no security, and that Deutch was known to leave memory cards with classified data lying in his car. Deutch used his influence to stop any further investigation and the CIA took no action until 1999, when it suspended his security clearances. He admitted finally the security breach and merely apologized.

3. In 1999 the Defense Department started its own investigation, and it appeared that in 1993 Deutch, as Defense Undersecretary, used unsecured computers at home and his America Online (!) account to access classified defense information. As Deputy Defense Secretary, he declined departmental requests in 1994 to allow security systems to be installed in his residence.

4. In 2000 Senator Charles Grassley asked the Justice Department to look into the case. There was no investigation.

5. In 2001 President Clinton pardoned Deutch. There were no comments.

Now, the question is: why is he still in the US if he's a "mole" under suspicion? I see only one explanation — he has a very powerful friend who can give orders to Attorney General and Secretary of Defense.

P.S. Professor Deutch is still at the Department of Chemistry, MIT. In March 2006, I asked him for an interview. As far as I know, he's still pondering that request.

CHAPTER 11. STRATEGIES

Every operation demands a set of original methods, especially if we are talk-ing about strategic intelligence. I just want to give you some idea what these methods (strategies) look like.

"Domino" or "chain reaction." A coup, revolution or civil war in one country provokes the same actions in other countries (neighbors).

"Sliding" strategy. Transformation of a secret operation into an open one: support of illegal opposition/coup.

"Restriction." You damage (limit) international and economic connections (projects) of the enemy.

"Monopoly." Special operation to keep country's monopoly or status as eco-nomic leader or special (nuclear) holder, or high tech producer. Includes actions to restrict the attempts of other countries to get strategic raw materials and modern weapons and technologies.

"Reverse effect." The government declares a certain goal and launches a military or special operation, but the result is something quite different, pos-sibly opposite. Examples: instead of separating (ethnic) group "A" from group "B" both of them are being exterminated; instead of peace and democracy in a certain region, power is being concentrated in one group and the opposition is being exterminated.

"Clash." You "clash" the government and opposition of a target country and support civil war until the country is ruined and you get it for free.

"Positive shock." A domestic operation; to save the government during a cri-sis, special service provokes artificial civil conflict or sabotage, imitation (ter-ror), and the government takes care of the "problem."

"Controlled crisis export"

"Sanitation border." "Fencing" the target country by enemies (neighbors).

"Alibi." You build a "chain" of evidence (witnesses) and move the investigation to a dead end.

"Passive sabotage." A very effective strategy used to cover up a major action like the assassination of a President or the destruction of several office towers. You just "do not see the bad guys" who are going to kill the President or blow up the city. In any case you win — the perpetrators are not sure you are watching them; you can arrest them if the object survives or liquidate them once the object is dead. You don't need a big conspiracy, you just give the order to ignore certain people until their plan materializes.

"Special tour." You help the target country to "build democratic institutions" (the government and local administrations) by sending official crews to help. Actually, they rule the country and that's a "hidden occupation."

"Mask." You mask your actual global plans (reforms) by another big action (war).

Other Strategies: Breaking Up the USSR

As an example, we can look at the strategies that were used to break up the USSR. This was political warfare on unprecedented scale, which means very aggressive use of political tools to achieve national objectives. It means a constant policy of taking political actions against the vital interests of another power. External strategies that were used to destroy the USSR included: economic exhaustion by the arms race, dollar intervention, prohibition to sell high-tech equipment to Soviet Union (official explanation — they could be used for military purposes; reality — they could be used to boost economic production), incentives to go for "dead end" economic projects, inducement to engage in a senseless war against Afghanistan, aggressive "anti-communist" propaganda.

Internal strategies used to destroy Soviet Union included: incentives and provocations (through local media and opposition parties) of national, religious and social conflicts; inducement into military conversion programs; encouragement of the disintegration of the Soviet republics under the appeal of illusory calls to undefined values like "democracy," "self-determination," and "freedom," instigation of corruption within the Kremlin; support of Soviet leader Gorbachev's utopian plan to "plant" democracy in the USSR.

As you understand by now, planned crowds etc. were also used extensively to force the government's hand. These techniques have also been used recently to weaken governements in Ukraine, Hungary and elsewhere.

Chapter 12. Presidential Security

The estimated cost of protecting the President, Vice President and their families alone is $356 million/year.

> "I guess there's always the possibility [of assassination], but that is what the Secret Service is for." —President John Kennedy
>
> "Trained pigs." "Stay ten yards away at all times." "If you want to remain on this detail, get your —— ass over here and grab those bags!" — First Lady Hillary Clinton on the Secret Service.

Four US Presidents have been killed:

1. Abraham Lincoln.

On April 14, 1865 during a performance of "Our American Cousin" at Ford's Theatre, John Booth killed Abraham Lincoln by shooting him in the back of the head. Leaping from the balcony to the stage, he broke his leg —but escaped. Federal troops found him hiding in a barn in Virginia, where they shot and killed him.

2. James Garfield.

On July 2, 1881 Charles Guiteau, who wanted to work for the President but wasn't accepted, shot James Garfield in the back at Union Station in Washington, DC. Garfield died eighty days later. Refusing to plead not guilty by reason of insanity, Guiteau was tried for murder, found guilty and hanged.

3. William McKinley.

On September 6, 1901 anarchist Leon Czolgosz shot William McKinley twice during a reception at the Pan-American Exposition in Buffalo, New York. He had concealed his revolver in a bandage and fired from only two feet away. McKinley died a week later from infection in one of the wounds. His killer confessed that he wanted to change the government; he was executed.

The next year, the Secret Service assumed full-time responsibility for protection of the President.

4. John F. Kennedy.

On November 22, 1963 JFK was assassinated in Dallas, Texas while campaigning, allegedly by Lee Harvey Oswald (see later chapters).

Six more US presidents were nearly killed:

1. Andrew Jackson.

On January 30, 1835 President Jackson went to the US Capitol to attend the funeral services of Congressman Davis. As the President filed past the casket and descended to the Capitol rotunda, Richard Lawrence, an unemployed house painter, fired at him point blank but a bullet failed to discharge from the gun barrel. Then Lawrence drew a second pistol and fired again, and again the gun failed to fire. A jury found Lawrence not guilty on grounds of insanity.

2. Harry Truman.

On November 1, 1950 two Puerto Rican nationalists, Oscar Collazo and Oriselio Torresola, attempted to assassinate President Truman, who was staying at the time in Blair House, across the street from the White House, due to White House renovations. They approached the house and tried to shoot their way inside, but were killed by White House police officers. President Truman was taking a nap upstairs.

3. Richard Nixon.

On February 22, 1974 Samuel Byck, an unemployed tire salesman with mental problems, attempted to hijack a plane from Baltimore-Washington International Airport. He intended to crash it into the White House hoping to kill the President. He stole a revolver from a friend and made a bomb out of 2 gallon jugs of gasoline and an igniter. He went to the airport, killed a police officer there, stormed aboard the plane and killed 2 pilots after they told him they couldn't take off until the wheel blocks were removed. Eventually, after Byck was shot and wounded by police officers, he committed suicide by shooting himself in the head.

4. Gerald Ford (two attempts).

On September 5, 1975, Lynette From, a follower of a cult leader Charles Manson, pointed a handgun at President Ford as he was shaking hands with well-wishers at Sacramento's Capitol Park. The weapon was loaded with 4 bullets but none was in the firing chamber. She was arrested and convicted of attempted assassination; she's serving life in prison.

On September 22, 1975 Sara Moore tried to assassinate President Ford outside the St. Francis Hotel in San Francisco. A psycho with revolutionary ideas she was once recruited by the FBI but her cover was blown. Then, in order to prove herself with her radical friends, she attempted to shoot Ford.

The President was saved by bystander Oliver Sipple, a former Marine Corps member who fought in Vietnam and was honorably discharged. He wrestled Sara Moore and grabbed the gun. She fired one shot which did not hit the President. Ford wrote a thank-you note to Sipple three days later, but never invited him to the White House. There is speculation that he was treated shabbily because he was alleged to be homosexual, and this severely affected his family.

5. Ronald Reagan.

On March 30, 1981 John Hinckley Jr. shot President Reagan, his Press Secretary James Brady, Secret Service agent Tim McCarthy and police officer Thomas Delehanty while they were leaving the Hilton Hotel in Washington, DC. Hinckley, a loser from a family of oil company owners, was obsessed with actress Jodi Foster, stalking her and developing ploys to get her attention, including by assassinating the US President. President Reagan was not hit directly but he was wounded in the chest on a ricochet — a stray bullet that bounced back from the bulletproof glass of the Presidential limousine hit him in the chest. Hinckley didn't attempt to flee and was arrested at the scene. At the trial he was found guilty by reason of insanity and confined at St. Elizabeth's Hospital in Washington, DC.

6. President George W. Bush.

On May 5, 2005 Vladimir Arutunyan threw a grenade at George W. Bush who was greeting a crowd (of about 15,000) on Freedom Square, Tbilisi, Georgia (a former Soviet republic) during an official visit. The grenade fell about 100 feet away from the tribune where the President was standing, but did not detonate. Early in the morning, before the US President appeared, thousands of local residents broke through the barriers and metal detectors and made their way to the city's central square waiting for Bush. Special agents and police officers of Georgia could not keep the crowd back, so they removed the barriers and let the people flow in without any inspection. Arutunyan was arrested two months later and sentenced to life in 2006.

Structure of the Secret Service

Director
Office of Inspection

Office of Administration: financial management personnel, administrative operations

Office of Protective Operations:
    Presidential Protective Division
    Vice-Presidential Protective Division
    Uniformed Division
    Western Protective Division
    Special Services Division
    Technical Security Division
    Communications Division
    Liaison Division

Technical Development and Planning

Office of Investigations:
    Special Investigations and Security Division
    Counterfeit Division

Treasury Security Force
    Fraud and Forgery Division
    Forensic Services Division
    Field Offices and Resident Agencies

Managing the Secret Service

The top priority in protecting the President's life must be organized and complete intelligence. Any information from any person from any country concerning the President's personal security has to be immediately analyzed, and immediate action has to be performed. This is the first priority for intelligence and counter-intelligence agencies and police as well as the Secret Service. If the system is organized properly, nobody could even get in a position to try to shoot. Of course, the safest thing is to restrict the President's routes to government buildings only; but he has to travel and he has to travel abroad, too. Still, the President should leave his Office only when he really has to.

Since the President has to be let out from time to time, the newer technique is to restrict where the onlookers may congregate, especially those who wish to take the opportunity to express dismay with Presidential policies. Thus we now see the evolution of "free speech corners" so that demonstrators are confined to specific areas far from the actual event where the President is appearing or the route he is transiting.

Practical Protection during Presidential Appearances

(1) The Secret Service has to have a top-secret plan of all visits, because the advance group has to come to the place at least a week ahead and cooperate with the field FBI offices and police (foreign special services if it's a visit abroad) paying attention to extremist groups and organizations. Officers and technicians

search the place, looking for possible explosives, radioactive, biological and chemical dangerous or poisonous stuff and weapons; they check the walls, floors and ceilings; check air and water in the area; install weapons and explosives detectors and stay at the place 24/7, using night vision devices, too. (Dogs are good helpers if there is any question of explosives.) You have to check nearby houses as well (there could be people with mental health problems or dangerous criminals). Remember, the President must not appear in open areas close to apartment buildings. And the President has to be able to reach the National Security Command Center at any time.

(2) If the President has to make a speech in open area there should be at least 3 security circles around him:

- up to 50 ft (personal bodyguards, weapons and explosives technicians)
- up to 200 ft (fast reaction anti-terror group)
- up to 1000 ft (support groups, snipers, police)

The security system includes both "open" and undercover groups (obvious security and people who play the crowd or service — drivers, waiters, cleaners — terrorists don't pay attention to them, as a rule). Each group follows its instructions strictly and avoids mess (personal bodyguards are in charge of immediate protection, anti-terror group has to fight and chase terrorists, etc.). Extra people always mean extra danger, so the most secure situation is when extra people have no access to the President at all and can't get into any of three circles. The guest list has to be triple checked to exclude anybody with criminal records who could compromise the leader. Reporters are there too and you have to tell them exactly where to wait (they have to be checked and kept separate after that), where to stand and what pictures (poses) to take; the President can't look stupid or funny. Inside the building watch when people applaud, stand up and sit down — terrorists prefer these situations to shoot or blow explosives.

When President moves through or along the crowd, "cut" it into pieces, guard him in circles, watch people who are carrying any objects (no flowers!) — they must not approach him; watch people with hands in their pockets, those who try to touch him, shake his hand, pass any object (gift, picture, photo). They must not be allowed to do that. If anybody behaves in a suspicious way, hold him tight (so he can't take out a gun) and "screw" him out of the crowd. In case of any attempt push the President to the ground, cover him and shoot immediately. Then leave the place as soon as possible and bring him to the hospital for a check up (even if he's OK).

Frequent Security Mistakes

The worst one — Secret Service and other agencies get inadequate intelligence information on a possible attempt or overlook important information, including anonymous letters and mail from psychos. (They must have information, even if it's "inside" the White House conspiracy. Agents have to memorize pictures of all the most dangerous persons who are wanted in the United States and people who were involved in attempted attacks on top politicians worldwide.)

The next two — extraneous people are allowed access to the President or extraneous people stay in the area close enough to shoot the President. In 1997, a France Press reporter took a picture of the Clintons dancing during their vacation on the Virgin Islands — they were dressed for the Caribbean and were happy in their privacy. Luckily, it was just a reporter, but what if it had been a sniper? What was the Secret Service doing? Then the picture was published worldwide and Hillary Clinton was furious — she didn't look attractive at all.

The last two major errors occur when (1) you can't identify the potential terrorists in the crowd and (2) you react too slowly or waste time evacuating the President.

Code Names of American Presidents

Harry Truman — "The General"
Dwight Eisenhower — "Providence"
John Kennedy — "Lancer"
Lyndon Johnson — "Volunteer"
Richard Nixon — "Searchlight"
Gerald Ford — "Passkey"
Jimmy Carter — "Deacon"
Ron Reagan — "Rawhide"
George Bush — "Timber-wolf"
Bill Clinton — "Eagle"

Part 3. Managing the Military

"This nation will remain a neutral nation. I shall say it again and again, and again. Your boys are not going to be sent into any foreign wars." — President Franklin D. Roosevelt, 1940

"The law of the strongest is the only international law." — M. K.

CHAPTER 13. COMMANDER-IN-CHIEF

The president is under constant reassure to make war, not peace, because:

(a) Successful military engagement enhances presidential popularity. All five Presidents who have run for re-election during a war have won.

(b) A quick war improves the electoral fortunes of the president's political party.

(c) War is good business, at least if you win, and at least if it does not drag on too long. It stimulates demand for a variety of manufactured goods and services (even if they are all destined to go down the drain) and is a powerful stimulus to all fields of scientific endeavor.

(d) War provides opportunities to direct lucrative contracts to companies and individuals who helped get the President elected, or who can help in the future; and to the constituents of select Senators and Congressmen for the same reasons.

(e) War usually pleases the Joint Chiefs (and their full support is important politically).

(f) War keeps down the unemployment figures.

(g) War is just one detail in a vast ongoing game of international strategy for domination; it is as much a financial operation as anything else.

(h) War unifies the country, and keeps the public's attention away from issues that might be controversial.

(i) War provides a rationale for the implementation of tighter legislation and the removal of certain freedoms that would never be tolerated in peacetime America.

At the same time, war is limited by political decisions and by public opinion. Initially the use of US forces spurs a "rally around the flag" effect that lifts the President's popularity and builds up support for the troops. But the American people are casualty averse and the positive effect lasts only until the number of casualties and the length of the engagement begin to wear on the public. Continued military action will then have a deleterious effect on presidential approval ratings as the war becomes increasingly unpopular.

In the long run, the destruction of such vast quantities of resources, and the diversion of so much of the nation's productive capacity away from actual goods and services for the real economy, are obviously immensely deleterious. Eventually, these downside effects will begin to dawn on even the best-manipulated electorate.

Keys to Success in War

- Income should be higher than expenses.
- Modern warfare is coalition warfare.
- Brainwash the nation first.
- Shut up politicians and reporters who talk too much about peace.
- The impact of the media on modern war is unprecedented and with media present in a war zone you are compressed by time to achieve success.
- The faster you finish the war, the lower the human cost.
- No hesitation, no mercy, no remorse.
- Try to cut all political and economic connections of the enemy (no weapons, no raw materials, no food, no medicine, no money from outside).
- Defeat the enemy entirely — destroy the economy, obliterate cultural centers and historical artifacts, steal technologies and scientists, divide the populace and lay the groundwork for future national, religious and territorial conflicts.
- If necessary, mask the war as a civil war of opposition and your victory as a victory of a "national army."
- If victory is not certain, try diplomatic pressure through other leaders and big business to stop the war.

Duties of the Commander-in-Chief

1. As President you are Commander-in-Chief, but your job is political decision making, not war management. You:

- lead all federal and state armed forces
- lead the US defense policy
- suggest a budget for the armed forces
- choose the leaders of the armed forces
- decide where the armed forces will be in the world
- abide by all laws about armed forces
- direct all war efforts
- protect the lives of Americans living in other countries

2. During wartime you have special powers and Congress must agree to any actions you take, including:

- placing limits on prices
- limiting the sale of food, clothes and other items
- having a control on war-related businesses
- limiting freedoms for the period of war

3. SIOP or Presidential nuclear command

The most classified business you will be briefed on about after you're elected is the Single Integrated Operational Plan (SIOP), which contains the possible US nuclear responses to a variety of attacks. Here's the procedure of Presidential nuclear command:

If the North American Aerospace Defense Command (NORAD) detects evidence of a possible nuclear attack against the United States, NORAD, the Strategic Air Command (SAC), the Pentagon's National Military Command Center and the Alternative National Military Command Center begin procedural steps to verify the authenticity of the attack. If NORAD and other units determine that the attack is real, you are informed of the attack and its characteristics. Then you have to consult with the Defense Secretary and Joint Chiefs of Staff and consider SIOP options. If a nuclear attack option is chosen, you have to transmit the launch codes that unlock the nuclear weapons and assure the officers in charge of the weapons that the launch order is authentic. You may also give authority to launch nuclear weapons to the Secretary of Defense.

Chapter 14. Strategy and Tactics in War

To win you must have clear knowledge and understanding of some basic and simple military notions, like strategy and tactics. And political decisions change strategies.

Strategy is the planning of campaigns, selecting the aims and solving the logistics problems connected with moving men and resources to their battle positions. Actually, strategy is how you use battles to win a war, while a tactic is how you use troops to win a battle. There's only one grand strategy — to win the war; and the President is very important here as a politician — he gives the orders to freeze the enemy's assets in American (and allies') banks and he builds up the international coalition. American military strategy in the 21st century has to be a global strategy, which means coalition building. We will not discuss nuclear strategy and tactics in depth, because we all hope that for the next 25 years at least the practical use of nuclear weapons will remain a matter of science fiction, something to hint at and suggest as a threat, but not to actually try. Please do not prove me wrong.

In general,

- Achieve absolute information dominance (exact knowledge of the enemy's positions).
- Modern war is all about bombing.

There are different kinds of strategies to win different battles:

Formal (general) strategy — a master plan for the use of military power in peace and war. For example, the US maritime strategy calls for keeping the sea lanes open worldwide in times of war, to provide forward deployments, to attack the enemy fleets, and to project naval firepower by a variety of means — aircraft, cruise missiles and traditional guns against an infinite variety of targets on land, sea and air.

Depending on the situation you can choose between broad strategies of limited and total war.

We call a war limited if at least one of the parties refrains from using all of its resources to defeat the enemy. Limits are put on wars by fear of the intervention of the opposition's nonbelligerent allies or by domestic opposition in one's own country (limited war in Vietnam where the United States had to stop short of provoking China's or Russia's direct involvement).

President Kennedy initiated a flexible response strategy, which is still a NATO's first choice — it suggests the weapons we use have to match the threat we see (no one is likely to "calm down" an enemy with nuclear weapons). NATO assumes a ranking of possible military reactions rather than a predetermined strategic plan.

Russia since 2000 boasts that it is matching the US escalation — "matching" is a military strategy which intimidates enemies by assuring them that their every move can be matched and overpowered (President Putin's favorite threat is a new mysterious submarine).

Watching America's second Iraq war, President Bush's intention to use an escalation strategy and expand the war makes no sense — we increase the army and the insurgents increase theirs. This is already a political threat, because 35% of our economy belongs to the Pentagon. The most effective choice would have been psychological warfare.

- Theatre strategy: involves the combination of operations in the air, on the land or the sea.
- Operational strategy: governs the functions of what is done or not done tactically.
- Tactical strategy: a series of engagements and battles that supports the operational campaign and governs the actions at the technical level.
- Technical strategy: the interaction between weapon systems (an example is the manner in which one tank maneuvers to engage and destroy another).

Any strategy has the following principles: cooperation, concentration, economy, surprise, maneuver, security, simplicity.

Insurgents use the strategy of a prolonged war because time works in their favor and inevitably lowers the enemy's morale, unites the native population around the insurgents, increases outside support, and encourages the anti-war movement worldwide.

The "strategic goal" defines the desired end result of the war (usually, a complete defeat of the enemy or enemy coalition) but it also includes a quick termination of the war and restoration of the status-quo. A strategic force (consisting of army groups, armies, corps and divisions of various branches of service) conducts a strategic mission in the course of war or a strategic operation (the mission must conform with the strategic goal). A strategic operation is the principal form of operation, and it may include one or more of the following types of military action: strategic offensive, strategic defensive, strategic counteroffensive, strategic redeployment. A strategic operation is the aggregate of interconnected operations by the combined forces (several army groups, strategic nuclear forces, strategic air armies, air defense forces, a naval fleet, airborne forces, national space assets; all of them act under a single unified plan and concept of operation, coordinated in aims, time and area to achieve strategic goals and missions).

Tactics

Tactics is the art of fighting a certain battle at sea, on land or in the air, as a part of a general (grand) strategy. It is the employment of units in combat. It includes the ordered arrangement and maneuver of units in relation to each other, the terrain and the enemy to translate potential combat power into victorious battles and engagements. The tactical level of war is the level at which battles and engagements are planned and executed to accomplish military objectives assigned to tactical units or task forces. The strategic and operational levels provide the context for the tactical operations. Without this context, tactical operations are reduced to a series of disconnected and unfocused actions. Engagements are linked to battles. One or more battles are linked to winning major operations and campaigns, leading to operational success, which can lead to strategic success.

Military tactics rest on fourteen elements:

(1) identification (ability to define and locate the opponent)

(2) administration (planning and analysis)

(3) concentration of efforts (against the enemy, where he is known to be weakest)

(4) security (intelligence and counter-intelligence)

(5) economy of force (to make the best use of all resources and in order to create and maintain a reserve)

(6) force protection (dispersing, camouflage, deception, electronic counter measures, exploiting night and prevailing weather, use of fortifications — entrenchments, over head protection, foxholes, revetting, vanguard)

(7) isolation (when the opponent is denied the ability to gain outside resources and assistance).

(8) suppression (the process of denying the opponent the freedom of movement and ultimately maneuver)

(9) maneuver (combination of movement and firepower to achieve a position of advantage which means the placing of strength against an opponent's weakness)

(10) flexibility (a capability to react to changing circumstances, especially by mobility, the rapid switching of fire-power and arrangement of sufficient resources)

(11) cooperation (with allies through secure links)

(12) offensive action (to win the initiative and throw an enemy off balance)

(13) destruction (physical destruction of resources or destruction of the opponent's will)

(14) troops motivation

Counter-Insurgency Tactics

Usually insurgents try to seize and keep the initiative, select targets that are not too big for them and avoid open confrontation with the army. The army has to gain initiative by fighting insurgents as often as possible to keep them off balance and force them into defensive by cordon, search and destroy operations and constant ground and airborne patrols. The military must seek out and destroy the insurgents' strongholds and infiltration routes, especially in the areas bordering other countries; and garrison major cities.

The military must pacify the population to dominate the territory continuously. The most important thing here is the winning of the psychological war — the insurgents could then be isolated and denied access to refuge, sustenance and information.

Firepower + Speed = Low Casualties

Staying Alive

There is no and there will be no such creature as the "soldier of tomorrow" loaded with computers who doesn't have to be skillful on his own; this is a scientistic fantasy of smart idiots wasting federal money, who never have been under fire amidst the hell of actual combat. Of course, technology has changed the character of modern war, but as the insurgents in Iraq have taught us, the rest of the world doesn't have to reach our level in military technology to fight — they can conduct urban guerilla warfare with whatever is at hand.

For a hundred years to come the best way to survive will still be to dig up a big, deep trench. The best computer is a loaded submachine gun, and the best techniques are

- the minor tactic of infantry: "fire and movement" — firing and moving, often in pairs, when one soldier fires to suppress or neutralize the enemy whilst the other moves either toward the enemy or to a more favorable position;
- basic drill (if you are under "effective fire"): run five-six steps, drop to the ground or into cover, crawl a few yards (or move under cover), observe, shoot identified targets within effective range, move, observe and shoot until you get another order;
- "overwatch": one small unit supports another while they execute fire and movement patrolling: reconnaissance patrol (used to collect information by observing the enemy and working with informants), fighting patrol (to raid or ambush a specific enemy not holding the ground; you need a platoon for a fighting patrol), clearing patrol (to ensure that newly occupied defensive position is secure), standing patrol (to provide early warning, security or to piquet some geographical feature such as dead ground).

Deserts

Successful desert operations require adaptation to heat and lack of water as temperatures may vary 136 degrees Fahrenheit in the deserts of Mexico and Libya to the bitter cold of winter in the Gobi (East Asia). Terrain varies from mountain and rocky plateau to sandy or dune terrain. The key to success in desert operations is mobility, though movement can easily be detected because of sand and dust signatures left due to the loose surface material (in an actual engagement, this may not be all that bad because a unit is obscured from direct fire while advancing, but the element of surprise may be lost). Moving at night is the best choice.

Attack helicopters are extremely useful there due to their ability to maneuver and apply firepower over a large battlefield in a short time. Suppression of enemy air defense has a high priority during offensive operations. The destruction of enemy antitank capabilities must also have a high priority due to the shock potential of armor in the desert.

No panic, no smoking, no alcohol (it dehydrates the body). Don't drink much liquid. Keep the gun clean from sand. Kill anybody for water and watch for water signs, like animal tracks and the birds' flight patterns.

Jungle

In the jungle you'll fight, most probably, guerrilla, not conventional forces. In general, jungle enemies can be expected to follow these tactical principles: maintain the offensive, stay close to the enemy to reduce the effects of his firepower, infiltrate at every opportunity, operate during periods of limited visibility, use surprise tactics (see Special forces).

In Latin America the most likely threat for the US are insurgent leftist movements. In Africa many of the conflicted factions struggle among themselves, due to political or ancient tribal differences, differences that may be stirred up by rival leaders in the "modern" political state, who in turn may be working (knowingly or not) in the interests of other, more developed, powers who benefit from the chaos. (These factions consist primarily of heavily armed with mortars and artillery guerrilla groups. There are active guerrilla movements in Southeast Asia, too).

The worst things (often exaggerated) in jungle combat are fear, malaria-carrying mosquitoes and snakes; also heat, thick vegetation and rugged terrain, especially for those who carry heavy weapons.

If bitten by a snake, follow these steps: remain calm but act swiftly, and chances of survival are good; immobilize the affected part in a position below the level of the heart; place a lightly constricted band 5 to 10 cm (2 to 4 inches) closer to the heart than the site of the bite (reapply the constricting band ahead of the swelling if it moves up the arm or leg). The constricting band should be placed tightly enough to halt the flow of blood in surface vessels, but not so tight as to stop the pulse; do not attempt to cut open the bite or suck out venom; seek medical help (if possible, the snake's head with 5 to 10 cm of its body should be taken to the medics for identification and a proper choice of anti venom).

The thick foliage makes ambush a constant danger, and that's why point, flank and rear security teams have to keep a force from being ambushed. These teams must be far enough away from the main body that if they make contact the whole force will not be engaged (use dogs, too). Successful jungle attacks usually combine dispersion and concentration. For example, a rifle company may move out in a dispersed formation so that it can find the enemy. Once contact is made, its platoons close on the enemy from all directions. Remember, jungle areas are ideal for infiltration because dense vegetation and rugged terrain limit the enemy's ability to detect movement. On the other side, it's difficult to detect the approach of an attacking enemy for the same reason. In the jungle the key weapons are infantry small arms, mortars and artillery.

Far North

Be ready for long hours of daylight and dust in summer, long nights and the extreme cold in winter, and the mud and morass of the transition periods of spring and autumn. The disrupting effects of natural phenomena, the scarcity of roads and railroads, the vast distances and isolation, and occasionally the lack of current maps combine to affect adversely but not totally restrict mobility, fire power, and communications.

The most suitable time for ground operations is from midwinter to early spring before the breakup of the ice. Early winter, after the formation of ice, is also favorable. Tracks in the snow, and fog created by a heat source, complicate the camouflage of positions. The blending of terrain features, lack of navigational aids, fog and blowing snow all combine to make land navigation extremely difficult. And don't eat the snow, and don't put weapons on the snow (especially after shooting).

Mountains

Mountain campaigns are characterized by a series of separately fought battles for the control of dominating ridges and heights that overlook roads, trails, and other potential avenues of approach. Operations generally focus on smaller-unit tactics of squad, platoon, company, and battalion size. Attacks in extremely rugged terrain are often dismounted, with airborne and air assaults employed to seize high ground or key terrain and to encircle or block the enemy's retreat. The mountainous terrain usually offers greater advantage to the defender and frontal attacks, even when supported by heavy direct and indirect fires, have a limited chance of success (the best thing is to use the envelopment). Infantry is the basic maneuver force in mountains. Mechanized infantry is confined to valleys and foothills, but their ability to dismount and move on foot enables them to reach almost anywhere in the area. The objective in mountainous areas of operations is normally to dominate terrain from which the enemy can be pinned down and destroyed.

If you're not a sniper, you have nothing to do there. Use grenades carefully (in winter time there's too much snow around). Keep in mind that low atmospheric pressure considerably increases the evaporation of water in storage batteries and vehicle cooling systems, and impairs cylinder breathing (consequently, vehicles expand more fuel and lubricant, and engine power is reduced by four to six percent for every 1,000-meters (3,300 ft) increase in elevation above sea level. You have to be used to the lack of oxygen. And don't drink or smoke while climbing. Be always ready to shoot. Watch open places and roads. Go parallel course when you chase the enemy. Shoot first if you see cut trees on your way.

MINES

Don't touch anything in the places the enemy just left — check for mines first. A minefield is a mortal surprise and you have to know how to breach and cross it: remove your helmet, rucksack, watch, belt, and anything else that may hinder movement or fall off, leave your rifle and equipment with another soldier in the team, get a wooden stick about 30 cm (12 in) long for a probe and sharpen one of the ends (do not use a metal probe), place the unsharpened end of the probe in the palm of one hand with your fingers extended and your thumb holding the probe, and probe every 5 cm (2 in) across a 1-meter area in front of you and push the probe gently into the ground at an angle less than 45 degrees, kneel (or lie down) and feel upward and forward with your free hand to find tripwires and pressure prongs before starting to probe, put enough pressure on the probe to sink it slowly into the ground and if the probe does not go into the ground, pick or chip the dirt away with the probe and remove it by hand, stop probing when a solid object is touched, remove enough dirt from around the object to find out what it is. If you found a mine, remove enough dirt around it to see what type of mine it is, mark it and report its exact location to your leader. Once a footpath has been probed and the mines marked, a security team should cross the minefield to secure the far side. After the far side is secure, the rest of the unit should cross.

Don't eat before the assault; if there is food in your system, you'll die if wounded in the belly.

WOUNDS

If you or another soldier is wounded, first aid must be given at once and the first step is to apply the four life-saving measures:

(1) Clear the airway, check and restore breathing and heartbeat. If he is not breathing, place him on his back and kneel beside his head, clear his airway and start mouth-to-mouth resuscitation and if necessary start external heart massage.

(2) Stop the bleeding. Look for both entry and exit wounds, as a bullet usually makes a smaller wound where it enters than where it exits.

(3) Prevent shock. Warning signs of shock are restlessness, thirst, pale skin and rapid heartbeat. Loosen the casualty's clothing at the neck, waist and wherever it restricts circulation. Keep him warm. Reassure him by being calm and self-confident. Put him in a comfortable position.

(4) Dress and bandage the wound.

EFFECTIVE SNIPERS

Camouflage yourself ten times before you make a single shot. Position yourself in a building (no rooftops or churches!), which offers a long-range fields of fire and all-round observation. Don't stay in places with heavy traffic!

You have to:

(a) Train your muscles to snap to the standard position for shooting.

(b) Train yourself to shoot while you stand, sit, lie, walk, run, jump, fall down; shoot at voices, shoot in a dark room, different weather and distance, day and night; shoot one object and a group; use one gun, two guns, gun and submachine gun.

(c) Move slowly to prevent accurate counter-attack, don't be a mark yourself.

(d) Kill officers and military leaders first (Attention, officers: don't walk in front of your soldiers!).

(e) Use suppressive fire to cover a retreat.

(f) Use rapid fire when the squad attempts a rescue.

(g) Shoot helicopters, turbine disks of parked jet fighters, missile guidance packages, tubes or wave guides of radar sets.

(h) At distances over 300 m attempt body shots, aiming at the chest; at lesser distances attempt head shots (the most effective range is 300 to 600 meters).

(i) Shoot from flanks and rear.

(j) Never approach the body until you shoot it several times.

(k) Careful: the object could be wearing a bulletproof vest.

(l) It's important to get to the place, but it's more important to get out alive.

(m) In hot weather bullets travel higher, in cold — lower; a silencer reduces the maximum effective range of the weapon. Wind poses the biggest problem — the stronger the wind, the more difficult it is to hold the rifle steady and gauge how it will affect the bullet's trajectory. (You must be able to classify the wind and the best method is to use the clock system. With you at the center of the clock and the target at 12 o'clock, the wind is assigned into three values: full, half and no value. Full value means that the force of the wind will have a full effect on the flight of the bullet, and these winds come from 3 and 9 o'clock. Half value means that a wind at the same speed, but from 1, 2, 4, 5, 7, 8, 10 and 11 o'clock, will move the bullet only half as much as a full-value wind. No value means that a wind from 6 or 12 o'clock will have little or no effect on the flight of the bullet.)

(n) if you work in terrain without any natural support, use your rucksack, sandbag, a forked stick, or you may build a field-expedient bipod or tripod.

COUNTER-SNIPER TACTICS

Active: direct observation by posts equipped with laser protective glasses and night vision devices; patrolling with military working dogs; calculating the trajectory; bullet triangulation; using decoys to lure a sniper; using another sniper; UAV (unmanned aerial vehicles).

Passive: limited exposure of the personnel (use concealed routes, avoid plazas and intersections, stay away from doorways and windows, move along the side of the street and not down the center, move in the shadows, move dispersed, avoid lighted areas at night, move quickly across open areas, avoid wearing obvious badges of rank, adapt screens on windows, use armored vehicles); use Kevlar helmet and bulletproof vest.

MILITARY TRICKS

- Use rapid dominance: technology + speed + information domination.
- Use artillery preparation. It is the artillery fire delivered before an attack to destroy, neutralize, or suppress the enemy's defense and to disrupt communications and disorganize the enemy's defense.
- Use deception especially before the first strike (air strike + artillery). Deception plays a key part in offensive operations and has two objectives: the first objective is to weaken the local defense by drawing reserves to another part of the battlefield. This may be done by making a small force seem larger than it is. The second objective is to conceal the avenue of approach and timing of the main attack.
- Imitate assault to make the enemy expose his positions and fire system.
- Use phony minefields to simulate live minefields. For example, disturb the ground so that it appears that mines have been emplaced and mark boundaries with appropriate warnings.
- Make a real minefield appear phony, or camouflage it. For example, once a real minefield is settled, a wheel or a specially made circular wooden tank track marker can be run through the field, leaving track or tire marks to lure the enemy onto live mines. Antipersonnel mines should not be sown in such a field until the track marks have been laid. Another method is to leave gaps in the mechanically laid field, run vehicles through the gaps, and then close them with hand-laid mines without disturbing the track marks.
- Use feint attack to draw defensive action towards the point under assault (it's usually used as a diversion and to force the enemy to concentrate more manpower in a given area so that the opposing force in another area is weaker).
- Issue false orders over the radio, imitate a tanks', fighters' and bombers' assault while preparing to retreat.
- Use dummy units and installations, phony radio traffic, movement and suppressive fires in other areas timed to coincide with the real attack.
- Use force multiplication by using decoy vehicles and use small convoys to generate dust clouds. Move trucks into and out of the area giving it the appearance of being a storage facility or logistic base.

- Simulate damage to induce the enemy to leave important targets alone. For example, ragged patterns can be painted on the walls and roof of a building with tar and coal dust, and covers placed over them.
- Stack debris nearby and wire any unused portions for demolition. During an attack, covers are removed under cover of smoke generators, debris scattered and demolitions blown. Subsequent enemy air photography will disclose a building that is too badly damaged to be used.
- Change positions at night time only.
- Use dispersal to relocate and spread out forces to increase their chances of survival.
- Imitate fake ballistic missiles divisions and military headquarters to entrap enemy's intelligence and sabotage groups.
- Use "sack" strategy ("cutting" enemy's army into separate groups).
- Use strategic bombing (the massive attack on cities, industries, lines of communication and supply).
- Simulate bombing of minor objects and attack important ones.
- Use counter-battery fire (detecting with counter-battery radars the source of incoming artillery shells and firing back), using mobile artillery pieces or vehicles with mounted rocket launchers to fire and then move before any counter-battery fire can land on the original position.
- Use airborne operations, when helicopters transport troops into the battle and provide fire support at battle sites simultaneously with artillery fire, keeping enemy off guard. Using helicopters is extremely important as they can be sent everywhere: to kill tanks and other helicopters, for aerial mine laying, for electronic warfare, for naval operations (anti-submarine and anti-ship patrols), to correct artillery and tactical fighters fire, for reconnaissance, command, control and communications, to insert special forces, to evacuate casualties (this helps maintain the morale of the troops), to carry supplies (missile systems, ammunition, fuel food, to escort convoys, for navigational help, to destroy battlefield radars, communications and radio relay systems, to seal gaps and protect flanks, for rear-area security, counter — penetration, rapid reinforcement of troops under pressure, raids and assaults behind enemy lines, air assault in offensive and defensive operations, to strengthen anti-tank defenses by inserting infantry anti-tank teams. Helicopters offer a strong tactical surprise and take a ground conflict into the third dimension, making the enemy's ground maneuvers impossible.

FIGHTING AN INSURGENCY

When fighting an insurgency: once you get intelligence, you have to bomb the area to "soften" insurgents and then send helicopters with special forces teams right away. Helicopters suppress and cut-off by fire insurgents trying to escape and the teams clear-up the remains. Transport helicopters must bring in troops rapidly from different bases and build-up numerically superior force which insurgents cannot match.

- Use joint bombers/fighters flights to bomb transportation, supply, bridges, railroads, highways, antiaircraft and radar sites.
- Watch out for tank ambushes!

- Use staged flanking maneuvers (actually, any smart maneuver mentally destroys the enemy).
- Keep close to the enemy in combat as his artillery could cut you off.
- Take care of flanks and rear zone security.
- Use staged attacks in different directions.

NAVAL TACTICS

- Use aircraft carriers to actively deny the enemy use of the seas, harbors and adjacent airspace, and project navy power under the sea, on the surface, in the air above and over land.
- The central weapon in modern naval combat is the missile, and the key to success is to destroy the launching platform before it fires, thus removing a number of missile threats in one go.
- Use submarines for surveillance and intelligence (using both unmanned aerial and undersea vehicles for special operations, carrying special forces teams and agents, for blocking enemy surface ships and submarines from using the seas. This may take place at strategic "choke points," along sea lanes or enemy ports. The goal is to destroy enemy surface ships, merchant vessels and submarines by torpedoes.)
- Submarines may also use mines to deny sea areas to enemy surface ships or submarines). To fight submarines use detection, identification, tracking and destruction of hostile submarines, which are the greatest threat to offensive operations. If a submarine is detected the issue is getting weapons in the water, even if they are not accurately targeted. Any efforts to distract it from attacking are made, including torpedo evasion maneuvers. (A general maneuver tactic is the zigzag.) A submarine usually relies on passive detection, not asking active sonar or a periscope observation. To determine where the unit is heading the submarine needs Target Motion Analysis; this requires several minutes of passive contact and if the contact starts to zigzag this process must restart. The most effective means of finding and destroying submarines is another submarine (hunter-killer) which operates independently.

OFFENSE

The offense is basic to combat operations, and has a number of undisputable advantages. The principal advantage is its possession of initiative, as having the initiative allows you to select the time, place, and specific tactics. You also have the time and opportunity to develop a plan and to concentrate your forces, and strike the enemy in unexpected ways at unexpected times and places. You can focus on attacking the right combination of targets, not necessarily the biggest or the closest.

Offensive operations aim at destroying or defeating an enemy. You may also conduct offensive operations to deprive the enemy of resources, seize decisive terrain, deceive or divert the enemy, develop intelligence, or hold an enemy in position. The offense is characterized by surprise, concentration, tempo and audacity. Execute violently without hesitation to break the enemy's will or destroy him. The four types of offensive operations are: movement to contact (to develop the situation and establish or regain contact), attack (to destroy or defeat enemy forces, seize and secure terrain, or both), exploitation (rapidly follows a successful attack and is designed to disorganize the enemy in depth) and pursuit (follows a successful exploitation and is designed to catch or cut off a hostile force attempting to escape, with the aim of destroying it).

You can also launch an attack to achieve special purposes and for that you use such subordinate forms of an attack as ambush, counterattack, demonstration, feint, raid and spoiling attack. An ambush is a form of attack by fire or other destructive means from concealed positions on a moving or temporarily halted enemy. It may include an assault to close with and destroy the engaged enemy force. In an ambush, ground objectives do not have to be seized and held. The two types of ambush are point ambush and area ambush. In a point ambush, a unit deploys to attack a single killing zone (it's the part of an ambush where firing is concentrated). In an area ambush, a unit deploys into two or more related point ambushes (a unit smaller than a platoon does not normally conduct an area ambush). A point ambush usually employs a line or an L-shaped formation. An area ambush is most effective when the enemy movement is largely restricted to trails or roads. (The area should offer several suitable point ambush sites. First, you select a central ambush site around which you can organize outlying ambushes. Then you must determine the enemy's possible avenues of approach and escape routes, and assign outlying point ambush sites to your subordinates to cover these avenues. Once they occupy these sites, they report all enemy traffic going toward or away from the central ambush site. These outlying ambushes allow the enemy to pass through their killing zone until you initiate the central ambush. Once the central ambush begins, the outlying ambushes prevent the enemy troops from escaping or entering the area).

A counterattack is a form of attack by part or all of a defending force against an enemy attacking force, with the general objective of denying the enemy his goal in attacking. You direct a counterattack (normally conducted from a defensive posture) to defeat or destroy enemy forces, exploit an enemy weakness, such as exposed flank, or to regain control of terrain and facilities after an enemy success. A unit conducts a counterattack to seize the initiative from the enemy through offensive action. A counterattacking force maneuvers to isolate and destroy a designated enemy force. It can attack by fire an engagement area to defeat or destroy an enemy force, restore the original position, or block an enemy penetration. Once launched, the counterattack normally becomes a decisive operation. A demonstration is a form of attack designed to deceive the enemy as to the location or time of the decisive operation by a display of force. Forces conducting a demonstration do not seek contact with the enemy. A feint is a form of attack used to deceive the enemy as to the location or time of the actual decisive operation. Forces conducting a feint seek direct fire contact with the enemy but avoid decisive engagement. The principal difference between these forms of attack is that in a feint you assign the force an objective limited in size and scope. Forces conducting a feint make direct fire contact with the enemy but avoid decisive engagement. Forces conducting a demonstration do not seek contact with the enemy. The planning, preparing, and executing considerations for demonstrations and feints are the same as for the other forms of attack.

A raid is a form of attack, usually small scale, involving a swift entry into hostile territory to secure information, confuse the enemy, or destroy installations. It ends with a planned withdrawal from the objective area on mission completion. A raid can also be used to support operations designed to rescue and recover individuals and equipment in danger of capture.

A spoiling attack is a form of attack that preempts or seriously impairs an enemy attack while the enemy is in the process of planning or preparing to attack. The objective of a spoiling attack is to disrupt the enemy's offensive capabilities and timelines while destroying his personnel and equipment, not to secure terrain. Conduct a spoiling attack whenever possible to strike the enemy while he is in assembly areas or attack positions preparing for his own offensive operation or is temporarily stopped.

Don't use a frontal assault — that's suicide. If you assault, you have to follow the ordered strategy of attrition (intense casualties producing and complete termination) or disintegration (to break up the opposing force by maneuvering). The primary task of military intelligence before assault is to discover the enemy's order of battle, because knowing exactly which units, with their special capabilities, are scheduled for combat in any theater can tell an intelligence analyst a good deal about the tactics and strategy which the enemy has planned. Here you have to use a triangular method which is a combination of secret agents, SIGINT and satellite observation.

The enemy must not get information about your operation — you have to know the counter-intelligence measures and practice camouflage techniques as well as noise and light discipline, use proper radiotelephone procedure, use the challenge and password properly, not take personal letters or pictures into combat areas and not keep diaries in combat areas, be careful when discussing military affairs, use authorized codes only, report any soldier or civilian who is believed to be serving or sympathetic with the enemy, report anyone who tries to get information about our operations, destroy all maps and important documents if capture is imminent, not discuss military operations in public areas. I recommend you to use all forms of maneuvers if you want to execute a successful offensive operation, like envelopment, turning movement, frontal attack, penetration and infiltration.

An envelopment is a form of maneuver in which an attacking force seeks to avoid the principal enemy's defenses by seizing objectives to the enemy rear to destroy the enemy in his current positions. At the tactical level, envelopments focus on seizing terrain, destroying specific forces, and interdicting withdrawal routes. Also, at the tactical level, airborne and air assault operations are vertical envelopes. Your decisive operation has to be focused on attacking an assailable flank — avoid the enemy's strength (his front) where the effects of his fires and obstacles are the greatest. I recommend envelopment instead of penetration or a frontal attack because the attacking force tends to suffer fewer casualties while having the most opportunities to destroy the enemy. An envelopment also produces great psychological shock on the enemy. (You can use also a pincer movement or double envelopment when the flanks of the enemy are attacked simultaneously in a pinching motion after the enemy has advanced towards the center of an army which is responding by moving its outside forces to the enemy's flanks, in order to surround it. At the same time, a second layer of pincers attacks on the more extreme flanks, so as to prevent any attempts to reinforce the target unit).

A turning movement is a form of maneuver in which the attacking force seeks to avoid the enemy's principle defensive positions by seizing objectives to the enemy rear and causing the enemy to move out of his current positions or divert major forces to meet the threat. A turning movement differs from an envelopment because the force conducting a turning movement seeks to make the enemy displace from his current locations, whereas an enveloping force seeks to engage the enemy in his current location from an unexpected direction.

An infiltration is another form of a "special" maneuver in which an attacking force conducts undetected movement through or into an area occupied by enemy forces to occupy a position of advantage in the enemy rear while exposing only small elements to the enemy defensive fires. Infiltration is also a march technique used within friendly territory to move forces in small groups at extended or irregular intervals. Infiltration occurs by land, water, air or a combination of means. Moving and assembling forces covertly through enemy positions takes a considerable amount of time. To successfully infiltrate, the force must avoid detection and engagement. Since this requirement limits the size and strength of the infiltrating force — and infiltrated forces alone can rarely win — infiltration is used in conjunction with and in support of the other forms of offensive maneuver.

A penetration is a form of maneuver in which an attacking force seeks to rupture the enemy defenses on a narrow front to disrupt the defensive system. Destroying the continuity of that defense allows the enemy's subsequent isolation and defeat in detail by exploiting the friendly forces. The penetration extends from the enemy's security area through his main defensive positions into his rear area. You have to employ a penetration when there is no assailable flank, enemy's defenses are overextended and weak spots are detected in the enemy's positions, or time pressures do not permit an envelopment.

A frontal attack is a form of maneuver in which an attacking force seeks to destroy a weaker enemy force or fix a larger enemy force in place over a broad front. At the tactical level, an attacking force can use a frontal attack to rapidly overrun a weak enemy force; it's usually used as a shaping operation in conjunction with other forms of maneuver.

STORMING THE CITY

The decision to attack a large city or major urban complex (more than 100,000 people) may be made at levels above the corps, based primarily on political and strategic considerations. Such vast areas are difficult to defend or attack in their entirety. The battle will proceed from the attack of smaller built-up areas leading to the central complex and will involve major forces. Elements of the attack force may be required to conduct the whole range of military operations, including attack, defense and retrograde.

The decision to attack a town or small city (3,000–100,000) will be normally made by corps or division commanders. The allocation of major forces and significant time are required to secure such objectives. Civilian casualties and significant collateral damage to structures usually accompany urban operations, so you must consider the political and psychological consequences of the storm. A hasty attack by heavy, mobile forces is preferred.

- Effective intelligence is 90% of success. Use sources like agents among the enemy's high ranking officers, prisoners of war, captured documents and maps, enemy's activity, local civilians (agents). Use intelligence and sabotage groups (through them you can deliver your fake plans and maps). You must know how the enemy usually defends a built-up area and the approaches to it, critical objectives within the built-up area that provide decisive tactical advantages, tactical characteristics of the built-up area and its structure. Information about the population will assist in determining where to attack, what firepower restrictions may be imposed, and what areas within the urban complex must be avoided to minimize destruction of life-support facilities and civilian casualties.
- Make the enemy attack you if possible, because if you attack first the victims calculation is 5:1.

- Train your troops to storm this certain city.
- Blockade the city completely.
- Attack the city from different points at the same time after intense artillery fire and bombing.
- Don't use tanks on narrow streets.
- Use 3 groups at each point.

    1. A "dead" assault group plus tanks (see above) moves fast to the center.

    2. The second group follows the first, and inside the city it fans out in all directions.

    3. A third group is on reserve in case the enemy counterattacks.

- Movement is very important for your survival in urban areas. To minimize exposure to enemy fire while moving do not silhouette yourself, stay low, avoid open areas as streets, alleys and parks (these are killing zones), select your next covered position before moving, conceal your movements by using smoke, buildings, rubble, or foliage, move rapidly from one position to another. Always cross a street rapidly. When you must move parallel to a building, use smoke for concealment and have someone to watch your move. Stay close to the side of the building, use shadows if possible, and stay low. Before moving around a corner, check out the area beyond to see if it is clear of obstacles and the enemy; look around the corner at ground level only enough to see around. When moving past a window on the first floor of a building, stay below the window level, when moving past a window in a basement, step or jump over it without exposing your legs. When moving in a building, do not silhouette yourself in doors and windows. When entering a building, take every precaution to get into it with minimum exposure to enemy fire and observation: select an entry point before moving, avoid windows and doors, use smoke for concealment, throw a hand grenade through the entry point before entering and quickly follow the explosion, enter at the highest level possible. Remember, limited visibility and night attacks are essential elements of the offense within an urbanized area, plus you will have problems with command and control, navigation, coordination of fire and friendly forces.
- Use paratroopers to capture important objects (airport, government buildings, military headquarters, port, railway station).
- Capture high buildings and place machine gunners and snipers on upper floors.
- Get all important cross-roads to maneuver troops and tanks.
- Block any highways!
- Watch out — there are mines everywhere.
- Watch underground communications — the enemy could stay in subway tunnels, sewage system.
- Don't waste time storming the buildings — blow up the walls and move forward.
- Soldiers in an urban environment are faced with ground direct fire danger in three dimensions — not just all-round fire but also from above (multi-story buildings) and from below (sewers and subways) and that's why, here, the most survivable systems, like tanks, are at great risk.
- In the streets use artillery and mortars to "soften" the enemy up before assault.
- House clearing: don't spare your grenades, move fast from room to room. Machinegunners from outside have to help the assault group with intense

fire on upper floors. The assault group always has to enter from the top floor. Shoot ceilings and floors, furniture and other hiding places.

You are not done even if the storm was a success, because right away you have to search the houses and buildings in the following way: divide the area to be searched into zones, and assign a search team to each. A team usually consists of a search element (to conduct the search), a security element (to encircle the area) and a reserve element (to assist, as required). Then search the buildings, underground and underwater areas using mine detectors. And it's necessary to establish checkpoints and roadblocks around the area.

- Remember: the enemy's defensive force is usually weaker on one flank than on the other — forces are being concentrated mostly on a threat coming from one particular direction, especially if there's no enough strength to keep all-round defense.
- During assault river crossing (at night only) use an engineer group, bank and assault groups. You must have air superiority and massive fire support. Having crossed, secure the exit bank.

POWs

In handling POWs (prisoners of war) follow the rules: search them as soon as they are captured and take their weapons and papers. When searching a POW, have one man guard him while another searches him. To search a POW, have him spread-eagle against a tree or wall, or get into a pushup position with his knees on the ground. Segregate POWs into groups by sex and into subgroups such as enlisted personnel, civilians and political figures — this keeps the leaders from promoting escape routes. Keep the groups segregated as you move them to the rear. Silence POWs and do not let them talk to each other — this keeps them from planning escape and cautioning each other on security. Speed POWs to the rear. Safeguard POWs when taking them to the rear and do not let anyone abuse them. Watch out for escape attempts and do not let them bunch up, spread out too far or start diversions. Attention: don't get out of your cover right away to accept surrender.

DEFENSE

Defensive operations defeat an enemy attack, buy time, economize forces, or develop conditions favorable for offensive operations. While the offense is the most decisive type of combat operation, the defense is the strongest type. The strengths of the defense include the defender's ability to occupy his positions before the attack and use the available time to prepare his defenses. Preparations end only when the defender retrogrades or begins to fight. The defender can study the ground and select defensive positions that mass the effects of his fires on likely approaches. He combines natural and manmade obstacles to cana-lize the attacking force into his engagement areas. The defender does not have to wait passively to be attacked — he has to seek ways of speeding attrition and weakening the attacking enemy forces before the initiation of close combat, ma-neuver to place the enemy in a position of disadvantage and attacks him at every opportunity, using his direct and indirect fires.

There are three basic types of defensive operations: the area defense, the mo-bile defense and the retrograde. The area defense concentrates on denying en-emy forces access to designated terrain for a specific time rather than destroying the enemy outright. The focus of the area defense is on retaining terrain where the bulk of the defending force positions itself in mutually supporting, prepared positions.

Effective Defensive Methods

Set anti-tank minefields and dummy positions, combine minefields with anti-tank ditches and natural obstacles, crater roads and blow up bridges. Start right away patrolling the zone, keeping fire and radio discipline.

Set roadblocks and ambushes with fire groups, put mines and booby traps and camouflage them well; choose ambush sites on regular enemy's routes, at the edge of the forest, at water points, approaches to your defensive positions (and choose withdrawal routes).

Choose your ground and depth, camouflage, organize all-round defense and food, water and ammunition supply and medical care. Keep reserve (and offen-sive spirit), be ready to reinforce or restore positions.

Support neighbors with fire, especially by cross-fire — the advantage of sup-porting one another is that it's difficult for an attacker to find a covered approach to any defensive position.

Sorry, but for security reasons you have often to remove or eliminate the nearby civilians.

Defending a house: use barricades, barbed wire and mines; fill chimney with barbed wire too; cover windows with sand bags or wire netting to keep out of grenades. Make holes through all internal walls to change positions fast; remove drainpipes, turn off gas and electricity. Organize escape route through a tunnel. Make grenade holes in the floors — it's easier to shoot through them.

If you withdraw from the area destroy anything that might be used by the enemy — crops, transportation, communications, industrial resources.

Mobile defense concentrates on the destruction or defeat of the enemy through a decisive attack by a striking force, defeating or destroying the enemy by allowing him to advance to a point where he is exposed to a decisive counterattack by the striking force. You have to steal the initiative; combine offense, defense and delay; maneuver and entrap the enemy; concentrate your armored reserve and use it in a combined offense with helicopters; start counterattack if attackers become vulnerable through exhaustion.

The retrograde involves organized movement away from the enemy. The retrograde is a transitional operation and it's usually a part of a larger scheme of maneuver designed to regain the initiative and defeat the enemy.

Special Forces

Maximum damage, minimum loss.

Special military operations have special requirements.

- Detailed planning and coordination that allow the special unit to discern and exploit the enemy's weakness while avoiding its strength.
- Decentralized execution, individual and unit initiative.
- Surprise, achieved through the unit's ability to move by uncommon means, along unexpected routes, over rough terrain, during poor weather and reduced visibility. Survivability, achieved by rapid mission accomplishment and a prompt departure from the objective area.
- Mobility, speed, and violence of execution (the speed at which events take place confuses and deceives the enemy as to the intent of the unit, and forces the enemy to react rather than to take the initiative).
- Shock effect, which is a psychological advantage achieved by the combining of speed and violence. The special unit strives to apply its full combat power at he decisive time and place, and at the point of the greatest enemy weakness.
- Multiple methods of insertion and attack, trying not to repeat operations thus decreasing the chance the enemy will detect a pattern. Deception, achieved by feints, false insertions, electronic countermeasures, and dummy transmissions.
- Audacity, a willingness to accept a risk.

Any special team member has to have experience in sniping, underwater swimming, conducting high-altitude, low-opening parachute operations, demolition, using all kinds of weapons, including man-portable air-defense system weapons. And there are some limitations, like limited capability against armored or motorized units in open terrain and no casualty evacuation capability.

Use special forces for:

(a) establishing a credible American presence in any part of the world

(b) conducting limited combat operations under conditions of chemical, nuclear or biological contamination

(c) surveillance and intelligence gathering using recruited agents too (local citizens who support your war or just work for money). To get to the area you have to use infiltration, the movement into the territory occupied by enemy troops, the contact is avoided.

(d) raids on the enemy's defense system

(e) ambush. Depending on terrain ambushes are divided into near (less than 50 meters, in jungle or heavy woods) and far (beyond 50 meters, in open terrain).

Raids consist of clandestine insertion, brief violent combat, rapid disengagement, swift deceptive withdrawal. The raid is used mostly to destroy command posts, communication centers and supply dumps, shipyards, electrical generation facilities, water pumping stations, phone lines, oil or natural gas pipelines, radio and TV stations, mountain passes or routes in restricted terrain, capture supplies and personnel, rescue friendly forces, distract attention from other operations, steal plans and code books, rescue prisoners of war, create havoc in the enemy's rear areas, blow railroads and bridges. By blowing bridges you block and delay the movement of personnel and supplies and by making railroads and certain routes temporary useless you change enemy's movement on to a small number of major roads and railway lines where it is more vulnerable to attack by other forces (especially air strikes).

Raids are normally conducted in the following phases: the team inserts or infiltrates into the objective area; the objective area is sealed off from outside support or reinforcement, to include the enemy air threat; any enemy force at or near the objective is overcome by surprise and violent attack, using all available firepower for shock effect; the mission is accomplished quickly before any surviving enemy can recover or be reinforced; the ranger force quickly withdraws from the objective area and is extracted. (The team can land on or near the objective and seize it before the enemy can react. Thus you avoid forced marches over land carrying heavy combat loads. If there is no suitable landing area near the objective, or the enemy has a strong reaction force nearby, the team has to land unseen far from the objective. It then assembles and moves to the objective).

Stages of an ambush:

1. Planning. You have to identify a suitable killing zone (a place where the ambush will be laid). It's a place where enemy units are expected to pass and which gives reasonable cover for the deployment execution and extraction phases of the ambush patrol. Ambush includes 3 main elements: surprise, coordinated fire of all weapons to isolate the killing zone and to inflict maximum damage and control (early warning of target approach, opening fire at the proper time, timely and orderly withdrawal). You can also plan a mechanical ambush, which consists of the mines set in series. Preparation. You have to deploy into the area covertly, preferably at night and establish secure and covert positions overlook-

ing the killing zone. Then you send two or more cut off groups a short distance from the main ambushing group into similarly covert positions — they have to give you early warning of approaching enemy by radio and, when the ambush is initiated, to prevent any enemy from escaping. Another group will cover the rear of the ambush position and thus give all-round defense to the ambush patrol. No smoking! Attention: you have to occupy the ambush site as late as possible — this reduces the risk of discovery. (While choosing an ambush site, pay attention to natural cover and concealment for your team, routes of entry and withdrawal, good observation and fields of fire, harmless-looking terrain, few enemy escape routes, terrain that will canalize enemy into the killing zone, and natural obstacles to keep him there.)

2. Execution. You must give a clear instruction for initiating the ambush. It should be initiated with a mass casualty producing weapon (mortars and machine guns) to produce a maximum shock effect and break the enemy's spirit to fight back (shock effect can cover unexpected defects in ambush, like ambushing a much larger force that expected). Then, after the firefight has been won, the ambush patrol has to clear the zone by checking bodies for intelligence and taking prisoners. After that you have to leave the area as soon as possible, by a pre-determined route.

3. Disruption of the government functions: recruitment of informants; terror and murders of political leaders and federal and local government chiefs, provoking strikes and mass disobedience; publishing illegal newspapers and literature; anti-government propaganda through illegal radio stations; involving locals in the guerrilla campaign.

4. Counter-guerilla. Typical missions which guerrillas conduct to accomplish their goals include: destroying or damaging vital installations, equipment or supplies; capturing supplies, equipment, or key governmental or military personnel; diverting government forces from other operations; creating confusion and weakening government morale.

GUERRILLAS' STRONG POINTS

Guerrillas are not normally organized or equipped for stand-and-fight type defensive operations. They prefer to defend themselves by moving, by dispersing into small groups, or by diverting the opponent's attention while they withdraw. Whenever possible, these operations are accomplished by offensive operations against the opponent's flank or rear. One of the most important needs of guerrilla forces is support, which can come from different sources — food can be stolen or supplied by political sympathizers, weapons can be gathered from raids on government installations or provided by a foreign power (as well as secret train-ing and indoctrination).

Start the war against guerrillas with intelligence. Usually, guerrillas have the following strengths:
- highly motivated leadership and simple organization. The basic guerrilla organization is an independent three- to five-men cell. The cells can be brought together for larger operations and dispersed later. Guerrillas are organized into cells for two reasons: first, it's security, second, it's for support (guerrillas must live off the land to a large degree, and small cells can support themselves more easily).
- strong belief in a political, religious, or social cause (most of them are fanatics)
- ability to blend with local population and perfect knowledge of environment
- strong discipline
- effective intelligence through penetration into the government agencies

Guerrillas also have the benefit of having limited responsibilities (they usu-ally don't have any responsibility to maintain normal governmental obligations toward society).

They can utilize a broad range of tactics, from terror and sabotage through conventional warfare. They don't hesitate to use bombings, kidnappings, mur-ders, torture, blackmail to press local authorities or provoke overreaction on the part of the government forces, so that the population will be alienated by the actions of government forces (it happens when they target government leaders). In cities guerrillas can disrupt public utilities and services by sabotage and the government may lose control of the situation; they can widely use snipers and explosives there. They can generate widespread disturbances, attack govern-ment offices, create incidents or massing crowds in order to lure the government forces into a trap.

Guerrillas have mobility. They usually disperse during their movements and unite near the target area. The most common techniques employed by them are the ambush, raid and small-scale attacks against security posts, small forces, fa-cilities and lines of communication, using mining, booby trapping and sniping. Targets are selected by the guerrilla based on an analysis of how much the elimi-nation of the target will disrupt the government, what the effect on the popu-lace will be, the risk of being killed or captured, and the amount of weapons or supplies which can be used (this analysis calls for timely intelligence, which is gained by active patrolling).

GUERRILLA WEAKNESSES
- mental and physical stress, caused by long periods of isolation in an unstable environment

- fear of criminal prosecution by the government, or of reprisals against friends and family
- feeling of numerical and technological inferiority of counter-guerrilla forces
- limited personnel and resources, and uncertain public base of support
- security problems about their base camps (they are usually not more than one day march from a village or town). If guerrillas receive support from external sources, they are faced with a problem of security for supply lines, transport means and storage facilities. Besides, you have to know their organization and plans, resources (arms, ammunition, food and medicine supply), leaders and their personalities, lines of communications, relations with civilian population, vulnerabilities. (Again, recruit, recruit and recruit!). You have to evaluate also the effects of terrain (including landing and pickup zones) and the weather effect on men, weapons, equipment, visibility and mobility.

Urban guerrilla warfare has its own peculiarities. Cities and towns are vulnerable to urban guerrilla because they are the focus of economic and political power. In many cases, public utilities can be disrupted and the government may appear to have lost control of the situation. The concentration of a large number of people in a relatively small area provides cover for the guerrilla. However, the insurgent may find support only in a certain areas of a town or a city. Anyway, the urban guerrilla lives in a community that is friendly to him or is too frightened to withhold its support or betray him. In a city the snipers and explosive devices can be placed everywhere. The availability of large numbers of people ensures that crowds can be assembled and demonstrations manipulated easily. The presence of women and children restricts counter-guerrilla force reactions, and excessive force may ensure a major incident that provides the guerrilla with propaganda. Publicity is easily achieved in an urban area because no major incident can be concealed from the local population even if it is not widely reported by the news media. Every explosion may be exploited to discredit the ability of the government to provide protection and control the guerrillas

TACTICAL COUNTER-GUERRILLA OPERATIONS

1. Encirclement, which is designed to cut off all ground routes for escape and reinforcement of the encircled force (darkness recommended) combined with combined with air assault, artillery and airborne troops. And — it's good to divide the enemy while encircling.

2. Search (of a village), which might be done in different ways:
- assemble inhabitants in a central location (if they are hostile) and then start the operation
- restrict inhabitants to their homes
- or control the heads of households (and take other family members to a central location) and then start the convoy security operation, which is one of your top priorities.

Think about ambushes and mines on the route all the time and place a strong attack element at the rear of the convoy where it has maximum flexibility in moving forward to attack guerrillas attempting to ambush the head or center of the convoy. At the first indication of an ambush vehicles have to move out of the killing zone (do not drive to roadsides or shoulders, which may be mined). A security team immediately returns fire from inside vehicles to cover dismounting personnel (if you have to stop) and then dismounts last under cover of the fire by those who dismounted first. Upon dismounting, personnel caught in a killing zone open fire and immediately assault toward the ambush force. Any movements of the troops and supplies are planned and conducted as tactical operations with effective front, flank and rear security.

3. Ambushes (see above).

4. Roadblocks and checkpoints (element of the checkpoint force has to be positioned and concealed at appropriate distance from the checkpoint to prevent the escape of any vehicle or person attempting to turn back).

5. Patrols, which are used to saturate areas of suspected guerrilla activity, control critical roads, maintain contact between villages and units, interdict guerrilla routes of supply and communication, provide internal security in rural and urban areas, locate guerrilla units and base camps. A patrol is a detachment sent out by a larger unit to conduct a combat or reconnaissance operation. There are three key principles to successful patrolling: detailed planning, thorough reconnaissance, all-round security.

Watch out: guerillas usually try to cut the lines of communications by mining roads, waterways and railways, or by ambushes located adjacent to them, blow up bridges and tunnels.

6. Crowd dispersal.

7. Assassination of the guerrilla leader.

8. Taking hostages to press guerrillas.

9. Organization of false guerrilla units.

Meanwhile the enemy will attempt to engage you in locations where your fire would endanger civilians or damage their property.

You have to match the size of the guerrilla unit. Employing a large force to counter a smaller one is inefficient because it compromises the chance of achieving surprise.

Psychological Operations

Psychological operations (PSYOP) in foreign internal defense include propaganda and other measures to influence the opinions, emotions, attitudes, and behavior of hostile, neutral, or friendly groups to support the achievement of national objectives. There are 5 major target groups for PSYOP:

1. Insurgents. The major PSYOP objective here is to discredit the insurgents and isolate them from he population. The most important direction of attack is against their morale. Themes should publicize and exploit differences between cadre, recruits, supporters, and the local population. Other themes might stress lack of support, isolation, homesickness, and hardship.

Amnesty programs are often useful in neutralizing insurgents, and they are most effective when they are well publicized, directed against lower ranking members of the insurgency, and offer sufficient reason and benefits for quitting the unit. These programs do, however, have several disadvantages: they recognize the insurgents as a legitimate political force, they forgo punishment of anyone accepting amnesty, and they increase the image of the insurgents' threat.

2. The population supporting the insurgents. You have to achieve withdrawal of support for the insurgents and a total defection. Propaganda should highlight the insurgents shortcomings, ultimate government victory, government successes, and the practical advantages of surrendering or of accepting amnesty.

3. The uncommitted population. The major mission here is to build national morale, unity, and confidence in the government. There should also be a major effort to win popular acceptance of the government force, and convince the people that government programs serve their interests, the government forces can protect them, ultimate government victory is assured.

4. Government personnel. When targeting government personnel, seek to maintain loyalties and develop policies and attitudes which will result in group members who will realize the importance of popular support, promote public welfare and justice, take action to eliminate the basic causes of the subversive insurgency, and protect the population. You have to indoctrinate the host country security and military forces regarding the importance of the civilian population support. When government personnel interact with neutral and non-hostile elements of the population, the emphasis should be positive and constructive.

5. Foreign audiences. There are two major groups to be addressed: neutral nations and hostile nations. For neutral nations, the purpose of psychological operations is to achieve friendly neutrality or active support for your side. For hostile powers, the major objective of these operations is to influence public opinion against involvement in supporting the insurgency.

Besides, you have to use psychological operations to establish and maintain a favorable image of our country. The themes most useful in establishing that image are that the US presence is requested by the host country government, it is legal and necessary, it is temporary, and it is advisory. Intelligence operations are facilitated by employing psychological operation media to inform the people that they should report to the proper authority information pertaining to strangers, suspicious persons, and guerrilla activities. Posters and leaflets provide definite instruction as to persons and places that are available to receive the information (indicate what rewards are available).

Chapter 15. The Future

The National Defense Strategy of the United States of America

This document was issued by the US Department of Defense in March, 2005. I can't resist telling you what I think of it.

A Defense Strategy for the 21st century:

> "We will give top priority to dissuading, deterring, and defeating those who seek to harm the United States directly, especially extremist enemies with weapons of mass destruction."

Wrong: US extremist enemies having weapons of mass destruction do not exist.

> "The United States will target eight major terrorist vulnerabilities [I'll cite just 3]:
> • ideological support key to recruitment and indoctrination
> • leadership
> • funds"

Wrong: Right now the Defense Department has nothing to do with these vulnerabilities.

> "The campaign to counter ideological support for terrorism may be a decade-long structure."

Wrong: First, again, the Defense Department currently now has nothing to do with such a "campaign." Second, you can't fight ideology — you can only substitute it.

> "We will focus our military planning, posture, operations, and capabilities on the active, forward, and layered defense of our nation, our interests and our partners."

Wrong: That is not a strategy; I don't know what it is.

"We will operationalize this strategy to address the spectrum of strategic challengers by setting priorities among competing capabilities."

Wrong: It's not a strategy. It's a bureaucratic puzzle.

The National Strategy for Victory in Iraq

This was issued by the US National Security Council, November, 2005.

"We will remain in Iraq as long as necessary, and not a day more."

Wrong: That's not a strategy. It's just 14 words put together.

"Victory in Iraq is defined in stages:
Longer term: Iraq is peaceful, united... and a full partner in the global war on terrorism. Iraq is the central front in the global war on terror."

Wrong: There is no "global war on terror." None.

"The political track: isolate enemy elements from those who can be won over the political process by countering false propaganda."

Wrong: It's too late. You could still change the situation if you had a live Department of State, but it's dead.

"Victory will be achieved, although not by a date certain. No war has ever been won on a timetable and neither will this one."

Wrong: You have no idea about military strategic planning. You have no strategy.

"Our mission in Iraq is to win the war. Our troops will return home when that mission is complete."

Wrong: You can't win a war if you have no strategy. It's nice that NSC staff clerks are familiar with Hollywood jargon, but that's not enough.

"Our mission in Iraq is clear. We're hunting down terrorists."

Wrong: War is not a "hunt."

"The terrorists regard Iraq as the central front in their war against humanity."

Wrong: You should not mix national military strategy and national brainwashing strategy.

"If we and our Iraqi partners fail in Iraq, the terrorists will have won a decisive victory over the United States."

Right: The fact that we have a National Security Council, which produced this garbage, is already the a decisive victory for the terrorists.

TREATY ON THE NON-PROLIFERATION OF NUCLEAR WEAPONS
(which seems to have faded from memory)

Signed at Washington, London and Moscow July 1, 1968

Ratification advised by US Senate March 13, 1969

Ratified by US President November 24, 1969

US ratification deposited at Washington, London and Moscow March 5, 1970

Proclaimed by US President March 5, 1970

Entered into force March 5, 1970

> The states concluding this Treaty, hereinafter referred to as the "Parties to the Treaty"... have agreed as follows:
> Article I
> Each nuclear-weapon State Party to the Treaty undertakes not to transfer to any recipient whatsoever nuclear weapons or other nuclear explosive devices or control over such weapons or explosive devices directly, or indirectly; and not in any way to assist, encourage, or induce any non-nuclear weapon State to manufacture or otherwise acquire nuclear weapons or other nuclear explosive devices, or control over such weapons or explosive devices.
> Article II
> Each non-nuclear-weapon State Party to the Treaty undertakes not to receive the transfer from any transferor whatsoever of nuclear weapons or other nuclear explosive devices or of control over such weapons or explosive devices directly, or indirectly; not to manufacture or otherwise acquire nuclear weapons or other nuclear explosive devices; and not to seek or receive any assistance in the manufacture of nuclear weapons or other nuclear explosive devices....
> Article IX
> This treaty shall be open to all States for signature. Any State which does not sign the Treaty before its entry into force in accordance with paragraph 3 of this article may accede to it at any time...

AMERICA'S NUMBER ONE "ENEMY" IS CHINA

Regardless how generous they have been in supplying cheap goods for the US consumer, the time is coming when the 1.3+ billion Chinese, too, will expect to have 2 cars, 3 TVs, a big kitchen, 3 or 4 marble baths, and a beachfront cottage with jacuzzi for themselves. The planet does not have enough resources to supply them, and pressure will grow for the US to consume only its fair share of petroleum, water and other raw materials. What then?

The Chinese army is by far the biggest in the world and totals 2.5 million members serving in four branches — ground forces (2 million troops), Air force, Navy and a strategic missile force.

China's Ground Forces:
    8,000 tanks
    4,000 armored vehicles
    25,000 artillery guns and multiple rocket launchers

Navy:
    74 submarines
    2 aircraft carriers (will be built by 2010)
    25 destroyers
    45 frigates
    90 guided missile boats
    9 torpedo boats
    238 patrol boats
    92 mine warfare
    88 amphibious warfare craft
    29 surveillance (including electronic reconnaissance, intelligence collection and space event)

Navy Air Force aircraft:
    45 bombers
    108 attack
    1300 fighters

Anti-Submarine Warfare:
    3 aerial refueling
    66 transport

Army Air Force:
    120 bombers
    525 attack
    1, 250 fighters
    180 reconnaissance
    14 tankers
    513 transports
    100 helicopters
    200 training
    169 aircraft (helicopters)
    ? unmanned aerial vehicles

China's estimated nuclear weapons stockpile, including nuclear gravity bombs, submarine-launched missiles, medium-range and intercontinental missiles, is about 400 nuclear warheads.

In times of crisis the army can be reinforced by a 1.5 million reserve militia force and one million more from the People's Armed Police.

Part 4. Still Want It?

Now that you have some idea what the President's job entails, and the implications of some of the actions you will be asked to take, the constraints that will hamper you in taking actions you think you'd like to take, and the tools at your disposal — you can make a responsible decision whether to go for it. Now, let's see what your chances are.

Chapter 16. Electability

Formal and Informal Considerations

The formal requirements for the Presidency, as the Constitution says, are simple: a candidate must be a natural-born US citizen, at least 35 years of age and a US resident for at least 14 years.

These formal requirements meet the technical minimum, but the informal and sometimes less apparent ones are equally important. You must have "political availability," which means political experience; be attractive (for political activists and general voting public); and project personal characteristics that enable the public to envision you as President.

Voters — and funders — must believe that you and only you deserve to represent them for the next four years.

Reality Check

If you pass the above tests, ask yourself five simple questions:

1. Am I a governor?
2. Am I a congressman?
3. Am I a senator?
4. Am I a cabinet member?
5. Am I a lawyer?

These are the jobs that put you closer to the Oval Office. How much difference does it make?

Seventeen US Presidents previously served as Governors: Thomas Jefferson, Martin Van Buren, William Harrison, John Tyler, James Polk, Andrew Johnson, Rutherford Hayes, Grover Cleveland, William McKinley, Theodore Roosevelt, William Taft, Woodrow Wilson, Calvin Coolidge, Franklin Roosevelt, Jimmy Carter, Ronald Reagan, Bill Clinton, George W. Bush.

Nineteen US Presidents were Congressmen: James Madison, John Adams, Andrew Jackson, William Harrison, John Tyler, James Polk, Millard Fillmore, Franklin Pierce, James Buchanan, Abraham Lincoln, Andrew Johnson, Rutherford Hayes, James Garfield, William McKinley, John Kennedy, Lyndon Johnson, Richard Nixon, Gerald Ford, George Bush.

Fifteen US Presidents were Senators: James Monroe, John Adams, Andrew Jackson, Martin Van Buren, William Harrison, John Tyler, Franklin Pierce, James Buchanan, Andrew Johnson, Benjamin Harrison, Warren Harding, Harry Truman, John Kennedy, Lyndon Johnson, Richard Nixon.

Six were Secretaries of State — Thomas Jefferson, James Madison, James Monroe, John Adams, Martin Van Buren, James Buchanan.

Two were Secretaries of War — Ulysses S. Grant and William Taft.

One was a Secretary of Commerce — Herbert Hoover.

And a full twenty-six US Presidents were lawyers: John Adams, Thomas Jefferson, James Madison, James Monroe, John Adams, Andrew Jackson, Martin Van Buren, John Tyler, James Polk, Millard Fillmore, Franklin Pierce, James Buchanan, Abraham Lincoln, Rutherford Hayes, James Garfield, Chester Arthur, Grover Cleveland, Benjamin Harrison, William McKinley, William Howard Taft, Woodrow Wilson, Calvin Coolidge, Franklin Roosevelt, Richard Nixon, Gerald Ford, Bill Clinton.

However, without wishing to dampen your enthusiasm, I must add that as of 2005, 8 Governors, 7 US Senators, 9 US Congressmen, 11 Mayors, 17 State Legislators and 11 judges have been violently attacked.

THE BILDERBERG GROUP

The Bilderberg Group is an annual invitation-only conference of around 100 guests, most of whom are usually influential politicians and big business. The title comes from the location of its first official meeting in 1954 in the Bilderberg Hotel, Arnhem, Netherlands. Its main office is now in Leiden, South Holland, the group's current Chairman is Etienne Davignon, a former Vice President of the European Commission. The original intention of the group was to further the understanding between Western Europe and North America through informal and closed for media and public meetings between powerful individuals. Of course, that's not what they are doing. If you look through the guests' lists, you can find some very popular names like David Rockefeller, Donald Rumsfeld and George Soros. Lists differ each year, but there's one name that remains there for years — Henry Kissinger, a former Secretary of State, who rules the Bilderberg Group and rules the world.

There are two more very interesting names and facts:

- Bill Clinton. The Arkansas Governor and presidential nominee went to Baden-Baden and attended the Conference from June 6 through 9, 1991.
- John Edwards. In the middle of his vice presidential campaign Senator Edwards, the running mate of 2004 presidential nominee Senator John Kerry, went to Stresa, Italy and attended the Conference from June 3 through 6, 2004.

What happened to these two? Bill Clinton was elected the US President in 1991. John Edwards got nothing, because his leader Kerry got nothing; but he is in the 2008 game and he is still very young.

It appears to be helpful to be invited to the Conference and blessed by Henry Kissinger if you want to run for President.

LIBERAL OR CONSERVATIVE — CHOOSING SIDES

The next step is to decide whether you want to be cast as a liberal (Democrat) or conservative (Republican). If you don't take a definite side, you will be labeled as a moderate liberal-conservative.

Moving towards 2008, the United States is divided as never before. If a Democrat is elected the US President, he will have to offer his Republican opponent the vice presidency — that's the only way to unite the nation.

Issues like those listed below, especially those with a strong emotional component, can be used to call certain groups of voters to your side, to tar-and-feather your rivals, and to deflect attention from complex issues where you might have more difficulty articulating a clear position without alienating other critical supporters.

You will be cast as a "liberal" if you:	You are a conservative if you:
1. Embrace national government resolutions to public problems.	1. State that the national government has grown too large.

2. Believe that the national government should intervene in the economy to ensure its health, to support social welfare problems to assist the disadvantaged, and to be tolerant of social change.	2. Insist the private sector needs less interference from the government, that social welfare programs should be limited and state and local governments should be able to make their own decisions, and that the nation's defense should be strengthened.
3. Identify yourself with pro-women's rights position, pro-civil rights policies, and opposition to increased defense spending.	3. Are not tolerant of gay rights laws.
4. Increase taxes.	4. Cut taxes.
5. Negotiate first and take military action only if sanctioned by the UN.	5. Work with the UN but take unilateral pre-emptive action to show the United States is not under anyone's thumb.
6. Block drilling for oil in Alaska.	6. Pursue this and other domestic oil sources.
7. Sign the Kyoto Treaty.	7. Don't sign environmental treaties.
8. Protect the rights of the accused first and foremost.	8. Provide maximum punishment and protect the rights of the victim first and foremost.
9. Allow doctor-assisted suicide.	9. Argue against any kind of suicide.
10. Scrap the missile defense program	10. Boost international military programs.
11. Increase age of initial retirement eligibility (e.g. 68 or 70); increase salary limits subject to tax.	11. Privatize; i.e. oblige citizens to handle their own retirement money and allow stock investments.
12. Propose 100% government-controlled reform.	12. De-regulate health care and introduce free market health care.
13. Maintain separation of church and state; stop faith-based government initiatives.	13. Introduce more religion in schools and public ceremonies; promote faith-based government initiatives.

CHAPTER 17. THE FIGHT FOR THE PRESIDENCY

Yes, the United States is huge. Yes, George Washington won election with 100% support; but for JFK 56% was just fine. Don't worry.

The whole process is your rotation inside a triangle:

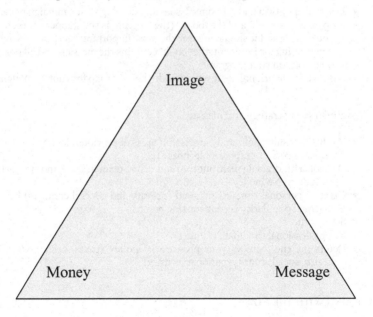

THINK IT OVER

Before you make a decision to run for President, you must determine for yourself if you can handle the Oval office:

- Are you willing to accept such a huge responsibility and put the rest of your life on hold ?
- Are you skilled in dealing with big groups of people ?
- Can you motivate the nation to action ?

Think about your biography, which is, of course, not perfect.

- Decide how are you going to impress Party leaders.
- Make intensive preliminary polling to determine your chances.
- Poll big demographic groups as well as smaller groups of people from selected demographic groups.

Determine the rationale for your candidacy. What is your political record?

- Delay announcing your candidacy until late in the year before the election to minimize expenditures and risk, avoid legal spending limits, avoid voter fatigue, avoid getting ensnarled in unnecessary controversies and contradictions.
- Carefully study applicable election laws before you start fundraising and spending.
- Write your campaign plan (strategic objective, tactical targets, key message, target audiences, methods of delivery, timing, your progress evaluation — polls).
- Learn the political and economic issues and develop your campaign message.
- Prepare the "speech" and the "book" (the "speech" is the standard speech that you deliver and it should answer the most important question — why are you running for President; the "book" contains the message and all possible questions on your program.
- Take a benchmark poll — it will provide the road map for your campaign.

Establish your strategy and message.

- Study the results, polls and "successful" areas of previous election.
- Establish a perfect graphic look (image).
- Develop a fundraising plan, put the fundraising team in place and start asking for money. No money — no campaign.
- Create a personal contacts pyramid (priority and general contacts) because personal popularity is your starting point.
- Set up offices.
- Get professional candidate training.
- Determine the focus of your presidential policy (taxes, crime, education, health, social security, national security).

WORKING WITH THE STAFF

Basic campaign staffers include:

1) campaign managers — they plan the campaign, organize and recruit the staff, supervise daily campaign operations, make priority contacts with key spe-

cial groups big business and big media, correct the strategy and make quick decisions. It has to be someone you trust completely.

2) campaign consultants-specialists in both direct (personal and public meetings) and indirect (media, advertising) campaigning

3) strategists

4) analysts

5) issues researchers

6) speechwriters

7) lawyer (interprets election and campaign reporting laws)

8) personal assistants (work on issues in foreign and domestic policy in cooperation with the whole team).

9) fundraisers (plan and execute fundraising events — dinners, parties, auctions, direct appeals through telephone and letters, receptions, computerized fundraising). Big business has to be approached by rich fundraiser only.

10) scheduler (determines events and locations — TV and radio talk shows, news — conferences, meetings with students and professors at college campuses and with professionals at their associations' annual meetings, special events and fundraisers especially with ethnic leaders in big cities, as well as festivals and big shows where celebrities demonstrate their support, large extravaganzas, meetings at civic clubs, farm warehouse auctions and special auctions, local civic events. Also, scheduler makes arrangements with local media before your visit and sends media the copies of your speech; insures that good crowd will attend the event and takes care of transportation arrangements). The purpose of the campaign planning and strategic scheduling is to draw press attention to the candidate for transmission to the voting public. That's natural — the candidate who has enough media attention has much better chances of recruiting public acceptance and raising campaign funds.

During the "invisible primary" which is the nomination campaign, you have to make visits to party organizations especially in pivotal states, such as the above mentioned Iowa and New Hampshire where you have to make as many handshaking and personal contacts as possible. Key staffers must travel with you.

FUNDRAISING

You are the #1 fundraiser yourself. You must have substantial financial support to compete. It was estimated early in 2007 that the major candidates for 2008 will spend ONE BILLION dollars in their campaigns. As they say, at that rate, pretty soon we're talking real money.

You must have an overall plan which outlines expenditures month by month. It is imperative to have even more money on hand at the end of the campaign for an advertising blitz when the voters are most attentive and the field of candidates has been winnowed out. Half of a campaign funds go to media.

Failing to do well in early caucus and primary contests means more than losing delegates — it means that contributions stop.

Your speeches have to be a fun, and match the meal and drinks — don't be heavy and too political.

Actually, you have to run two campaigns (a political campaign and a fundraising one) and you must win both; if you raise less money than your opponent, you lose, because you don't have enough money to inform, influence, and motivate your voters.

If you are a Senator or a Congressman, you already have an advantage in money (free postage on mail sent to your constituents, automatic media coverage) and you can use your congressional staff to assist your campaign. Besides, you are interviewed by reporters for free as an elected official.

You can also ask your political party for a contribution to your campaign. Party money can be given in two ways — as a "direct" contribution or as a "coordinated" expenditure. Direct contributions are funds given by the party to candidates to do with as they please. Coordinated expenditures are made for such services as polling and TV advertising, but the party has a say how the money is spent.

Then you have to ask PACs (political action committees) to fund your campaign, too. PACs are special-interest groups which consist of people who pool their money in order to contribute it to candidates or political party committees who share their political, social, religious or economic views. PACs include corporations, trade unions, professional associations and groups composed of political conservatives or liberals, or people who share the same ideological views on women's rights, gun control, the environment, civil rights, etc. Remember the "women factor": there are more women than men in our country, women are more likely to be registered to vote, and among registered voters women are more likely to vote.

An additional source of money is "soft money" contributions. "Soft money" is supposed to be used for the party-building activities, but often ends up supporting the campaigns of individual candidates.

The key rules in fundraising are:

- find some "fat cats," quick
- go where the money is
- get fundraisers with lots of rich friends

- get money from those who usually contribute

And the most important strategy is to raise big money for yourself and prevent big money from being spent against you. Early fundraising is crucial to a campaign because of the high costs organization and the need to demonstrate viability. The best states for fundraising are California, New York, Florida, Texas, which supply half of all campaign donations. Go right ahead and raise money in New York and spend in Iowa and New Hampshire.

To finish well in pre-nomination popularity contests ("straw polls") you have to appear daily in TV ads, and prime-time news coverage — after the primaries media "label" winners and losers and that affects voters and contributors a lot. Media, especially the most influential "The New York Times" and "Washington Post" (their publications influence decisions on which news stories will be carried on TV channels), have to take you as a very serious contender.

Geography

Due to the winner-take-all electoral college system, in which the leading vote-getter in a state wins all of that state's electoral votes, you MUST win as many large states as possible rather than build up strength in states where you are weak.

You have to win a majority (270 of the 538 electoral votes) and for that, concentrate on visits to the most populous states — California, New York, Texas, Florida, Pennsylvania, Illinois, Ohio, Michigan, New Jersey, North Carolina, and Georgia (54+33+32+25+23+22+21+18+15+14+13 = 270).

Work closely with your party activists and supporters among Senators, Representatives, Governors, Mayors, ethnic and religious groups leaders, big business, celebrities, unions leaders.

Determine the states in which you are the strongest and then build you campaign on that basis. Republicans have usually done well in recent years in the Midwest, West and South (Tennessee, Kentucky, Texas, Oklahoma). Democrats win in the Northeast industrial base, Mid-Atlantic and Pacific Coast. New York City is a very important factor because the most active, influential and rich people live there.

Chapter 18. Meet the Electorate: Basic Information and the 2004 Election State by State

Alabama (Heart of Dixie, Camellia State).

9 electoral votes

State motto: We dare defend our rights.

Population: 4,500,752 [2003 est.].

Racial distribution: 71.1% white, 26.0% black, 0.5% Native American, 0.7% Asian, 1% Hispanic [2000].

Chief industries: pulp and paper, chemicals, electronics, apparel, textiles, primary metals, lumber and wood products, food processing, oil and gas exploration.

10 largest cities: Birmingham, 242,820; Montgomery, 201,568; Mobile, 198,915; Huntsville, 158,216; Tuscaloosa, 77,906; Hoover, 62,742; Dothan, 57,737; Decatur, 53,929; Auburn, 42,987; Gadsden, 38,978 [2000]

2004 election: Bush 1,176,394 (63%) Kerry 693,933 (37%)

Alaska (The Last Frontier).

3 electoral votes

State motto: North to the future.

Population: 648,818 [2003 est.].

Racial distribution: 69. 3% white, 3. 5% black, 15. 6% Native Americans, 4.0% Asian, 2.1% Hispanic [2000].

Chief industries: petroleum, tourism, fishing, mining, forestry, transportation, aerospace.

10 largest cities: Anchorage, 260,283; Juneau, 30,711; Fairbanks, 30,224; Sitka, 8,835; Ketchikan, 7,922; Kenai, 6,942; Kodiak, 6,334; Bethel, 5,471; Wasilla, 5,469; Barrow, 4,581 [2000]

2004 election: Bush 190,889 (61%) Kerry 111,025 (36%)

Arizona (Grand Canyon State).

10 electoral votes

State motto: Ditat Deus (God enriches).

Population: 5,580,811 [2003 est.].

Racial distribution: 75. 5% white, 3.1% black, 5.0% Native American, 1.8% Asian, 25. 3% Hispanic [2000].

Chief industries: manufacturing, construction, tourism, mining, agriculture.

10 largest cities: Phoenix, 1,321,045; Tucson, 486,699; Mesa, 396,375; Glendale, 218,812; Scottsdale, 202,705; Chandler, 176,581; Tempe, 158,625; Gilbert, 109,697; Peoria, 108,364; Yuma, 77,515 [2000]

2004 election: Bush 1,104,294 (55%) Kerry 893,524 (44%)

Arkansas (The Natural State, The Razorback State).

6 electoral votes

State motto: Regnat Populus (The people rule).

Population: 2,725,714 [2003 est.].

Racial distribution: 80.0% white, 15. 7% black, 0.8% Native American, 0.8% Asian, 3.2% Hispanic [2000].

Chief industries: manufacturing, agriculture, tourism, forestry.

10 largest cities: Little Rock, 183,133; Fort Smith, 80,268; North Little Rock, 60,433; Fayetteville, 58,047; Jonesboro, 55,515; Pine Bluff, 55,085; Springdale, 45,798; Conway, 43,167; Rogers, 38,829; Hot Springs, 35,750 [2000]

2004 election: Bush 572,898 (54%) Kerry 469,953 (45%)

California (Golden State).

55 electoral votes

State motto: Eureka (I have found it).

Population: 35,484,453 [2003 est.].

Racial distribution: 59. 9% white, 6. 7% black, 1.0% Native American, 10.9% Asian, 4. 7% Hispanic [2000].

Chief industries: agriculture, tourism, apparel, electronics, telecommunications, entertainment.

10 largest cities: Los Angeles, 3,694,820; San Diego, 1,223,400; San Jose, 894,943; San Francisco, 776,733; Long Beach, 461,522; Fresno, 427,652; Sacramento, 407,018; Oakland, 399,484; Santa Ana, 337,977; Anaheim, 328,014 [2000]

2004 election: Kerry 6,745,485 (54%) Bush 5,509,826 (45%)

Colorado (Centennial State).

9 electoral votes

State motto: Nil Sine Numine (Nothing without providence).

Population: 4,550,688 [2003 est.].

Racial distribution: 82.2% white, 3.8% black, 1.0% Native American, 2.2% Asian, 17.15% Hispanic [2000].

Chief industries: manufacturing, construction, government, tourism, agriculture, aerospace, electronics, equipment.

10 largest cities: Denver, 554,636,; Colorado Springs, 360,890; Aurora, 276,393; Lakewood, 144,126; Fort Collins, 118,652; Arvada, 102,153; Pueblo, 102,121; Westminster, 100,940; Boulder, 94,673; Thornton, 82,384 [2000]

2004 election: Bush 1,101,255 (52%) Kerry 1,001,732 (47%)

Connecticut (Constitution State, Nutmeg State).

7 electoral votes

State motto: Qui Transtulit Sustinet (He who transplanted still sustains).

Population: 3,483,372 [2003 est.].

Racial distribution: 81. 6% white, 9.1% black, 0.3% Native American, 2. 4% Asian, 9. 4%Hispanic [2000].

Chief industries: manufacturing, retail trade, government (aircraft engines and parts, submarines, helicopters), services, finances, insurance, real estate.

10 largest cities: Bridgeport, 139,529; New Haven, 123,626; Hartford, 121,578; Stamford, 117,083; Waterbury, 107,271; Norwalk,82,951; Danbury, 74,848; New Britain, 71,538; West Hartford, 63,589; Greenwich, 61,101 [2000]

2004 election: Kerry 857,488 (54%) Bush 693,826 (44%)

Delaware

3 electoral votes

State motto: Liberty and independence.

Population: 817,491 [2003 est.].

Racial distribution: 74. 6% white, 19.2% black, 0.3% Native American, 2.1 5 Asian, 4.8% 4.8% Hispanic [2000].

Chief industries: chemicals, agriculture, finance, poultry, shellfish, tourism, auto assembly, food processing, transportation equipment.

10 largest cities: Wilmington, 72,664; Dover, 32,135; Newark, 28,547; Milford, 6,732; Seaford, 6,699; Middletown, 6,161; Elsmere, 5,800; Smyrna, 5,679; New Castle, 4,862; Georgetown, 4,643 [2000].

2004 election: Kerry 200, 152 (53%) Bush 171,660 (46%)

Florida (Sunshine State).

27 electoral votes

State motto: In God we trust.

Population: 8,684,715 [2003 est.].

Racial distribution: 65.1% white, 28. 7% black, 0.3% Native American, 2.1% Asian, 5. 3% 5. 3% Hispanic [2000].

Chief industries: tourism, agriculture, manufacturing, construction, services, international trade.

10 largest cities: Jacksonville, 735,617; Miami, 362,470; Tampa, 303,447; St. Petersburg, 248,232; Hialeah, 226,419; Orlando, 185,951; Fort Lauderdale, 152,397; Tallahassee, 150,624; Hollywood, 139,357; Pembroke Pines, 137,427 [2000].

2004 election: Bush 3,964,522 (52%) Kerry 3,583,544 (47%)

Georgia (Empire State of the South, Peach State).

15 electoral votes

State motto: Wisdom, justice and moderation.

Population: 8,684,715 [2003 est.].

Racial distribution: 65.1% white, 28. 7% black, 0.3% Native American, 2.1% Asian, 5. 3% 5. 3% Hispanic [2000].

Chief industries: services, manufacturing, retail trade.

10 largest cities: Atlanta, 416,474; Augusta-Richmond County, 199,775; Columbus, 182,291; Savannah, 131,510; Athens-Clarke County, 101,489; Macon, 97,255; Roswell, 79,334; Albany, 76,939; Marietta, 58,748; Warner Robins, 48,804 [2000].

2004 election: Bush 1,914,254 (58%) Kerry 1,366,149 (41%)

Hawaii

4 electoral votes

State motto: The life of the land is perpetuated in righteousness.

Population: 1,257,608 [2003 est.].

Racial distribution: 24. 3 white, 1.8% black, 0.3% Native American, 41. 6% Asian, 7.2%, 7.2% Hispanic [2000]. Chief industries: tourism, defense, sugar, pineapple.

10 largest cities: Honolulu, 371,657; Hilo, 40,759; Kailua, 36,513; Kaneohe, 34,970; Waipahu, 33,108; Pearl City, 30,976; Waimalu, 29,371; Mililani Town, 26,608; Kahului, 20,146; Kihei, 16,749 [2000].

2004 election: Kerry 231,108 (54%) Bush 194,191 (45%)

Idaho (Gem State).

4 electoral votes

State motto: Esto Perpetua (It is perpetual).

Population: 1,257,608 [2003 est.]

Racial distribution: 91.0% white, 0.4% black, 1. 4% Native American, 0.9% Asian, 7. 9% Hispanic [2000].

Chief industries: manufacturing, agriculture, tourism, lumber, mining, electronics.

10 largest cities: Boise, 185,787; Nampa, 51,867; Pocatello, 51,466; Idaho Falls, 50,730; Meridian, 34,919; Coeur d'Alene, 34,514; Twin Falls, 34,469; Lewiston, 30,904; Caldwell, 25,967; Moscow, 21,291 [2000].

2004 election: Bush 409,235 (69%) Kerry 181,098 (30%)

Illinois (Prairie State).

21 electoral votes

State motto: State sovereignty — national union.

Population: 12,653,544 [2003 est.].

Racial distribution: 73. 5% white, 15.1% black, 0.2% Native American, 3. 4% Asian, 12. 3% Hispanic [2000].

Chief industries: services, manufacturing, travel, wholesale and retail trade, finance, insurance, real estate, construction, health care, agriculture.

10 largest cities: Chicago, 2,896,016; Rockford, 150,115; Aurora, 142,990; Naperville, 128,358; Peoria, 112,936; Springfield, 111,454; Joliet, 196,221; Elgin, 94,487; Waukegan, 87,901; Cicero, 85,616 [2000].

2004 election: Kerry 2,891,550 (55%) Bush 2,345,946 (44%)

Indiana (Hoosier State).

11 election votes)

State motto: Crossroads of America.

Population: 6,195,643 [2003 est.].

Racial distribution: 87. 5% white, 8. 4% black, 0.3% Native American, 1.0% Asian, 3. 5% 3. 5% Hispanic [2000].

Chief industries: manufacturing, services, agriculture, government, wholesale and retail trade, transportation and public utilities.

10 largest cities: Indianapolis, 791,926; Fort Wayne, 205,727; Evansville, 121,582; South Bend, 107,789; Gary, 102,746; Hammond, 83,048; Bloomington, 69,291;

Muncie, 67,430; Anderson, 59,734; Terre Haute, 59,614 [2000].

2004 election: Bush 1,479,438 (60%) Kerry 969,011 (39%)

Iowa (Hawkeye State).

7 electoral votes

State motto: Our liberties we prize, and our rights we will maintain.

Population: 2,944,062 [2003 est.].

Racial distribution: 93. 9% white, 2.1% black, 0.3% Native American, 1. 3% Asian, 2.8% Hispanic [2000].

Chief industries: agriculture, communications, construction, finance, insurance, trade, services, manufacturing.

10 largest cities: Des Moines, 198,682; Cedar Rapids, 120,758; Davenport, 98,359; Sioux City, 85,013; Waterloo, 68,747; Iowa City, 62,220; Council Bluffs, 58,268; Dubuque, 57,686; Ames, 50,731; West Des Moines, 46,403 [2000].

2004 election: Bush 751,957 (50%) Kerry 741,898 (49%)

Kansas (Sunflower State).

6 electoral votes

State motto: Ad Astra per Aspera.

Population: 2,944,062 [2003 est.].

Racial distribution: 86.1% white, 5. 7% black, 0.9% Native American, 1.7% Asian, 7.0% 7.0% Hispanic [2000].

Chief industries: manufacturing, finance, insurance, real estate, services.

10 largest cities: Wichita, 344,284; overland Park, 149,080; Kansas City, 146,868; Topeka, 122,377; Olathe, 92,962; Lawrence, 80,098; Shawnee, 47,996; Salina, 45,679; Manhattan, 44,831; Hutchinson, 40,787 [2000].

2004 election: Bush 736,456 (62%) Kerry 434,993 (37%)

Kentucky (Bluegrass State).

8 electoral votes

State motto: United we stand, divided we fall.

Population: 4,117,827 [2003 est.].

Racial distribution: 90.1% white, 7. 3% black, 0.2% Native American, 0.7% Asian, 1. 5% 1. 5% Hispanic [2000].

Chief industries: manufacturing, services, finance, insurance and real estate, retail trade, public utilities.

10 largest cities: Lexington-Fayette, 260,512; Louisville, 256,231; Owensboro, 54,067; Bowling Green, 49,296; Covington, 43,370; Hopkinsville, 30,089; Frankfort, 27,741; Henderson, 27,373; Richmond, 27,152; Jeffersontown, 26,633 [2000].

2004 election: Bush 1,069,439 (60%) Kerry 712,733 (40%)

Louisiana (Pelican State).

9 electoral votes

State motto: Union, justice and confidence.

Population: 4,496,334 [2003 est., pre-Katrina].

Racial distribution: 63. 9% white, 32. 5% black, 0.6% Native American, 1.2% Asian, 2. 4% Hispanic [2000].

Chief industries: wholesale and retail trade, tourism, manufacturing, construction, transportation, communication, public utilities, finance, insurance, real estate, mining.

10 largest cities: New Orleans, 484,674; Baton Rouge, 227,818; Shreveport, 200,145; Lafayette, 110,257; Lake Charles, 71,757; Kenner, 70,517; Bossier City, 56,461; Monroe, 53,107; Alexandria, 46,342; New Iberia, 32,623 [2000].

2004 election: Bush 1,102,169 (57%) Kerry 820,299 (42%)

Maine (Pine Tree State).

4 electoral votes

State motto: Dirigo (I direct).

Population: 1,305,728 [2003 est.].

Racial distribution: 96. 9% white, 0.5% black, 0.6% Native American, 0.7% Asian, 0.7% Hispanic [2000].

Chief industries: manufacturing, agriculture, fishing, services, trade, government, finance, insurance, real estate, construction.

10 largest cities: Portland, 64,249; Lewiston, 35,690; Bangor, 31,473; South Portland, 23,324; Auburn, 23,203; Brunswick, 21,172; Biddeford, 20,942; Sanford, 20,806; Augusta, 18,560; Scarborough, 16,970 [2000].

2004 election: Kerry 396,842 (54%) Bush 330,201 (45%)

Maryland (Old Line State, Free State).

10 electoral votes

State motto: Fatti Maschli, Parole Femine (Manly deeds, womanly words).

Population: 5,508,909 [2003 est.].

Racial distribution: 64.0% white, 27. 9% black, 0.3% Native American, 4.0% Asian, 4. 3% 4. 3% Hispanic [2000].

Chief industries: manufacturing, biotechnology and information, technology, services, tourism.

10 largest cities: Baltimore, 651,154; Frederick, 52,767; Gaithersburg, 52,613; Bowie, 50,269; Rockville, 47,388; Hagerstown, 36,687; Annapolis, 35,838; College Park, 24,657; Salisbury, 23,743; Cumberland, 21,518 [2000]

2004 election: Kerry 1,334,493 (56%) Bush 1,024,703 (43%)

Massachusetts (Bay State, Old Colony).

12 electoral votes

State motto: Ense Petit Placidam Sub Libertate Quietem (By the sword we seek peace, but peace only under liberty).

Population: 6,433,422 [2003 est.].

Racial distribution: 84. 5% white, 5. 4% black, 0.2% Native American, 3.8% Asian, 6.8%Hispanic [2000].

Chief industries: services, trade, manufacturing.

10 largest cities: Boston, 589,141; Worcester, 172,648; Springfield, 152,082; Lowell, 105,167; Cambridge, 101,355; Brockton, 94,304; New Bedford, 93,768; Fall River, 91,938; Lynn, 89,050; Quincy, 88,025 [2000].

2004 election: Kerry 1,803,800 (62%) Bush 1,071,109 (37%)

Michigan (Great Lakes State, Wolverine State).

17 electoral votes

State motto: Si Quaeris Peninsulam Amoenam, Circumspice (If you seek a pleasant peninsula, look about you).

Population: 10,079,985 [2003 est.].

Racial distribution: 80.2% white, 14.2% black, 0.6% Native American, 1.8% Asian, 3. 3% 3. 3%Hispanic [2000].

Chief industries: manufacturing, services, tourism, agriculture, forestry/lumber.

10 largest cities: Detroit, 951,270; Grand Rapids, 197,800; Warren, 138,247; Flint, 124,943; Sterling Heights, 124,471; Lansing, 119, 128; Ann Arbor, 114,024; Livonia, 100,545; Dearborn, 97,775; Westland, 86,602 [2000].

2004 election: Kerry 2,479,183 (51%) Bush 2,313,746 (48%)

Minnesota (North Star State, Gopher State).

10 electoral votes

State motto: L'etoile du Nord (The star of north).

Population: 5,059,375 [2003 est.].

Racial distribution: 89. 4% white, 3. 5% black, 1.1% Native American, 2. 9% Asian, 2. 9%, 2. 9% Hispanic [2000].

Chief industries: agribusiness, forest products, mining, manufacturing, tourism.

10 largest cities: Minneapolis, 382,618; St. Paul, 287,151; Duluth, 86,918; Rochester, 85,806; Bloomington, 85,172; Brooklyn Park, 67,338; Plymouth, 65,894; Eagan, 63,557; Coon Rapids, 61,607; Bumsville, 60,220 [2000].

2004 election: Kerry 1,445,014 (51%)   Bush 1,346,695 (48%)

Mississippi (Magnolia State).

6 electoral votes

State motto: Virtute et Armis (By valor and arms).

Population: 2,881,281 [2003 est.].

Racial distribution: 61. 4% white, 36. 3% black, 0.4% Native American, 0.7% Asian, 1. 4%Hispanic [2000].

Chief industries: warehousing, & distribution, services, manufacturing, government, wholesale and retail trade.

10 largest cities: Jackson, 184,256; Gulfport, 71,127; Biloxi, 50,644; Hattiesburg, 44,779; Greenville, 41,663; Meridian, 39,968; Tupelo, 34,211; Southhaven, 28,977; Vicksburg, 26,407; Pascagoula, 26,200 [2000].

2004 election: Bush 684,981 (60%) Kerry 457,766 (40%)

Missouri (Show Me State).

11 electoral votes

State motto: Salus Populi Suprema Lex Esto (The welfare of the people shall be the Supreme Law)

Population: 5,704,484 [2003 est.].

Racial distribution: 84. 9% white, 11.2% black, 0.4% Native American, 1.1% Asian, 2.1%, 2.1% Hispanic [2000].

Chief industries: agriculture, manufacturing, aerospace, tourism.

10 largest cities: Kansas City, 441,545; St. Louis, 348,189; Springfield, 151,580; Independence, 113,288; Columbia, 84,531; St. Joseph, 73,890; Lee's Summit, 70,700; St. Charles, 60,321; St. Peter's, 51,381; Florissant, 50,497 [2000].

2004 election: Bush 1,455,713 (53%) Kerry 1,259,171 (46%)

Montana (Treasure State).

3 electoral votes

State motto: Oro y Plata (Gold and silver).

Population: 917,621 [2003 est.].

Racial distribution: 90.6% white, 0.3% black, 6.2% Native American, 0.5% Asian, 2.0%, 2. 0% Hispanic [2000].

Chief industries: agriculture, timber, mining, tourism, oil and gas.

10 largest cities: Billings, 89,847; Missoula, 57,053; Great Falls, 56,690; Butte-Silver Bow, 34,606; Bozeman, 27,509; Helena, 25,780; Kalispell, 14,223; Havre, 9,621; Anaconda-Deer Lodge County, 9,417; Miles City, 8,487 [2000].

2004 election: Bush 266,063 (59%) Kerry 173,710 (39%)

Nebraska (Cornhusker State).

5 electoral votes

State motto: Equality before the law.

Population: 1,739,291 [2003 est.].

Racial distribution: 89. 6% white, 4.0% black, 0.9% Native American, 1.3% Asian, 5. 5% Hispanic [2000].

Chief industries: agriculture, manufacturing.

10 largest cities: Omaha, 390,007; Lincoln, 225,581; Bellevue, 44,382; Grand Island, 42,940; Kearney, 27,431; Fremont, 25,174; Hastings, 24,064; North Platte, 23,878; Norfolk, 23,516; Columbus, 20,971 [2000].

2004 election: Bush 512,814 (66%) Kerry 254,328 (33%)

Nevada (Sagebrush State, Battle Born State, Silver State).

5 electoral votes

State motto: All for our country.

Population: 2,241,154 [2003 est.].

Racial distribution: 75.2% white, 6.8 black, 1. 3% Native Americans, 4. 5% Asian, 19. 7% Hispanic [2000].

Chief industries: gaming, tourism, mining, manufacturing, government (aerospace products), retailing, warehousing, trucking.

10 largest cities: Las Vegas, 478,434; Reno, 180,480; Henderson, 175,381; North Las Vegas, 115,488; Sparks, 66,346; Carson City, 52,457; Elko, 16,708; Boulder City, 14,966; Mesquite, 9,389; Fallon, 7,536 [2000].

2004 election: Bush 418,690 (51%) Kerry 397,190 (48%)

New Hampshire (Granite State).

4 electoral votes

State motto: Live free or die.

Population: 1,287,687 [2003 est.].

Racial distribution: 96.0% white, 0.7% black, 0.2% Native American, 1. 3% Asian, 1. 7% Hispanic [2000].

Chief industries: tourism, manufacturing, agriculture, trade, mining.

10 largest cities: Manchester, 107,006; Nashua, 86,605; Concord, 40,687; Derry, 34,021; Rochester, 28,461; Salem, 28,112; Dover, 26,884; Merrimack, 25,119; Londonderry, 23,236; Hudson, 22,928 [2000].

2004 election: Kerry 340,511 (50%) Bush 331,237 (49%)

New Jersey (Garden State).

15 electoral votes

State motto: Liberty and prosperity.

Population: 8,638,396 [2003 est.].

Racial distribution: 72. 6% white, 13. 6% black, 0.2% Native American, 5. 7% Asian, 13. 3% Hispanic [2000].

Chief industries: pharmaceuticals/drugs, telecommunications, biotechnology, printing & publishing.

10 largest cities: Newark, 273,546; Jersey City, 240,055; Paterson, 149,222; Elizabeth, 120,568; Edison, 97,687; Woodbridge, 97,203; Dover, 89,706; Hamilton, 87,109; Trenton, 85,403; Camden, 79,904 [2000].

2004 election: Kerry 1,911,430 (53%) Bush 1,670,003 (46%)

New Mexico (Land of Enchantment).

5 electoral votes

State motto: Crescit Eundo (It grows as it goes).

Population: 1,874,614 [2003 est.].

Racial distribution: 66.8% white, 1. 9% black, 9. 5% Native American, 1.1% Asian, 42.1% Hispanic [2000].

Chief industries: government, services, trade.

10 largest cities: Albuquerque, 448,607; Las Cruces, 74,267; Santa Fe, 62,203; Rio Rancho, 51,765; Roswell, 45,293; Farmington, 37,844; Alamogordo, 35,582; Clovis, 32,667; Hobbs, 28,657; Carlsbad, 25,625 [2000].

2004 election: Bush 376,930 (50%) Kerry 370,942 (49%)

New York (Empire State).

31 electoral votes

State motto: Excelsior (Ever upward).

Population: 19,190,115 [2003 est.].

Racial distribution: 67. 9% white, 15. 9% black, 0.4% Native American, 5. 5% Asian, 15.1% Hispanic [2000].

Chief industries: manufacturing, finance, communications, tourism, transportation, services.

10 largest cities: New York, 8,008,278; Buffalo, 292,648; Rochester, 219,773; Yonkers, 196,086; Syracuse, 147,306; Albany, 95,658; New Rochelle, 72,182; Mount Vernon, 68, 381; Schenectady, 61,821; Utica, 60,651 [2000].

2004 election: Kerry 4,314,289 (59%) Bush 2,962,567 (40%)

North Carolina (Tar Heel State, Old North State).

15 electoral votes

State motto: Esse Quam Videri (to be rather than to seem).

Population: 8,407,248 [2003 est.].

Racial distribution: 72.10% white, 21. 6% black, 1.2% Native American, 1. 4% Asian, 4. 7% Hispanic (2000).

Chief industries: manufacturing, agriculture, tourism.

10 largest cities: Charlotte, 540,828; Raleigh, 276,093; Greensboro, 223,891; Durham, 187,035; Winston-Salem, 185,776; Fayetteville, 121,015; Cary, 94,536; High point, 85,839; Wilmington, 75,838 [2000].

2004 election: Bush 1,961,166 (56%) Kerry 1,525,849 (44%)

North Dakota (Peace Garden State).

3 electoral votes

Population: 633,837 [2003 est.].

Racial distribution: 92. 4% white, 0.6% black, 4. 9% Native American, 0.6% Asian, 1.2% Hispanic [2000].

Chief industries: agriculture, mining, tourism, manufacturing, telecommunications, energy, food processing.

10 largest cities: Fargo, 90,599; Bismarck, 55,532; Grand Forks, 49,321; Minot, 36,567; Mandan, 16,718; Dickinson, 16,010; Jamestown, 15,527; West Fargo, 14,940; Williston, 12,512; Wahpeton, 8,586 [2000].

2004 election: Bush 196,651 (63%) Kerry 111,052 (36%)

Ohio (Buckeye State).

20 electoral votes

State motto: With God, all things are possible.

Population: 11,435,798 [2003 est.].

Racial distribution: 85.0% white, 11. 5% black, 0.2% Native American, 1.2% Asian, 1. 9% Hispanic [2000].

Chief industries: manufacturing, trade, services.

10 largest cities: Columbus, 711,470; Cleveland, 478,403; Cincinnati, 331,285; Toledo, 313,619; Akron, 217,074; Dayton, 166,179; Parma, 85,655; Youngstown, 82,026; Canton, 80,806; Lorain, 68,652 [2000].

2004 election: Bush 2,859,764 (51%) Kerry 2,741,165 (49%)

Oklahoma (Sooner State).

7 electoral votes

State motto: Labor Omnia Vincit (Labor conquers all things).

Population: 3,511,532 (2003 est.).

Racial distribution: 76.2% white, 7. 6% black, 7. 9% Native American, 1. 4% Asian, 5.2% Hispanic (2000).

Chief industries: manufacturing, mineral and energy exploration and production, agriculture, services.

10 largest cities: Oklahoma City, 506,132; Tulsa, 393,049; Norma, 95694; Lawton, 92,757; Broken Arrow, 74,859; Edmond, 68,315; Midwest City, 54,088; Enid, 47,045; Moore, 41,138; Stillwater, 39,065 [2000].

2004 election: Bush 959,792 (66%) Kerry 503,966 (34%)

Oregon (Beaver State).

7 electoral votes

State motto: She flies with her own wings.

Population: 3,559,596 [2003 est.].

Racial distribution: 86. 6% white, 1. 6% black, 1. 3% Native American, 3.0% Asian, 8. 0% Hispanic [2000].

Chief industries: manufacturing, services, trade, finance, insurance, real estate, government, construction.

10 largest cities: Portland, 529,121; Eugene, 137,893; Salem, 136,924; Gresham, 90,205; Beaverton, 76,129; Hillsboro, 70,186; Medford, 63,154; Springfield, 52,864; Bend, 52,029; Corvallis, 49,322 [2000].

2004 election: Kerry 943,163 (52%) Bush 866,831 (48%)

Pennsylvania (Keystone State).

21 electoral votes

State motto: Virtue, liberty, and independence.

Population; 12,365,455 [2003 est.].

Racial distribution: 85. 4% white, 10.0% black, 0.1% Native American, 1.8% Asian, 3.2% Hispanic [2000].

Chief industries: agribusiness, advanced manufacturing, health care, travel and tourism, depository institutions, biotechnology, printing and publishing, research and consulting, trucking and warehousing, transportation, by air, legal services, engineering and management.

10 largest cities: Philadelphia, 1,517,550; Pittsburgh, 334,563; Allentown, 106,632; Erie, 103,717; Upper Darby, 81,821; Reading, 81,207; Scranton,76,415; Bethlehem, 71,329; Lower Merion, 59,850; Bensalem, 58,434 [2000].

2004 election: Kerry 2,938,095 (51%) Bush 2,793,847 (49%)

Rhode Island (Little Rhody, Ocean State).

4 electoral votes

State motto: Hope.

Population: 1,076,164 [2003 est.].

Racial distribution: 85.0% white, 4. 5% black, 0.5% Native American, 2. 3% Asian, 8. 7% Hispanic [2000].

Chief industries: services, manufacturing.

10 largest cities: Providence, 173,618; Warwick, 85,808; Cranston, 79,269; Pawtucket, 72,958; East Providence, 48,688; Woonsocket, 43,224; Coventry, 33,668; North Providence, 32,411; Cumberland, 31,840; West Warwick,29,581 [2000].

2004 election: Kerry 259,760 (60%) Bush 169,046 (39%)

South Carolina (Palmetto State).

8 electoral votes

State motto: Dum Spiro Spero (While I breathe, I hope).

Population: 4,147,152 [2003 est.].

Racial distribution: 67.2% white, 29. 5% black, 0.3% Native American, 0.9% Asian, 2. 4% Hispanic [2000].

Chief industries: tourism, agriculture, manufacturing.

10 largest cities: Columbia, 116,278; Charleston, 96,650; North Charleston, 79,641; Greenville, 56,002; Rock Hill, 49,765; Mount Pleasant, 47,609; Spartan-burg, 39,673; Sumter, 39,643

2004 election: Bush 937,974 (58%) Kerry 661,699 (41%)

South Dakota (Coyote State, Mount Rushmore State).

3 electoral votes

State motto: Under God, the people rule.

Population: 764,309 [2003 est.].

Racial distribution: 88. 7% white, 0.6% black, 8. 3% Native American, 0.6% Asian, 1.4% Hispanic [2000].

Chief industries: agriculture, services, manufacturing.

10 largest cities: Sioux Falls, 123,975; Rapid City, 59,607; Aberdeen, 24,658; Waretown, 20,237; Brookings, 18,504; Mitchell, 14,558; Pierre, 13,876; Yankton, 13,528; Huron 11,893; Vermillion, 9,765 [2000].

2004 election: Bush 232,584 (60%) Kerry 149,244 (39%)

Tennessee (Volunteer State).

11 electoral votes

State motto: Agriculture and commerce.

Population: 5,841,748 [2003 est.].

Racial distribution: 80.2% white, 16. 4% black, 0.3% Native American, 1.0% Asian, 2.2% Hispanic [2000].

Chief industries: manufacturing, trade, services, tourism, finance, insurance, real estate.

10 largest cities: Memphis, 650,100; Nashville-Davidson, 569,891; Knoxville, 173,890; Chattanooga, 155,554; Clarksville, 103,455; Murfreesboro, 68,816; Jackson,59,643; Johnson City, 55,469; Kingsport, 44,905; Franklin, 41,842 [2000].

2004 election: Bush 1, 384,375 (57%) Kerry 1,036,477 (43%)

Texas (Lone Star State).

34 electoral votes

State motto: Friendship.

Population: 22,118,509 [2003 est.].

Racial distribution: 71.0% white, 11. 5% black, 0.6% Native American, 2. 7% Asian, 32. 0% Hispanic [2000].

Chief industries: manufacturing, trade, oil and gas extraction, services.

10 largest cities: Houston, 1,953,631; Dallas, 1,188,580; san Antonio, 1,144,646; Austin, 656,562; El Paso, 563,662; Fort Worth, 534,694; Arlington, 332,969; Corpus Christi, 277,454; Plano, 222,030; Garland, 215,768 [2000].

2004 election: Bush 4,526,917 (61%) Kerry 2,832,704 (38%)

Utah (Beehive State).

5 electoral votes

State motto: Industry.

Population: 2,351,467 [2003 est.].

Racial distribution: 89.2% white, 0.8% black, 1. 3% Native American, 1. 7% Asian, 9. 0% Hispanic [2000].

Chief industries: services, trade, manufacturing, government, transportation, utilities.

10 largest cities: Salt Lake City, 181,743; West Valley City, 108,896; Provo, 105, 166; Sandy, 88,418; Orem, 84,324; Ogden, 77,226; West Jordan, 68,336; Layton, 58,474; Taylorsville, 57,439; St. George, 49,663 [2000].

2004 election: Bush 663,742 (72%) Kerry 241,199 (26%)

Vermont (Green Mountain State).

3 electoral votes

State motto: Freedom and unity.

Population: 619,107 [2003 est.].

Racial distribution: 96.8% white, 0.5% black, 0.4% Native American, 0.9% Asian, 0.9% Hispanic [2000].

Chief industries: manufacturing, tourism, agriculture, trade, finance, insurance, real estate, government.

10 largest cities: Burlington, 38,889; Essex, 18,626; Rutland, 17,292; Colchester, 16,986; South Burlington, 15,814; Bennington, 15,737; Brattleboro, 12,005; Hartford, 10,367; Milton, 9,479; Barre, 9,291 [2000].

2004 election: Kerry 184,0676 (59%) Bush 121,189 (39%)

Virginia (Old Dominion).

13 electoral votes

State motto: Sic Semper Tyrannis (Thus always to tyrants).

Population: 7,386,330 [2003 est.].

Racial distribution: 72. 3% white, 19. 6% black, 0.3% Native American, 3. 7% Asian, 4. 7% Hispanic [2000].

Chief industries: services, trade, government, manufacturing, tourism, agriculture.

10 largest cities: Virginia Beach, 425,257; Norfolk, 234,403; Chesapeake, 199,184; Richmond, 197,790; Newport News, 180,150; Hampton, 146,437; Alexandria, 128,283; Portsmouth, 100,565; Roanoke, 94,911; Lynchburg, 65,269 [2000].

2004 election: Bush 1,716,959 (54%) Kerry 1,455,742 (46%)

Washington (Evergreen State).

11 electoral votes

State motto: Alki (By and by).

Population: 6,131,445 [2003 est.].

Racial distribution: 81.8% white, 3.2% black, 1. 6% Native American, 5. 5% Asian, 7. 5% Hispanic [2000].

Chief industries: advanced technology, aerospace, biotechnology, international trade, forestry, tourism, recycling, agriculture and food processing.

10 largest cities: Seattle, 563,374; Spokane, 195,629; Tacoma, 193,556; Vancouver, 143,560; Bellevue, 109,569; Everett, 91,488; Federal Way, 83,259; Kent, 79,524; Yakima, 71,845; Bellingham, 67,171 [2000].

2004 election: Kerry 1,510,201 (53%) Bush 1,304,894 (46%)

West Virginia. (Mountain State).

5 electoral votes

State motto: Montani Semper Liberi (Mountaineers are always free).

Population: 5,472,299 [2003 est.].

Racial distribution: 95.0% white, 3.2% black, 0.2% Native American, 0.5% Asian, 0.7% Hispanic [2000].

Chief industries: manufacturing, services, mining, tourism.

10 largest cities: Charleston, 53,421; Huntington, 51,475; Parkersburg, 33,099; Wheeling, 31,419; Morgantown, 26,809; Weirton, 20,411; Fairmont, 19,097; Beckley, 17,254; Clarksburg, 16,743; Martinsburg, 14,972 [2000].

2004 election: Bush 423,778 (56%) Kerry 326,541 (43%)

Wisconsin (Badger State).

10 electoral votes

State motto: Forward.

Population: 5,472,299 [2003 est.].

Racial distribution: 88. 9% white, 5. 7% black, 0.9% Native American, 1.,7% Asian, 3. 6% Hispanic [2000].

Chief industries: services, manufacturing, trade, government, agriculture, tourism.

10 largest cities: Milwaukee, 596,974; Madison, 208,054; Green Bay, 102,313; Kenosha, 90,352; Racine, 81,855; Appleton, 70,087; Waukesha, 64,825; Oshkosh, 62,916; Eau Claire, 61,704; West Allis, 61,254 [2000].

2004 election: Kerry 1, 489,504 (50%) Bush 1,478,120 (49%)

Wyoming (Equality State, Cowboy State).

3 electoral votes

State motto: Equal rights.

Population: 501,242 [2003 est.].

Racial distribution: 92.1 white, 0.8% black, 2. 3% Native American, 0.6% Asian, 6. 4% Hispanic [2000].

Chief industries: mineral extraction, oil, natural gas, tourism and recreation, agriculture.

10 largest cities: Cheyenne, 53,011; Casper, 49,644; Laramie, 27,204; Gillette, 19,646;Rock Springs, 18,708; Sheridan, 15,804; Green River, 11,808; Evanston, 11,507; Riverton, 9,310; Cody, 8,883 [2000].

2004 election: Bush 167,629 (69%) Kerry 70,776 (29%)

District of Columbia

3 electoral votes

District motto: Justitia Omnibus (Justice for all).

Population: 563,384 (2003 est)

Racial distribution: 30.8% white, 60.0% black, 0.3% Native Americans, 2. 7% Asian, 7. 9% Hispanic.

Chief industries: government, service, tourism.

2004 election: Kerry 202,970 (90%) Bush 21,256 (9%)

Chapter 19. Campaign Planning

The most important event in the election process is the National Convention, not only because the eventual finalist candidate is actually nominated but because after that the campaign's audience increases (more than twice as many people vote in general elections as participate in the nomination process). You have to decide how to win the support of these new voters as well as to appeal to people who identify with the other party and partisans who backed losing candidates for the nomination.

The Press and Your Press Officer

The press officer (contacts media, takes care of newspapers, radio and TV ads) — the person who markets you — is the boss of advance team that takes care in each state of a total exclusively positive press coverage. To my mind, the best choice for this position is a former journalist with good wide connections to media. He prepares press releases and press kits and schedules interviews and press conferences with the positive vision and attitude reporters (press or media kits contain your photos, a brief biography, campaign position papers, printed brochures and names of contacts for additional information).

The technique in good paid advertising is to go with those ideas, arguments, thoughts, themes and believes in which people are already inclined to believe or ready to accept. There's no difference between commercial and political advertising — you just substitute a car or shampoo for a human being.

Modern presidential campaigns center on "media events" — staged public appearances, during which reporters can talk with you and take pictures (if you have too much money, you can organize media wave — a very large amount of political advertising on TV). Then, the "walking tours" must be scheduled when you, followed by reporters, photographers and TV crews visit potential supporters.

Simultaneously your aide sets up press conferences, selects interviews, and background briefings. You have to talk to press 24/7 and everywhere on the campaign bus, train or plain, hotel, etc. A good thing is — you get free media coverage and people trust it more than paid coverage, like TV and radio commercials. You are most likely to win if you obey these rules:

- If you can manipulate the media — you manipulate the nation (sorry, it's harder to manipulate free coverage).
- The media makes the election, not the voters.
- A Presidential campaign does not allow for privacy.
- Newspapers put emphasis on issues; TV on image, style and ability to communicate.
- Never lie to reporters; they will make sure it backfires on you sooner or later.
- If an influential newspaper, radio or TV station endorses you, you have their supporters, readers, listeners and viewers.
- People remember much better what they see, not what they read; if they don't see you on TV, you don't exist.
- TV talks to 98% of Americans and takes your message — and other messages about, or against, you — immediately, straight to the nation.
- TV, not your political party, is the #1 channel of communication between you and the public.
- Your political party is nothing but a service center and a money machine. Parties divide the nation while your message has to be one of unity.
- Take it seriously if *The New York Times* takes your opponent seriously.
- It's important to know what your opponent is saying to reporters privately, "not for attribution."
- If you live in a heavily populated state like New York, California or Texas, you start the presidential election campaign with much better coverage.
- Never fight the media, as the Nixon administration did — they kept a list of Nixon's critics (famous reporters), so they could be targeted for harassment, accused of income tax evasion, etc. What happened then? The reporters felt like heroes, Nobel Prize winners. Better target them for buttering up, and feed them lots of stories with a spin in your favor instead.

POLLS AND YOUR POLLSTER

A pollster works through newspapers, Internet, telephone surveys, person-to-person surveys, mailed questionnaire to selected voters. He provides voters behavior research and analyze past election data. He has to tell you how well-known you are, how well you perform, what are the voters' preferences.

You should poll voters in each state in proportion to that state's share of the national vote. (You must have at least one polling company on payroll.)

Polling is of extreme importance in presidential campaign because it's the tool to correct your strategy, determine "positive" local areas and supportive voters and work with them, it tests the nation's attitude to your personality and your issues and that means you can calibrate your message and calculate your success. The most important thing about polls is that they play indicator and identify support or hostility. And the golden rule here is: you have to ask the right question if you want to get a useful answer.

At the same time polling is one of the most expensive elements of a modern campaign because now you have to receive information on too many groups and issues, including groups with specific economic, ethnic, religious, geographic, educational, occupational and residential characteristics and how those characteristics affect attitudes about a wide range of policy issues.

Polls also help you:

- to decide whether to run or not
- improve your recognition and image
- target opposition's weakness
- formulate media ads

Your pollster has to pinpoint blocks of voters (swing districts) who are undecided and who might be persuaded to vote for you.

Experience shows that 40% of public attention go to social problems, 40% — to economy and 20% — to international matters, but if the United States is at war, the situation is different and national security turns into a top priority for everyone. And watch out for campaign spies — keep polls analysis and media plan secret.

Practical Polls to Use until Election Day

"Benchmark" — surveys of the whole nation which provide basic information about your chances and the nation's political preferences (it's your "presidential decision maker").

"Follow-up" — surveys are used to gather more data about particular concerns raised in initial benchmark surveys. They are conducted state by state and are used in planning campaign strategy.

"Panel" — surveys are used to refine strategy further by re-interviewing previous respondents to determine opinion shifts on specific issues within various demographic categories. They are supplemented by continuous "tracking polls" that measure fluctuations in general voter support for the candidate across time.

"Special group" — used to poll the debate results. Selected groups of voters watch candidate debates and register their "positive " or "negative" feelings toward the candidate's specific statements or actions. After that analysts tabulate and analyze the reactions of the whole groups.

OTHER CRITICAL PERSONNEL

"Image makers" — political consultants who sell your public image as a clear, simple, portrait-like characterization, acceptable to all groups.

"Hit men" — campaign consultants who are experts on negative advertising, designed to "kill" your opponents.

"Field staff" (in target cities mostly). The most important person at any local office is the coordinator — he establishes organization and contacts influential people and political activists. Coordinators must be appointed to each special interests group (women, minorities, unions, college students, public interest activists, the professionals)

"Local volunteers" are needed to work in the offices and the streets. Your family has to take an active part in your campaign, too. Your wife and kids are your visual image makers

"Running Mate." Your running mate belongs to your staff too — it has to be your best choice. This person should be compatible with you in age, intellect, political views, and be of approximately the same height. He is selected to balance the national ticket in terms of geography, religion, ideology, government experience and political style. You have to appeal to the broad electorate, while your running mate appeals to specific groups. He serves to reinforce — or break down — the electorate's attitudes toward you. If you have little domestic or foreign policy, or Washington experience, a running mate with that experience can reassure voters. And he has to give voters the impression your policy will be continued unchanged in case you die during your presidency or in case he is elected the US President himself after your two terms in the Office.

CAMPAIGN TIPS

Never behave as if you think you are God's gift to mankind.

Be presidential — look calm, sincere, knowledgeable, fatherly and open.

Be electable — prove to the nation that you are the best choice.

No one has ever been elected the US President without winning the New Hampshire primary.

Primaries direct financial backers to a promising candidate.

Voters judge you by your friends — appear with popular politicians, big business, labor and interest groups leaders, and show business celebrities.

Choosing a Strategy

Any strategy is good if it helps you to win support of a majority of people chosen by the state parties to be delegates to the national convention.

Your choice of a strategy depends on your current position.

(A) If you are an incumbent, you have to stress that the American people's life improved a lot during your first term. You can count on successful start because you are guaranteed to be known actually to every American, and the Oval Office lends you credibility and respect. It's of vital importance to have economic accomplishments — in such a case well-timed announcements of government statistics on the economy or of plans for domestic initiatives can also help you. Listen, I didn't tell you this, but you have to manipulate (stimulate) the economy during the election year with tax cuts that can help reduce unemployment, and with social programs financing.

Of course, you'll have to pay for it, but that will happen after you are re-elected. And a good thing is — an improved economy erases voters' bad memories of past years. Then, try to avoid too aggressive campaigning — it's a sign of weakness. Make official appearances in carefully controlled settings. Influence media coverage with official presidential actions and use "pork barrel" politics to appeal to specific constituents.

You can also benefit from the nation's reluctance to reject a tested national leader for an unknown newcomer. And if you start important foreign policy initiatives, it will guarantee you continued media coverage.

If you have poor chances to be re-elected, you can play the "national security" card:
- find a US "enemy"
- start a media psychosis (see propaganda tricks and brainwashing)
- concentrate power (special services) to establish a total legal control on the nation
- provoke an international conflict, restricted or full-scale war
- send a message: "If you are against the President, you are against America!"

(B) If you are a challenger, you have to convince the public they don't live better than they did 4 years ago, or, if the economy is OK, point out mistakes that were made in the foreign policy. Or make up some social issue that will get passions inflamed and hijack the headlines.

The job is tough if you challenge a President who is popular — first, you have to break down his positive image; second, you have to portray yourself as a much better replacement. You have no choice but to start with the "outsider" strategy

— you present a "fresh face" to voters weary of the current political situation (in such a case you have to attack administration in a very aggressive manner). Plus, you must give quick response to your opponent's charges (get advance copies of his speeches through friends in the media).

Then, show yourself as a smart and diplomatic person using a special "triangular" strategy, when you, like majority of the voters, place yourself between liberal and conservative positions. Evaluate situation — you may need "early knockout," when front-runners hope to use their early strength in polls, fundraising and endorsements into decisive primary victories at the beginning of the primary season. The hope is that the candidate will build such an impressive early lead that the competition quickly drops out. And a "shift" is the most popular thing with challengers — if the President is good in national security, they point out to the problems in economy, if he's good on the economy, they point out to the problems in national security — very simple. (Watch his mistakes anyway — you can benefit from them. Bill Clinton would never have run for President in 1992 if someone from the Bush White House hadn't called him in 1990 and asked him not to run. That phone call was one of the dummest political moves of the 20th century, because it convinced Clinton that they thought he had a good chance if he did run for Office.)

Be simple, identify with "ordinary people" and no matter what tell the voters your parents or your grandparents "were like them — regular people, not millionaires." You can even say "Feb-uary" and "nuc-ular," and see if they forget you were educated at Yale.

Finally, you must know some very popular and efficient dirty tricks, like "negative campaigning" or "black PR." To make a long story short: no matter what your opponent says or what decent people think about negative campaigning, "black PR" works! Use it to turn a rumor or a fact into a serious political scandal; respond to and neutralize the opponent's attacks (using "black PR") fast, before they are broadcasted or published.

It works best through intermediates (persons and organizations not connected directly to your campaign). You must have a very detailed file on your opponent (negative research) and then start spreading negative and all kinds of compromising data from his personal and political life. If he is or was elected official (Senator, Governor, Mayor), you can point out his mistakes and actions which were not popular. People must know in detail (get your staff to read a few books) the negative sides of his life, program and terrible consequences of his election. Remember also that a rumor repeated twice turns into a fact, especially if you start a "whispering campaign" in Congress.

A "negative ID" trick is my favorite: you identify your opponent with a totally unacceptable (for the voters) viewpoint, like: "There are those who want to stop the war on international terror and you know who they are!"

DEBATES

Debates are very important because they offer the only all-national event at which candidates can be judged. You and your opponent will be under huge stress as you both must operate simultaneously at the focus of attention of each other and of all elements of electorate. Debates are, actually, head-to-head confrontations with two main aspects: the pre-debate negotiations over whether there will be a debate, and the post-debate analysis of who did how well. The debates offer nothing new for the public and the basic strategy is to hope your opponent will make a mistake. (President Ford made one in 1976, saying that: "There is no Soviet domination of Eastern Europe." People just didn't want to hear it. Richard Nixon was very wrong in 1960 trying to debate on substance, while his opponent, John F. Kennedy, concentrated on style and on presenting the correct presidential image.)

While preparing for to win the debates you must:

- have a detailed file on your opponent and study all his speeches and statements; ask yourself: "What does he have that I don't have?"
- train to answer all possible questions
- be ready to demonstrate deep knowledge of issues and your presidential bearing to a nationwide audience
- repeat your message but keep in mind that image is more important than ideas while you debate — people want to see your good looks, good clothes and nice smile.

And here are the debating "don'ts":

- Don't attack first — that's a sign of weakness.
- Don't be over-polite — a little showmanship appeals to voters.
- Don't be too aggressive — it will ruin your image as a future President.
- Don't answer the questions too fast — that implies you are not thinking.

Follow the rules and you win:

- Don't rush, no negative emotions, no sudden gestures (extra gestures mean that you are not sure what you are saying is correct).
- Avoid anxiety reactions — speech errors, moistening of lips, perspiring, shifting eye movements, body jerks. Gesturing with fingers apart communicates weakness, while gesturing with fingers tightly together communicates power.
- Look at your opponent with intense concentration — it gives the attitude of command and comfort in the situation.
- Don't touch anything while you talk.
- Don't disappoint people — speak in a clear and simple way.

- You restrict your influence if you sit.
- Answer a question you want to answer, no matter what question was asked.
- If you give better answers, you are the better candidate.

Immediately after the debates your press officer has to give the media his biased impression and explain why you won the debates. Your pollster has to watch the polls results.

Here's a short excerpt of the first John F. Kennedy–Richard Nixon debate on September 26, 1960. There were five debates altogether, but Kennedy actually won the presidency with this one. One could say it is more a speech than a part of a debate. It worked. Note Kennedy's perfect tactic of delivering a strong (strategic) messages that turn his opening statement into a presidential speech:

> Senator Kennedy: Mr. Smith [the moderator], Mr. Nixon. In the election of 1860, Abraham Lincoln said the question was whether this nation could exist half-slave and half-free. In the election of 1960, and with the world around us, the question is whether the world will exist half-slave and half-free, whether it will move in the direction of freedom, in the direction of the road that we are taking, or whether it will move in the direction of slavery. I think it will depend in great measure upon what we do here in the United states, on the kind of society that we build, on the kind of strength that we maintain... The kind of country we have here, the kind of society we have, the kind of strength we build in the United States will be the defense of freedom. If we do well here, if we meet our obligations, if we're moving ahead, then I think freedom will be secure around the world. If we fail, freedom fails. Therefore, I think the question before the American people is: are we doing as much as we can do? Are we as strong as we should be? Are we as strong as we must be if we're going to maintain our independence, and if we're going to maintain and hold out the hand of friendship to those who look to us for assistance, to those who look to us for survival? I should make it very clear that I do not think we're doing enough, that I am not satisfied as an American with the progress that we're making. This is a great country, but I think it could be a greater country; and this is a powerful country, but I think it could be a more powerful country. I'm not satisfied to have fifty per cent of our steel-mill capacity unused. I'm not satisfied when the United States had last year the lowest rate of economic growth of any major industrialized society in the world. Because economic growth means strength and vitality; it means we're able to sustain our defenses; it means we're able to meet our commitments abroad...
>
> I saw cases in West Virginia, here in the United States, where children took home part of their school lunch in order to feed their families; I don't think we're meeting our obligations toward those Americans. I'm not satisfied when the Soviet Union is turning out twice as many scientists and engineers as we are... I'm not satisfied when I see men like Jimmy Hoffa — in charge of the largest union in the United States — still free... I'm not satisfied until every American enjoys his full constitutional rights. If a Negro baby is born — and this is true also of Puerto Ricans and Mexicans in some of our cities — he has about one-half as much chance to get through high school as a white baby. He has about a third as much chance to get through college as a white student. He has about a third as much chance to

be a professional man, about half as much chance to own a house. He has about — four times as much chance that he'll be out of work in his life as the white baby. I think we can do better...

I know that there are those who say that we want to turn everything over to the government. I don't at all... I don't believe in big government, but I believe in effective government. And I think that's the only way that the United States is going to maintain its freedom... The reason Franklin Roosevelt was a good neighbor in Latin America was because he was a good neighbor in the United States... I want people in Latin America and Africa and Asia to start to look to America; to see how we're doing things; to wonder what the president of the United States is doing; and not to look at Khrushchev or look at Chinese Communists. That is the obligation upon our generation...

...I come out of the Democratic party, which in this century has produced Woodrow Wilson and Franklin Roosevelt and Harry Truman... Mr. Nixon comes out of the Republican Party. He was nominated by it. And it is a fact that through most of these last twenty-five years the Republican leadership has opposed federal aid for education, medical care for the aged, development of the Tennessee Valley, development of natural resources. I think Mr. Nixon is an effective leader of his party. I hope he would grant me the same. The question before us is: which point of view and which party do we want to lead the United States?

Mr. Smith: Mr. Nixon, would you like to comment on that statement?

Mr. Nixon: I have no comment.

Speaking in Public

First things first — you have to know your own nation well. Here is a popular classification of American voters:

1. Entrepreneurs. Traditional Republicans driven by free enterprise economic concerns.

2. Moralists. Less affluent populist Republicans driven by moral issues, such as abortion.

3. New Dealers. Older traditional Democrats who are pro-government but socially conservative.

4. Sixties Democrats. Mainstream Democrats highly tolerant of varying lifestyles with strong beliefs in social justice.

5. Partisan poor. Low-income, mainly black, who believe in the Democratic Party as a vehicle for social change.

6. Passive poor. The older God-and-Country Democrats who have a strong faith in America and an uncritical attitude toward its institutions but favor social spending.

7. By-standers. Those who are mainly young, white and poorly educated and who show almost no interest in politics.

8. Upbeats. Young, optimistic moderates who lean toward the Republicans.

9. Disaffected. Middle-aged, pessimistic working class who, even though they have Democratic roots, lean toward the Republicans.

10. Seculars. Affluent and highly educated but lacking religious convictions; committed to personal freedom and peace.

11. Followers. Poor, young, uninformed blue-collar workers with little religious commitment and limited interest in politics.

PROMISES

Your aides have to determine the "theme of the day" and brief you about the day's events and issues. To get elected you must promise economic growth with low inflation and balanced budget no matter how grave the economic situation is — Americans, like Russians, still believe in wonders.

Don't be too specific on issues and tell people they elect their way, not a candidate. Cite the Bible. Don't look too intellectual. State repeatedly that you're not going to divide the nation into supporters and enemies, Democrats and Republicans, "my voters and other voters" — be a leader to all. (But first, to win the nomination you must appeal to the more liberal sections of your party if you are Democrat, and to more conservative sections if you belong to Republicans). Think well on this tactic.

Don't talk much; transform your thoughts into examples and slogans. Never say you want power, even if you want to save the nation in crisis. Never talk down on big business. Promise federal financing, especially in economic downturns. Remember, voters are extremely sensitive to tax-cut proposals and which social segment would benefit from them. The middle class brings you victory, so promise tax cuts for these people, with tax increases for the wealthy and high unemployment rates. Even if the economy is OK, point out the signs of coming crisis and promise to change the situation fast. Keep talking about problems, though it's hard to win if the incumbent President runs for re-election with balanced budget and economic growth. You can be liberal on domestic issues, but you have to be conservative on national security (defense and foreign affairs).

WHAT TO TALK ABOUT WHERE

> Iowa, New Hampshire — farm problems, energy costs, trade issues
> Northern "rustbelt" states — industrial concerns
> Southern states — defense and social issues
> New York State — unemployment

Eat the food typical of the region where you campaign, and use these tactics:

- "Join the crowd" — this reinforces people's natural desire to be on the winning side and it is used to convince the audience that your program is an expression of the nation's desire for change, and it is in their best interest to join;
- "Provoke disapproval" — persuade a target audience to disapprove your opponent's message by suggesting that the message is popular with groups hated, feared or held in contempt by the target audience;
- "Inevitable victory" — invite those who have not yet joined you to "join the majority";
- "Neuro-linguistic programming" — you will be elected if you can do this better than your opponent and program the whole nation for a positive reaction.

People always try to avoid anything and anybody unpleasant; and people are always looking for pleasant things and other pleasant people, somebody they want to meet again and again or at least see on TV. Everybody wants to be a winner; and to be a winner brings pleasure and self respect. Just convey this sense to the nation:

"Vote for me and you win!" or

"Vote for me or you lose!"

"The choice is yours!"

Now, you have to be the first to install this program in the voters' minds and the other candidate has no chance.

THE 2004 PRESIDENTIAL ELECTION

WHO VOTED FOR WHOM

	Bush (Republican)	Kerry (Democrat)
Popular vote	51%	48%
Electoral College	274	252
White males	61%	38%
African Americans	11%	89%
Hispanics	42%	55%
Married women	54%	45%
Veterans	57%	42%
First-time voters	45%	54%
Not married	40%	59%
Those for whom terrorism was the most important issue	86%	14%
Those for whom moral values was the most important issue	79%	18%

PART 5. LEARNING FROM THE PAST

Chapter 20. Learning from Past Presidents

1. George Washington (1789-1797)

Quotes

"There is scarcely any part of my conduct which may not be hereafter drawn into precedent."

"To be prepared for war is one of the most effectual means of preserving peace."

Actions
- was inevitable choice of the nation and was unanimously elected the President having the nonpartisan reputation needed to transcend sectional and ideological conflicts, so that the United States would have time to establish effective government institutions and gain the trust of the people
- established national bank
- favored a federal government
- believed that the young nation had to avoid alliance entanglements if it were to survive and remain united during its early years

Scandals
- according to the story spread by political opponents, the Secretary of Treasury, Alexander Hamilton, was his illegitimate son
- a rumor was spread that he had stolen over $4,000 from the federal government by deliberately overdrawing his salary.

2. JOHN ADAMS (1797-1801). FEDERALIST.

Quotes

"I'm old, old, very old, and I shall never be very well [not] while in this office, for the drudgery is too much for my years and strength."

"The happiness of society is the end of government."

"Whoever would found a state, and make proper laws for the government of it, must presume that all men are bad by nature."

Actions

- avoided full-scale war with France and finally concluded a treaty of peace and commerce
- pushed for judicial reforms and appointed more than 200 new judges, attorneys, clerks and marshals

Scandals

- was accused of having sent General Thomas Pinckney to England to obtain four mistresses — two for Adams and two for Pinckney. His reaction: "I do declare, if this be true, General Pinckney has kept them all for himself and cheated me out of my two.

3. THOMAS JEFFERSON (1801-1809). DEMOCRAT — REPUBLICAN.

Quotes

"One man with courage is a majority."

"Do you permit a slave to be a more of a gentleman than you are?" (Jefferson, when his grandson ignored a slave who bowed to him.)

Actions

- worked with Congress to cut the government budget and federal taxes
- was strong advocate of westward expansion
- struck a deal with French Emperor Napoleon to buy Louisiana (Louisiana Purchase) for $15 million and thus won re-election

Scandals

- had (or was accused of having) affairs with several married women as well as with one of his slaves, Sally Hemings

4. JAMES MADISON (1809-1817). DEMOCRAT-REPUBLICAN.

Quotes

"The truth is that all men having power ought to be mistrusted."

"The problem to be solved is, not what form of government is perfect, but which of the forms is least imperfect."

"Politics is the business of men." — First Lady Dolly Madison (Hillary Clinton's icon)

Actions

- demilitarized US–Canadian border
- insisted on increased funds to strengthen the army

5. JAMES MONROE (1817-1825). DEMOCRAT-REPUBLICAN.

Quotes

"The American continents... are hence forth not to be considered as subjects for future colonization by any European powers."

Actions

- obtained Florida from Spain
- settled boundary disputes with Britain over Canada
- supported the antislavery position
- authored the Monroe Doctrine, which opposed European intervention in the Western Hemisphere and became a cornerstone of our foreign policy — "Hands off Latin America"!

6. JOHN QUINCY ADAMS (1825-1829). DEMOCRAT-REPUBLICAN.

Quotes

"May our country be always successful, but whether successful or otherwise, always right."

"I pray to Heaven to bestow the Best of Blessing on THIS HOUSE and All that shall Hereafter Inherit it. May none but Honest and Wise Men ever rule under this Roof."

"My whole life has been a succession of disappointments. I can scarcely recollect a single instance of success that I ever undertook. I have no plausible motive to live."

"The world will retire from me before I shall retire from him."

Actions

- expanded executive powers (it was strongly opposed)
- tried (and failed) to stimulate the economy by the construction of a federally funded system of roads and roads and implementation of high protective tariffs
- opposed slavery
- admitted that he was not a popular President with the nation

7. ANDREW JACKSON (1827-1839). DEMOCRAT-REPUBLICAN.

Quotes

"I was born for the storm. Calm does not suit me. I try to live my life as if death might come at any moment."

"I know what I am fit for. I can command a body of men in a rough way; but I am not fit to be President."

Actions

- introduced "spoils system," rewarding party members with government posts
- deposited federal funds in so-called pet-banks, those directed by Democratic bankers, rather than in the Bank of the United States
- in 1832, killed the Congressional caucus for nominating Presidential candidates and substituted the National Convention
- ordered army and naval forces to Charleston when South Carolina refused to collect imports under his protective tariff
- became the first President to be the target of an assassination attempt

Scandals

- during presidential election was called an adulterer and a bigamist because his wife, Rachel, had not been legally divorced from her first husband when she married Jackson.

8. MARTIN VAN BUREN (1837-1841). DEMOCRAT.

Quotes

"As for the Presidency, the two happiest days of my life were those of my entrance upon the office and my surrender of it."

Actions

- instituted the independent treasury system

- promoted the moderate course of allowing slavery to continue where it existed but blocking its extension

9. WILLIAM HARRISON (1841). WHIG.

Caught pneumonia during the inauguration and died after only one month in office.

10. JOHN TYLER (1841-1845). INDEPENDENT.

Quotes

"Popularity, I have always thought, may be compared to a coquette — the more you woo her, the more apt is she to endure your embrace."

Actions

- used a special strategy and proposed in his State of the Union message to the effect that the Texas annexation from Mexico might be approved by a simple majority of both houses. The proposal was controversial because such a method of granting congressional consent would ignore the constitutional provision requiring a two-thirds vote by the Senate for approval of treaties. However, his strategy worked and an important legislative precedent was set. He signed the bill into law three days before leaving office.

11. JAMES POLK (18445-1849). DEMOCRAT.

Quotes

"No President who performs his duty faithfully can have any leisure. The Presidency is not a bed of roses."

"I am heartily rejoiced that my term is so near its close. I will soon cease to be a servant and will become a sovereign."

"I disposed of all the business on my table down to the minutes detail, and at the close of the day left a clean table for my successor."

Actions

- re-established the independent treasury system originated by van Buren
- started the Mexican War which ended with California and New Mexico annexation
- stimulated free trade and the US economy by greatly reducing the tariffs

12. ZACHARY TAYLOR (1849-1850). WHIG.

Quotes

"The idea that I should become President seems to me too visionary to re-quire a serious answer. It has never entered my head, nor is it likely to enter the head of any other person."

"God knows I have tried to do my honest duty. But I have made mistakes. My motives have been misconstrued and my feelings have been outraged."

Actions

- as a general, lacked political experience
- resumed the "spoils system"
- worked to admit California as a free state

13. MILLARD FILLMORE (1850-1853). WHIG.

Quotes

"God knows I detest slavery, but we must endure it."

"It is not strange... to mistake change for progress"

Actions

- signed the Fugitive Slave Law
- opposed the efforts to overthrow Spanish rule in Cuba

14. FRANKLIN PIERCE (1853-1857). DEMOCRAT.

Quotes

"The storm of frenzy and faction must inevitably dash itself in vain against the unshaken rock of the Constitution."

[After leaving office] "There's nothing left but to get drunk."

Actions

- believed that slavery was constitutional
- supported the controversial Kansas-Nebraska Act, which left the question of slavery in the new territories of Kansas and Nebraska to popular vote, and that turned Kansas into a war zone ("Bleeding Kansas")

15. JAMES BUCHANAN (1857-1861). FEDERALIST, LATER — DEMOCRAT.

Quotes

"There is nothing stable but Heaven and Constitution."

"To avoid entangling alliances has been a maxim of our policy since the days of Washington, and its wisdoms no one will attempt to dispute."

"If you are as happy, my dear sir, on entering this house as I am leaving it and returning home, you are the happiest man in the country" [to his successor Abraham Lincoln].

Actions

- favored popular sovereignty on slavery and choice by state constitutions (believed people in the Southern states had the constitutional right to own slaves)

Scandals

- awarded government contracts to his campaign sponsors only. Finally, the Congress formally censured him on June 13, 1860 and helped next President, Abraham Lincoln, win the elections.

16. ABRAHAM LINCOLN (1861-1865). REPUBLICAN.

Quotes

"If slavery is not wrong, nothing is wrong."

"There is time for all who need me."

"People who like this sort of thing will find this sort of thing they like."

Actions

- On September 22, 1862, five days after the Battle of Antietam, Lincoln announced that slaves in territory then in rebellion would be free January 1, 1863, the date of the Emancipation Proclamation.

17. ANDREW JACKSON (1865-1869). DEMOCRAT.

Quotes

"Honest conviction is my courage; the Constitution is my guide."

Actions

- proclaimed amnesty to all Confederates if they would ratify the 13th Amendment abolishing slavery.

18. ULYSSES S. GRANT (1869-1877). REPUBLICAN.

Quotes

"It was my fortune, or misfortune, to be called to the office of Chief Executive without any previous political training."

"I have never advocated war except as a means of peace."

Actions

- supported the ratification of the Fifteenth Amendment giving blacks the right to vote
- peacefully settled disputes with Great Britain

Scandals

"Black Friday" scandal. In 1869 financier Jay Gould tried to corner the New York City gold supply in order to make a super profit out of artificially high prices. Through Grant's brother-in-law he convinced the President not to sell the federal government gold if the prices go up. The prices went up and Grant finally understood he's been manipulated and on Friday, September 24, the federal government dumped $ 4 million worth of gold onto the market.

19. RUTHERFORD HAYES (1877-1881). REPUBLICAN.

Quotes

"Nothing brings out the lower traits of human nature like office seeking. "
"I am tired of this life of bondage, responsibility, and toil."

Actions

- proposed civil service reforms, alienating those favoring "spoils system" and advocated repeal of the Tenure of Office Act restricting Presidential power to dismiss officials.

20. JAMES GARFIELD (1881). REPUBLICAN.

Quotes

"Whoever controls the volume of money in any country is absolute master of all industry and commerce."

Actions

- tried to fight corruption

On July 2, 1881 was shot and died on September 19, 1881.

21. CHESTER ARTHUR (1881-1885). REPUBLICAN.

Quotes

"If it were not for reporters, I would tell you the truth."

"There doesn't seem to be anything else for ex-President to do but go into the country and raise big pumpkins."

Actions

- signed major civil service reform legislation

22 AND 24. GROVER CLEVELAND (1881-1889 AND 1893-1897). DEMOCRAT.

Quotes

"Sometimes I wake at night in the White House and rub my eyes and wonder if it is not all a dream."

"It is the responsibility of the citizens to support their government. It is not the responsibility of the government to support its citizens."

Actions

- enlarged the civil service and vetoed many pension raids on the Treasury
- a severe economic depression and labor troubles racked his administration, but he refused to interfere in business matters

Scandals

- during his presidential campaign it was revealed that he had fathered an illegitimate child ten years earlier. He was one of several men dating the same woman, a department store worker from Buffalo, New York. When she became pregnant, she named Cleveland as the father because all the other men were married. Cleveland agreed to pay child support.

23. BENJAMIN HARRISON (1889-1893). REPUBLICAN.

Quotes

"We Americans have no commission from God to police the world."

"The White House is my jail."

Actions

- sharply raised tariffs, providing protection to some US industries but raising prices for many consumer goods
- initiated Pan American Union

25. WILLIAM MCKINLEY (1897-1901). REPUBLICAN.

Quotes

"That's all a man can hope for during his lifetime — to set an example — and when he is dead, to be an inspiration for history."

"I have no enemies. No one would wish to hurt me."

Actions

- negotiated an agreement with European nations that established an "Open Door" policy toward China, under which all nations doing business with China would enjoy equal trading rights

26. THEODORE ROOSEVELT (1901-1909). REPUBLICAN.

Quotes

"To announce that there must be no criticism of the President, right or wrong, is not only unpatriotic, but is morally treasonable to the American public."

"Speak softly and carry a big stick."

"No President has enjoyed himself as much as I have enjoyed myself."

"I can do no further harm to the Constitution."

Actions

- fought corruption of politics by big business
- mediated (1905) the peace between Japan and Russia, for which he won the Nobel Peace Prize
- abetted the 1903 revolution in Panama that led to US acquisition of territory for the Panama Canal
- fought for US intervention in World War I

27. WILLIAM TAFT (1909-1913). REPUBLICAN.

Quotes

"Politics, when I am in it, makes me sick."

"The personal side of politics has always been funny to me, but nothing has been quite as funny as to have a man's career wrecked by a jealous wife."

"I am glad to be going. This [the White House] is the loneliest place in the world."

Actions

- continued Roosevelt's trust-busting (90 antitrust suits in four years)
- instituted the Department of Labor
- drafted the Amendments calling the direct election of the Senators and the income tax
- instituted a "dollar diplomacy" — the policy sought to use investments and trade to expand US influence abroad, especially in Latin America

28. WOODROW WILSON (1913-1921). DEMOCRAT.

Quotes

"If you want to make enemies, try to change something."

"I of all people must observe the laws."

"We grow great by dreams. All big men are dreamers. "

Actions

- protected American interests in revolutionary Mexico and fought for American rights on the high seas
- oversaw the creation of the Federal Reserve system, cut the tariffs and developed a reputation as a reformer
- tried to mediate an end to the World War I and called for a "peace without victory" that would end the fighting and the establishment of a League of Nations, an international body that would prevent and settle disputes between members

29. WARREN HARDING (1921-1923) REPUBLICAN.

Quotes

"Our most dangerous tendency is to expect too much of government, and at the same time do for it too little."

"I never find myself with my work completed. I don't believe that there is a human being who can do all the work there is to be done in the President's office."

"I am not fit for this office and should never have been here."

Actions

- stressed a return to "normalcy" and worked for tariff revision and the repeal of excess profits law and high income taxes
- did not prevent corruption in his administration

Scandals

- his close friend, a Director of the Veterans Bureau, pocketed as much as $250 million of the federal government money and fled to Europe.

30. CALVIN COOLIDGE (1923-1929). REPUBLICAN.

Quotes

- "There is no dignity so impressive, and no independence so important, as living within your means."
- "The business of America is business."
- "One of the most important accomplishments of my administration has been minding my own business."

Actions

- opposed the League of Nations and the soldiers' bonus bill, which was passed over his veto
- substantially reduced the national debt
- twice voted the farm bill, which would have provided relief to financially hard-pressed farmers
- supported hands-off policy toward business activities
- re-established diplomatic relations with Mexico

31. HERBERT HOOVER (1929-1933). REPUBLICAN.

Quotes

"Absolute freedom of the press to discuss public questions is a foundation stone of American liberty"

"If a man hasn't made a fortune by age forty, he isn't worth much."

"My friends have made the American people think me a sort of superman, able to cope successfully with the most difficult and complicated problems. They expect the impossible of me and should there arise conditions with which the political machinery is able to cope, I will be the one to suffer."

Actions

- tried (and failed) to fight Great Depression through limited public works projects, increased government loans to banks and businesses, reductions in the already low income tax, personal appeals to industry to maintain wages and production levels and opposing benefit programs to help the poor

32. FRANKLIN ROOSEVELT (1933-1945). DEMOCRAT.

Quotes

"A good leader can't get too far ahead of his followers."

"These Republican leaders have not been content with attacks on me, on my wife, or on my sons. No, not content with that, they now include my little dog, Fala. Well, of course, I don't resent the attacks, and my family doesn't resent the attacks — but Fala does resent them! His Scotch soul was furious. He has not been the same dog since." — FDR presidential election campaign speech in 1944, after Republicans falsely accused him of sending a destroyer to pick up his Scotch terrier dog, Fala, which allegedly had been left behind on a distant island during a wartime visit).

Actions

- greatly expanded the federal government's regulation of business

- promoted legislation establishing the Social Security systems
- was openly hostile to fascist governments before World War II and launched a lend-lease program on behalf of the Allies
- won unprecedented (and un-repeated) third term
- with Winston Churchill wrote a declaration of "a permanent system of general security" to be followed after Nazi defeat (the Atlantic Charter) and urged the Four Freedoms (freedom of speech, of worship, from want, from fear), August 9, 1941.

33. Harry Truman (1945-1953). Democrat.

Quotes

"When you get to be President, there are all those things, the honors, the twenty-one gun salutes, all those things. You have to remember, it isn't for you. It's for the Presidency."

"You cannot stop the spread of an idea by passing a law against it. "

"A pessimist is one who makes difficulties of his opportunities, and optimist is one who makes opportunities of his difficulties."

Actions

- authorized the first uses of the atomic bombs against Japanese civilians (Hiroshima and Nagasaki, August 6 and 9, 1945), bringing World War II to a rapid end. Some researchers have concluded the war was in its final days anyway but there was a desire to test the new weaponry on a highly unpopular race.
- was responsible for what came to be called the Truman Doctrine (to prop up nations such as Greece and Turkey, threatened by Communist takeover)
- broke a Soviet blockade of West Berlin with a massive airlift
- when communist North Korea invaded South Korea (June 1950), he won UN approval for a "police action" and sent in forces under Gen. McArthur

34. Dwight Eisenhower (1953-1961). Republican.

Quotes

"I never saw a pessimistic general win a battle."

"Things are more like they are now than they ever been before."

Actions

- favored the "free market system" vs. government price and wage controls
- kept government out of labor disputes
- reorganized the defense establishment and promoted missile programs
- sped the end of the Korean War
- advocated the "open skies" policy of mutual inspection with the USSR
- sent US troops into Little Rock, AR, in September 1957, during the segregation crisis

35. JOHN F. KENNEDY (1961-1963). DEMOCRAT.

Quotes

"If we cannot end now our differences, at least we can help make the world safe for diversity."

Actions

- negotiated on October 22, 1962, with the Soviet Union to avoid a nuclear catastrophe on terms opposed by some of his aides. Moscow dismantled its missile bases in Cuba; apparently US warheads aimed at Russia were concomitantly removed from Turkey, though little is said about that.
- defied Soviet attempts to force the Allies out of Berlin
- created the Peace Corps
- supported civil rights and expanded medical care for the aged
- greatly developed space exploration

Scandals

- the Kennedy family had personal connections with the mafia boss Sam Giancana
- the President and his brother Robert were involved with Marilyn Monroe
- JFK also had sexual liaisons with dozens of other women, including Ellen Rometsch, a part-time model and a prostitute. In July 1963, FBI counterespionage division opened an investigation into her as a possible STAZI (East Germany) spy. She was deported back to Germany in August 1963 and was reportedly paid to keep her mouth shut.

36. LYNDON JOHNSON (1963-1969). DEMOCRAT.

Quotes

"Freedom is not enough. You do not wipe away the scars of centuries by saying: now, you are free to go where you want, do as you desire, and choose the leaders you please. You do not take a man who for years has been hobbled by chains, liberate him, bring him to the starting line of a race, saying, "You are free to compete with all others," and still justly believe you have been completely fair. This is not enough to open the gates of opportunity. "

"A President's hardest task is not to do what is right, but to know what is right."

"The thing I feared from the first day of my Presidency was actually coming true" (after Robert Kennedy declared that he would challenge Johnson in 1968 primary).

Actions

- won passage of major civil rights, anti-poverty, aid to education and health-care (Medicare, Medicaid)legislation — the "Great Society" program

- escalated senseless war in Vietnam

Scandals

Slept with numerous women (mostly from Texas). Nothing happened.

37. RICHARD NIXON (1969-1974). REPUBLICAN.

Quotes

"I'm an introvert in an extrovert's profession."

"I like the job I have, but if I had to live my life over again, I would like to have ended up a sports writer."

"I'm glad I'm not Brezhnev. Being the Russian leader in Kremlin. You never know if someone's tape recording what you say."

"What really hurts is if you try to cover it up. I can categorically say that no one on the present White House staff, no one in this administration, presently employed, was involved in this very bizarre incident" (on Watergate break-in).

"When the President does it, that means it's not illegal."

A Joke

Just after President John Kennedy's inauguration in 1961, presidential aide Ted Sorensen and Republican candidate Richard Nixon met and the discussion turned eventually to Kennedy's inaugural address.

"I wish I had said some of those things," said Nixon.

"What part? " asked Sorensen, proud of his speech-writing. "That part about 'Ask not what your country can do for you...?'"

"No," commented Nixon. "The part that starts, 'I do solemnly swear...'"

Actions

- as a "new federalist" sought to shift responsibility to state and local governments
- altered relations with Communist China
- pursued détente with the Soviet Union
- began a gradual withdrawal from Vietnam

Scandals

The "Watergate" scandal. On June 17, 1972 five men were arrested in the act of breaking into the headquarters of the Democratic National Committee, which was located at the Watergate Hotel, Washington, DC (they intended to plant listening devices). Nixon tried to use CIA to block FBI investigation. Then Nixon blamed six members of his staff for the break-in and fired them. Nixon fired the Attorney General and Deputy Attorney General who refused to fire the special prosecutor. By 1974 twenty-nine people had been indicted, pleaded guilty or had been convicted of Watergate related crimes.

38. GERALD FORD (1974-1977). REPUBLICAN.

Quotes

"A government big enough to give you everything you want is a government big enough to take everything you have."

Vicci Carr (a singer of Mexican origin): "What's your favorite Mexican dish?" Gerald Ford: "You are." [A talk at the White House reception.]

Actions
- vetoed 48 bills in his first 21 months in office, mostly in the interest of fighting high inflation
- continued to pursue détente

Scandals
- pardoned President Nixon for any federal crimes he might have committed

39. JIMMY CARTER (1977-1981). DEMOCRAT.

Quotes

"We must adjust to changing times and still hold to unchanging principles."

"I have often wanted to drown my troubles, but I can't get my wife to go swimming."

Jimmy Carter: "I have looked upon a lot of women with lust. I've committed adultery in my heart many times." [*Playboy* interview, 1976]

"In his heart he knows your wife" [bumper sticker following the interview].

Actions
- played a major role in the negotiations leading to the 1979 peace treaty between Israel and Egypt
- won passage of new treaties with Panama providing for US control of the Panama Canal to end in 2000

Scandals

"Billygate": It was revealed that his brother, Billy Carter, had received $220,000 from the Libyan government as an initial payment on a $500,000 loan. It was one of the reasons Carter lost re-election to Ronald Reagan.

40. RONALD REAGAN (1981-1989). REPUBLICAN.

Quotes

"Recession is when your neighbor losses his job, depression is when you lose yours, and recovery will be when Jimmy Carter loses his!"

"America is too great for small dreams."

"Politics is supposed to be the second oldest profession. I have come to realize that it bears a very close resemblance to the first."

"We've heard a great deal about Republicans fat-cats — how the Republicans are the party of big contributions. I've never able to understand why a Republican contributor is a fat-cat and a Democratic contributor of the same amount of money is a public-spirited philanthropist."

"I don't know I could do this job if I were not actor."

"My fellow Americans, I'm pleased to tell you today that I've signed legislation that will outlaw Russia forever. We begin bombing in five minutes" (testing microphone before broadcast in 1984).

Actions

- successfully forged a bipartisan coalition in Congress, which led to enactment of his program of large-scale tax cuts, cutbacks in many government programs, and a major defense buildup
- signed a Social Security reform bill designed to provide for the long-term solvency of the system and signed into law a major tax-reform bill
- at the 1987 meeting with Soviet leader Gorbachev signed a historic treaty eliminating short- and medium-range missiles from Europe
- made every effort to win Cold War and eliminate the USSR as a communist state (which was the biggest mistake an American President could ever make. After the Soviet Union collapsed, China took its place and now we are approaching the next war which, after several phases of economic power plays, looks likely to become very hot, rather than cold).

Scandals

The "Iran-Contra" affair in which the CIA secretly sold weapons to Iran, a country that supported anti-American terrorism, while in exchange Iran used its influence to secure the release of two Americans who were being held hostage by the pro-Iranian "Hezbollah" group in Lebanon. Then it was revealed that between $10 and $30 million from the Iranian arms sales had been diverted by some National Security Council members, including the President's National Security Advisor John Poindexter, to help support the Contras, resistance fighters trying to oust Nicaragua's elected leftist government. Reagan supported the Contras, but Congress had eliminated funding for that cause. Throughout the investiga-

tion Reagan insisted he knew nothing about the affair. Finally, he made a statement which deserves its place in history:

"A few months ago, I told American people I did not trade arms for hostages.
My heart and best intentions still tell me this is true, but the facts and evidence
tell me it is not." [Bravo, Hollywood!].

41. GEORGE H.W. BUSH (1989-1993). REPUBLICAN.

Quotes

"If anyone tells you that America's best days are behind her, they are looking
the wrong way."

"It's no exaggeration to say that the undecideds could go one way or
another."

Actions

- faced a severe budget deficit annually, struggled with military cutbacks in
  light of reduced cold war tensions
- vetoed abortion-rights legislation
- supported Soviet democratic reforms and Eastern Europe democratization
- reacted to Iraq's August 1990 invasion of Kuwait by sending our forces to the
  Persian Gulf area and assembling a UN-based coalition, including NATO
  and Arab League members (after a month-long war allied forces retook
  Kuwait)

42. WILLIAM CLINTON (1993-2001). DEMOCRAT.

Quotes

"There is nothing wrong in America that can't be fixed with what is right in
America."

"All I've been asked by the press about a woman I didn't sleep with and a
draft I didn't dodge."

Jim Lehrer: "You had no sexual relationship with this young woman [Monica Lewinsky]?

Bill Clinton: "What I am trying to do is to contain my natural impulses and
get back to work" [01. 21.1998]

"It depends on what meaning of the word "is" is. If the — if he — if "is" means
never has been, that's not — that is one thing. If it means there is none, that was
a completely true statement" [8.17.1998].

"I think most Americans who are watching this tonight, they'll know what
we're saying, they'll get it, and they'll feel that we have been more than candid.
And I think what the press has to decide is, are we going to engage in a game of

'gotcha'? " (answering the "60 Minutes" question on his sexual relations with Jennifer Flowers).

"He's out of ideas and out of time" (on his opponent George H. W. Bush).

Actions

- won passage of a measure to reduce the federal budget deficit (1993)
- won Congressional approval of the North American Free Trade Agreement (NAFTA)
- sent troops to Bosnia to help "implement a peace settlement" which led to the dismemberment of the Slavic nation of Yugoslavia and the establishment of a Moslem nation (Bosnia) in the heart of Europe, and split Catholic Slovenia and Croatia from Orthodox Christian Serbia. Slovenia and Croatia (like Poland, Hungary and Czechia) were then given a head start against Romania and Bulgaria (never mind Serbia) in joining the capitalist Western circuit
- in 1999, the United States, under Clinton joined other NATO nations in an aerial bombing campaign that induced Serbia to withdraw troops from the Kosovo region where they had been terrorizing ethnic Albanians

Scandals

- Travelgate: In May, 1993 seven career employees from the White House Travel Office were abruptly fired, apparently in order to direct more lucrative bookings toward travel agents close to the Clintons.
- Fund-raising. During the 1996 presidential election both President Clinton and Vice President Gore acted illegally by raising funds by entertaining guests overnight in the White House and by using official government phones to make fund-raising calls. Several Democratic fund-raisers were indicted for various infractions and one pleaded guilty to illegal fund-raising from foreign nationals.
- Filegate. In June 1996 it was revealed that the White House personnel security office had requested 700 confidential FBI files on Republicans, including such eminences as former Secretary of State James Baker and a former National Security Advisor Brent Scowcroft.
- Whitewater. There were many questions of financial and legal improprieties around a failed land development deal, known as Whitewater, in which Clintons were involved while he was Governor of Arkansas. Kenneth Starr, independent counsel, conducted a lengthy investigation and found plenty of evidence of criminal activity, but not against the Clintons.
- Chinagate. (see "Which Service is the Best.")
- Monica Lewinsky and impeachment. In 1995, an intern at the White House engaged President Clinton in sexual play and confided details to her friend Linda Tripp, who in January 1998 brought their recorded telephone conversations to the above-mentioned Kenneth Starr. In September 1998 Starr sent to the House of Representatives his report, wherein eleven possibly impeachable offenses were identified, including perjury before a grand jury, obstruction of justice and abuse of power. Clinton made a desperate attempt to divert public attention from the scandal and ordered on December 17, 1998 the bombing of Iraq. The House of Representatives impeached Clinton by approving two articles — perjury before a grand jury and obstruction of justice. On February 12, 1999, the Senate rejected both articles; the first article received forty-five "yes," the second — fifty "yes").

RESULTS OF PRESIDENT CLINTON'S SENATE IMPEACHMENT TRIAL
(For each article of impeachment a two-thirds majority of 67 votes is required to convict)

Article 1. Perjury before the grand jury			
Republicans	Democrats	Total	
guilty	45	0	45
not guilty	10	45	55
Article 2. Obstruction of justice.			
Guilty	50	0	50
Not guilty	5	45	50

43. GEORGE W. BUSH (2001-). REPUBLICAN

Quotes

"It's clearly a budget. It's got a lot of numbers in it."

"If you are sick and tired of the politics of cynicism and polls, and principles, come and join this campaign."

"We will bring terrorists to justice, or we will bring justice to terrorists. Either way, justice will be done."

Actions

On September 11, 2001 faced with national security total crisis, when two hijacked jetliners crashed into twin towers of the World Trade Center in New York City with 3000 employees killed; another jet struck the Pentagon and the fourth crashed in rural Pennsylvania.

After that in a "war against terrorism" the US military attacked and deposed the Taliban regime in Afghanistan, which was sheltering leaders of the Al-Qaeda terrorist network, which was supposedly responsible for the attacks. The war is still going on, with no clear victory in sight.

In March 2003, the United States aided mainly by forces of Great Britain launched an air and ground war against Iraq and deposed the elected, if dictatorial, regime of President Saddam Hussein. The regime was accused of harboring weapons of mass destruction (which were not there). The war is still going on as of this writing and a stable, if tightly controlled, nation has been dragged into a civil war that may yet manage to disrupt the entire region for decades to come.

PRESIDENTIAL LAST WORDS

Thomas Jefferson: "I resign my spirit to God, my daughter to my country."

John Adams: "This is the last of Earth! I am content."

Andrew Jackson: "I hope to see you all in Heaven, both white and black, white and black."

Ulysses S. Grant: "Water."

Grover Cleveland: "I have tried so hard to do the right."

William McKinley: "It is God's way; his will, not ours, be done."

Theodore Roosevelt: "Put out the light."

Woodrow Wilson: "I'm a broken machine, but I'm ready."

Franklin Roosevelt: "I have a terrific headache!"

Dwight Eisenhower: "I've always loved my wife. I've always loved my children, I've always loved my grandchildren. And I've always loved my country."

PART 6. WHERE DOES THE CIA FIT IN

The United States has witnessed an ongoing series of major mysteries starring the CIA, many characterized by never-ending news stories, multiple conflicting cover stories, revised stories, recanted stories, and deathbed confession stories. In these and other major incidents, what role did the CIA (and other intelligence agencies from the US, our allies, and our enemies) play, and whose agendas were they promoting?

In 2005, President Bush used the emergency climate fostered in the aftermath of 9/11 to inaugurate a controversial change in the hierarchy of US intelligence agencies, such that all sixteen agencies that are formally part of the "US Intelligence Community," including the hallowed CIA, were unified under one director of national intelligence. As the Christian Science Monitor reported on February 18, 2005, "some human rights groups have alleged that [the new Director] Negroponte knew about and did not disapprove of the activities of Honduran death squads funded and partly trained by the CIA." In other words, while he might be expected to rein in the CIA he is more likely comfortable with CIA-style operations, including "passive sabotage." Indeed, what if in practice it's not that the CIA has been reined in but the CIA gaining the upper hand? You could say that the CIA has more or less run the White House since former CIA director George H. W. Bush was named Vice President in 1980.

As President, you'll need to give this some thought. You might not be as free to act as you think you are.

What Happened to Them?

Whenever somebody investigating an important murder or kidnapping starts to get close to the truth, a hue and cry goes out labeling him a conspiracy freak or an attention-seeker. Of course, some murders *are* the result of a conspiracy or, if you prefer, a complex and highly-coordinated plan. For professionals, this sort of business is normal and we use terms like "case" or "file."

There is no possible scenario explaining the JFK assassination, for instance, that would not qualify as a "conspiracy theory." That does not mean the scenario is wrong. While some details in the following analyses may be off target, the approach and questions are on target for anyone seeking the truth about what happened.

Since criminology was part of my education at a special counter-espionage school and I understand perfectly well what kind of operation is behind the fact and what crime is behind the evidence, I offer some analysis not found in the many hundreds of books that struggle to untangle this mystery, some analysis that might answer a few questions in the minds of the Kennedy family and many others.

Case 1. Heinrich Muller.

GESTAPO Chief, convicted war criminal. Last seen April 24, 1945

Question 1. What was the GESTAPO doing during World War II?

> "The head of the Jewish section in the GESTAPO, and the man directly responsible for carrying out the mass extermination program against the Jews by GESTAPO, Obersturmbannfuehrer Eichmann, estimated in his report to Himmler that 2,000,000 Jews had been killed by shootings, mainly by the Einsatz Groups of the SIPO during the campaign in the East. This did not include the estimated 4,000,000 sent by the GESTAPO for extermination in annihilation camps." — The International Military Tribunal, Nurnberg, 1946, Volume II, Chapter XV, p. 282

Question 2. What happened to Heinrich Muller? US government agency officers would not approve my private investigation of GESTAPO crimes and Heinrich Muller's post-war activity. That in itself is a strong suggestion that Muller was secretly transferred to the USA and put to work for the CIA. And it's even understandable — the "cold war" needed his experience.

Question 3. Why hasn't Henry Kissinger, the leader of the Bilderberg group and one of the most influential US politicians, who knows the CIA perfectly well, said anything about it?

Case 2. Marilyn Monroe.

Movie star, drug addict, unbalanced personality with four suicide attempts, sex maniac, a very lonely person with unhappy family history and a "Communist" according to her FBI and CIA files.

Date of death: August 5, 1962, murdered.

Official version: Suicide with barbiturates overdose — which flies in the face of the evidence. Why?

On August 1, 1962 Marilyn Monroe signed a $1 million contract with 20th Century Fox. Four days later she "committed suicide." Despite physical autopsy and toxicological tests, it's still not clear how she was killed; and given her links to the Kennedys as well as crime leaders and others there are plenty of theories as to who needed her dead, and why. In this way, her story resembles that of JFK's murder.

The evidence allows for the following possibilities, and others as well, which need not be mutually exclusive:

- Mafia boss Sam Giancana killed Monroe to set up Robert Kennedy, who had publicly declared war on organized crime
- Joseph Kennedy, the two brothers' father, hired Giancana to kill Monroe because she was pregnant with Robert's child and tried to blackmail him
- The CIA killed Monroe to get even with JFK for the Bay of Pigs fiasco (because her death could compromise him)
- Fidel Castro had her killed to send a message to JFK, who had given orders for the assassination of the Cuban leader
- JFK gave the order to kill Monroe, because she knew too much about his murky activities, and then he was killed by "Italian friends" of her former husband Joe DiMaggio.
- [my view] Marilyn had information on plans for the JFK assassination, and a lot of people needed to have her silenced

Now, once again — what was Robert Kennedy looking for in her house that day? If Senator Edward Kennedy helps me to answer the question, we might come very close to "cracking" the case.

I hate when big, strong, healthy men kill a woman and that's against all the rules — don't kill kids and women. Trust me, one day I'll get those guys — dead or alive.

Case 3. John F. Kennedy.

35th American President
Date of death: April 4, 1963, murdered; shot by snipers.
Reason: His decision to liquidate the CIA.

Like Marilyn Monroe, John Kennedy was a sex maniac and that kind of activity can upset a lot of people; that alone could have provided a motive for murder, when you take a look at the endless list of his partners beginning with movie stars like Marilyn Monroe, Sophia Loren, Audrey Hepburn, Judy Campbell, Jayne Mansfield, and finishing with his wife's press secretary, his own secretaries and regular prostitutes like the above mentioned Ellen Rometsch. Everybody who starts an "investigative" book on this case dreams of putting a final dot and giving the ultimate explanation.

What is a conspiracy? It's when you ask a simple question and nobody wants to answer it. Besides, if you ask the wrong questions you get the wrong answers, as with the Warren Commission. Let's ask some good questions and answer them ourselves. Actually, it doesn't matter who was shooting — Oswald or a can of soda. I have different questions.

Question 1. What would have happened if the snipers missed the target or Kennedy survived, being merely wounded? A sniper is a human being — he makes mistakes.

Answer. Quite possibly, Kennedy would have won the 1964 Presidential election and then conceivably his brothers, Robert and Edward, would keep the Oval Office until 1984 (count the years for yourself). No war in Vietnam. The CIA would have been shut down. The FBI and Pentagon would have been "cleaned up" and "cleaned out."

This leads to Question 2. Why would the CIA, FBI and big business behind them, not to mention others who had their eye on the Oval Office, take such a huge risk?

There was no risk at all — they used the passive sabotage method (See "Strategies"); there was no "huge conspiracy with hundreds of people involved."

Question 3. Why was Kennedy murdered in public?

President Kennedy was a sick man, taking a lot of different pills every day. He had Addison's disease which, in addition to susceptibility to infection can cause weakness, weight loss and low blood pressure; so he was taking cortisone. For his back pain Dr. Max Jacobson injected him (and Jackie) with a mixture of unspecified (!) multivitamins, hormones, steroids, enzymes, and animal organ cells. Kennedy also used cocaine, marijuana, hashish and even LSD, especially during dates with women, including prostitutes — for many people this was not a secret. There were enough opportunities to stage a death in private.

But this had to be a public execution with a very clear message for the next Presidents — "Don't touch the CIA!" and it worked. Bill Clinton was ready to follow Kennedy and fight CIA, "a state inside a state," but Jackie Kennedy gave him a nice tip. Hillary Clinton says so in her book, *Living History*: "Jackie... she never came out and said it, but she meant that he [Bill Clinton] might also be a target. 'He has to be very careful,' she told me."

"Very careful."

Question 4. What was the rush?

Something extraordinary happened that forced the plotters' hand and I think most probably it was Kennedy's decision to name Martin Luther King as his running mate. President talked about it with his brother Robert and his assistants — O'Brien and O'Donnell, and then there was a leak.

Question 5. Were any witnesses liquidated?

Curiously, John Kennedy and Bill Clinton are the only US Presidents whose names have been linked by the media and by self-proclaimed investigators to multiple natural and unnatural (suspicious) deaths. With Kennedy it's clear — numerous persons died under peculiar circumstances after he was assassinated and there's a possibility that at least many of them were liquidated. Two thousands authors worldwide have written irresponsibly on this topic because they have no idea what is a professional staged murder — explaining that "most people out of the popular list of 101 died of a heart attack" — that tells you nothing as to whether it was a natural death or a murder. And never mind dates — it doesn't matter when a certain witness was killed, a day or ten years after the assassination — it depends on whether a victim talks or not. Besides, if one hundred people connected to such a case die unexpectedly, whether in one day or one year, it's suspicious, don't you think?

Let's have a look at a few names on the above-mentioned "mystery deaths" list:

- Karen Kupcinet, the daughter of an L. A. TV host. Unidentified sources reported that she screamed into the telephone that JFK would be killed (murdered in Los Angeles on 11. 24.1963)
- Jack Zangetty, a motel manager in Oklahoma, who told friends about three assassins scheduled to kill Kennedy (murdered, 1963).
- C. D. Jackson, *Life* magazine executive who decided to purchase the Zapruder film that belied the official story (heart attack, 1964).
- Hank Killian, husband of a Ruby employee (murdered, 1964).
- Bill Hunter, reporter who visited Ruby's apartment on November 24, 1963 and talked to Ruby's attorney, as well as to one of his friends and a roommate (killed in accidental shooting, 1964).
- Jim Koethe, reporter who was together with Bill Hunter (murder in a fight with a gay lover).

There are literally several dozen of others, many of whom died prematurely and, in some cases, just as they were due to speak to the committee investigating JFK's murder. See *Conspiracy in Camelot* by Dr. Jerry Kroth for a more complete list.

Ultimate questions.

The US Congress closed to the public 40,000 documents on the case, promising to de-classify them in 40 years. In 2003 the US Congress (no doubt, under Senator Edward Kennedy's pressure), called for another 40 years. Why? What's behind all the above mentioned names? I wish we could live long enough to find out.

President Bill Clinton visited President Kennedy's grave on the first day of his first presidency. Yet President Clinton, for whom President Kennedy was an idol and an icon, did nothing during his 8-year-long chaos at the White House to gain access for us to the above mentioned documents. Why?

And one more "why": why did President Johnson order a halt to the investigation on "Numec" and "Permindex" companies right after JFK was killed? Those two companies allegedly delivered 280 kilograms of stolen uranium to Israel, and Kennedy controlled the investigation himself.

Case 4. Martin Luther King, Jr.

Pastor, prominent black civil rights leader.

Date of death: April 4, 1968, murdered; shot by a sniper.

Reason: Political popularity and his decision to campaign for the US President

Question 1: What is the US military best kept secret? The "Alpha 184" team.

On April 4, 1968, Martin Luther King, Jr. was shot dead on the Lorraine Motel balcony in Memphis, Atlanta. In a room in a house across the street the FBI found fingerprints of a Missouri penitentiary fugitive, James Earl Grey, a professional armed robber. He fled to Great Britain but was arrested in June and extradited to the United States. He was sentenced to 99 years and died in 1998, claiming until his last days he was a patsy.

In 1967, a year before King was shot, Military Intelligence formed part of the US Army Intelligence Command (USAINTC) based at Fort Holobird, Maryland. Its task was to collect information on American citizens, including civil rights leaders. USAINTC took control of seven of the eight existing Military Intelligence Groups (MIGs) in the continental United States and Germany. The eighth, the 902nd, was under the command of the Army's Assistant Chief of Staff for Intelligence Major General William Yarborough (in 1966-1968), the founder of Green Berets. MIGs were responsible for audio and visual surveillance and coordinated their work with FBI and CIA. The above mentioned 902nd MIG was a most secretive organization, inside of which there existed the "Operation Detachment Alpha 184" team. On April 4, 1968 it was deployed in Memphis.

Any further questions would have to be asked of the Defense Department.

Case 5. SPECIAL.

Name: Pope John Paul II (born Karol Wojtyla).

Date of assassination attempt: May 13, 1981; shot by a gunman.

Reason: Pope's intent to investigate the illegal activity of the Vatican Bank.

On May 13, 1981 Pope John Paul II was shot and critically wounded by Mehmet Agdca, a Turkish gunman, as he entered St. Peter's Square to address the audience. Agdca was caught and sentenced to life imprisonment. In 1983 John Paul II visited the prison and spoke privately with Agdca for 20 minutes, and after that made a statement: "What we talked about will have to remain a secret between him and me. I spoke to him as a brother whom I have pardoned and who has my complete trust."

An Italian parliamentary commission, after its own investigation, concluded that the Soviet Union was behind the attempt, in retaliation for Pope's support to "Solidarity," the Polish anti-Communist workers' movement. Its report stated that the Bulgarian secret service was utilized to prevent the Soviet Union's role from being uncovered, but during his 2002 visit to Bulgaria the Pope himself declared that this country had nothing to do with the assassination attempt. Unless a lone, mad Turk picked up the gun on a whim, there was a conspiracy involved. Who was behind it, and why?

File 1. The Vatican Bank, the first partner.

The Vatican Bank (Institute for Religious Works) is the central bank of Roman Catholic Church; its CEO reports directly to a committee of cardinals and to the Pope. It's known that in the 1990s the Bank invested over $10 billion in foreign companies. In 1968, due to a change in Italian financial regulations which would have mandated more transparency — it began to appear that the Bank was laundering money for big business. (The Bank was supposed to funnel all profits directly and immediately to charity.) To prevent a public scandal Pope Paul VI enlisted Michele Sindona as papal finance advisor to sell off assets and move money overseas. Sindona had been chiefly responsible for the massive influx of money when he began processing the Gambino crime family's heroin money (taking a 50% cut) through a shell corporation "Mabusi." This was accomplished with the help of another banker, Roberto Calvi, who managed the Banco Ambrosiano. Both Sindona and Calvi where members of "Propaganda Due" (P2) Masonic Lodge and close friends to its headmaster, the neofascist Licio Gelli, who worked for "Gladio"(see file #3). Sindona was poisoned in 1986 in prison in Italy, and we'll talk about Calvi too, don't worry. When Pope John Paul I succeeded Pope Paul VI on August 26, 1978 he ordered Cardinal Jean Villot, papal Secretary of State and Head of papal Curia, to investigate the Vatican Bank operations. Just

33 days later, after informing Villot that he was going public with the scandal (and firing Villot, among others), John Paul I died. The official cause of death was "possibly associated to a myocardial infarction" (heart attack), though no autopsy was performed.

On October 22, 1978, Karol Wojtyla, 58, was inaugurated as Pope John Paul II. The youngest pope in Roman Catholic Church history, he thought he would strengthen his position first; but the explosive situation with the Vatican Bank impelled him to act.

File 2. Banco Ambrosiano, the second partner.

The Vatican Bank was the above mentioned Banco Ambrosiano's main shareholder and knew well that its Chairman, Roberto Calvi, was funding P2. In 1981 police raided the office of P2 Grandmaster Licio Gelli and found evidence against Calvi, who was arrested and sentenced to four years in jail. However, he was released pending an appeal, and kept his position in the bank. On May 13, 1981, Pope John Paul II was shot in Rome, and survived. In 1982 it was discovered that Ambrosio Bank could not account for $1,287 billion. Calvi fled Italy on a false passport. His personal secretary, Graziella Corrocher, left a note denouncing Calvi before jumping from her office window to her death. On June 17, 1982, Calvi's body was found hanging beneath Blackfriars Bridge in London. His suit was stuffed with rocks and a brick had been placed in his trousers. The British police treated his death as suicide, but after 1992 exhumation concluded it was a murder. In 2003 City of London Police reopened the investigation.

File 3. "Gladio," the third partner.

Mehmet Agdca was a member of the "Grey Wolves," an ultra-nationalist Turkish terror organization, infiltrated by "Gladio" — a CIA and NATO sponsored super-secret paramilitary terror organization in Italy with branches all over Western Europe. "Gladio" was a part of a clandestine "stay-behind" operation to counter communist influence after World War II, but like all other branches was actually never used "to resist Soviet influence or invasion." Still, the structures exist even now (what for?). "Gladio's" existence was acknowledged in 1990 by the head of the Italian government, Giulio Andreotti. Further investigations revealed links to neo-fascists, the mafia and law-breaking P2 Masonic Lodge. The following was passed on November 22, 1990.

European Parliament Resolution on the "Gladio" Affair

> A. Having regard to the revelation by several European governments of the existence for 40 years of a clandestine parallel intelligence and armed operations organization in several Member States of the Community,

B. Whereas for over 40 years this organization has escaped all democratic controls and has been run by the secret services of the states concerned in collaboration with NATO,

C. Fearing the danger that such clandestine network may have interfered illegally in the internal political affairs of Member States or may still do so,

D. Whereas in certain Member States military secret services (or uncontrolled of branches thereof) were involved in serious cases of terrorism and crime as evidenced by various judicial inquiries,

E. Whereas these organizations operated and continue to operate completely outside the law, since they are not subject to any parliamentary control and frequently those holding the highest government and constitutional posts are kept in the dark as to these matters,

F. Whereas the various "Gladio" organizations have at their disposal independent arsenals and military resources which give them an unknown strike potential, thereby jeopardizing the democratic structures of the countries in which they are operating or have been operating,

G. Greatly concerned by the existence of decision-making and operational bodies which are not subject to any form of democratic control and are of a completely clandestine nature at a time when greater Community cooperation in the field of security is a constant subject of discussion,

1. Condemns the clandestine creation of manipulative and operational networks and calls for a full investigation into the nature, structure, aims and all other aspects of these clandestine organizations or any splinter groups, their use for illegal interference in the internal political affairs of the countries concerned, the problem of terrorism in Europe and the possible collusion of the secret services of Member States or third countries;

2. Protests vigorously at the assumption by certain US military personnel at SHAPE and NATO of the right to encourage the establishment in Europe of a clandestine intelligence and operational network;

3. Calls on the governments of the Member States to dismantle all clandestine military and paramilitary networks;

4. Calls on the judiciaries of the countries in which the presence of such military organizations has been ascertained to elucidate fully their composition and modus operandi and to clarify any action they may have taken to destabilize the democratic structure of the Member States;

5. Requests all the Member States to take the necessary measures, if necessary by establishing parliamentary committees of inquiry, to draw up complete list of organizations active in this field, and at the same time to monitor their links with the respective state intelligence services and their links, if any, with terrorist action groups and/or other illegal practices;

6. Calls on the Council of Ministers to provide full information on the activities of these secret intelligence and operational services;

7. Calls on its competent committee to consider holding a hearing in order to clarify the role and impact of the 'Gladio' organization and any similar bodies;

8. Instructs its President to forward this resolution to the Commission, the Council, the Secretary-General of NATO, the governments of the Member States and the United States Government.

By now the following code names of other "Gladio" branches are known:

SDRA8 — in Belgium

ABSALON — in Denmark

TD BJD — in Germany

LOK — in Greece

Stay-Behind — in Luxemburg

I&O — in Netherlands

ROC — in Norway

AGINTER — in Portugal

P26 — in Switzerland

Counter-Guerrilla — in Turkey

OWSGV — in Austria

The code names of the branches in France, Finland, Spain and Sweden remain unknown. In 1996, five years after the Soviet Union collapsed, Austrian President Thomas Klestil and Chancellor Franz Vranitsky insisted that they knew nothing of the existence of the secret, illegal CIA-NATO army and they demanded that the United States launch a full-scale investigation into the violation of Austria's neutrality, which was denied by President Bill Clinton. Was Mr. Clinton covering terrorists who tried to kill the Pope?

Case 6. Robert Kennedy.

US Senator and 1968 Presidential candidate, President Kennedy's brother.

Date of death: June 5, 1968, murdered. Method: Shot in Los Angeles Ambassador Hotel kitchen pantry one minute after leaving a ballroom celebration of winning the California Democratic presidential primary; the official story has it that the shooter was a Palestinian immigrant, Sirhan Sirhan, a psycho and a loser. There was zero security — an obvious sign of "passive sabotage."

Reason: Robert Kennedy stated that an investigation of JFK's assassination would be one of the most important issues if he was elected to the Oval Office.

Case 7. Ronald Brown.

US Commerce Secretary.

Date of death: April 3, 1996, murdered. Method: staged air crash. Another 34 passengers also died, mostly businessmen and officials from the Commerce Department, along with Jim Lewek, a CIA analyst; Lee Jackson, Treasury Dept, Niksa Antonioni, photographer; Dragica Lendic Bebek, interpreter; Nathaniel Nash, New York Times reporter, and the crew. According to my take on the evidence, Brown was most probably killed on board the plane before the crash and that means that his death was "double guaranteed."

Soon after the crash dispatcher at Croatia's airport "committed suicide," supposedly because he felt guilty about the crash (no doubt it was a staged suicide).

Reason: In 1993 Vice President Gore and Russian Prime Minister Chernomyrdin signed a 20-year $12 billion deal under which Russia would ship its weapons-grade uranium to the United States (the actual value of such an amount of weapons-grade uranium, Russian experts calculate, would have been $12 trillion. They call this supersecret agreement one of the "crimes of the century." Questions abound in any multibillion bribe with a former Russian President and a former US President involved. Ronald Brown most probably knew too much and tried to press Bill Clinton. (Besides, Brown was already under investigation by a special investigator and was about to be indicted with 54 others — and he spoke publicly of his willingness to "make a deal" with the prosecutors. Once the background to the situation is known, it becomes apparent he was not talking about the IRS. In a moment we'll also look at several Russians who tried to investigate this crime and died mysteriously in Russia.)

Bill Clinton in his over 1,000-page memoir *My Life* (2004) wrote nothing about this "deal of a century."

> "In the afternoon [April, 3, 1993] we [Clinton and Russian President Yeltsin] agreed on a way to institutionalize cooperation, with a commission headed by Vice President Gore and Russian Prime Minister Victor Chernomyrdin. The idea was developed by Strobe [Talbott] and Georgi Mamedov, the Russian Deputy Foreign Minister, and it worked better than any of us could have imagined, thanks largely to the consistent and concentrated efforts made over the years by Al Gore and his Russian counterparts in working through a host of difficult, contentious problems" [p. 507].

(What did you make of that? Nothing?)

> "On January 30 [1996], Prime Minister Victor Chernomyrdin of Russia came to the White House for his sixth meeting with Al Gore. After they finished their commission business, Chernomyrdin came to see me to brief me on events in Russia and Yeltsin's prospects for reelection" [p. 697].

(Again — nothing).

Questions:

What idea was "developed" by Talbot?

What extremely secret commission was "headed by Gore and Chernomyrdin"?

Why Mr. Clinton was so happy that "it worked better than any of us could have imagined"?

What "difficult and contentious problems" were Al Gore and others working through?

What "commission business" did Al Gore and his partner finish on January 30, 1996?

File 1. Why did this secret Commission appear right after Bill Clinton entered the Oval Office in 1993 and what was the "business" President Clinton still doesn't want to talk about?

At their summit meeting in Vancouver, in April 1993, President Clinton and President Yeltsin created the U.S.–Russian Joint Commission on Economic and Technological Cooperation. Since then it has become known as the Gore–Chernomyrdin Commission (GCC), after its co-chairmen US Vice President Al Gore and Russian Prime Minister Victor Chernomyrdin. The Commission's original mandate was to support cooperation between the United States and Russia in the areas of space, energy and high technology.

In fact it was a ruse to mask work on a non-proliferation agreement to convert highly enriched uranium (HEU) taken from dismantled Russian nuclear warheads into low-enriched uranium (LEU) fuel to be sold to customers in the USA and worldwide through the USEC (United States Enrichment Company). USEC was created in 1993 as a government corporation with the mission to restructure the US government's uranium enrichment operation and to prepare it for sale to the private sector. (On April 26, 1996 Bill Clinton signed into law the USEC Privatization Act.) The HEU Agreement required the United States to purchase through USEC 500 metric tons, $12 billion worth, of HEU. Yes, that's the market price, but President Yeltsin sold nearly the whole stock of Russia's military uranium for one thousandth of its actual cost in terms of petroleum equivalent — one ton of military grade uranium is equivalent to 100 million tons of oil — or several Persian Gulfs). President Clinton was very interested in a contract and personally asked President Yeltsin to keep to its terms.

File 2. What documents we are talking about?

a. Gore–Chernomyrdin September 1–2, 1993 Russian-American Agreement on HEU deal. (The full document is not available).

b. Gore–Chernomyrdin January 6, 1996. The Russian Ministry of Atomic Energy and the US Department of Energy agreed to create a Russian-American Consortium on fuel elements to develop environmentally safe and marketable fuel cell power sources.

c. Gore–Chernomyrdin February 8, 1997. Memorandum of Cooperation in the Field of Research on Fundamental Properties of Matter. In a prelude to the U.S.–Russian summit in Helsinki, Gore and Chernomyrdin met in Washington to sign a joint statement on nuclear materials security and continued to make progress on other arms control related matters, such as implementation of the 1993 HEU Agreement.

File 3. Dead Russians.

Three Russian statesmen tried to investigate the Gore–Chernomyrdin deal — Ruvim Nureyev, Lev Rokhlin, Yuri Shchekotchikhin. All of them are dead now.

1. Ruvim Nureyev. The Russia Chief Inspector for Nuclear and Radiation Safety, who strongly opposed the deal, was found dead on the railroad tracks in June 1996. The incident was described as a suicide.

2. Lev Rokhlin. The Russian State Duma Deputy Lieutenant General Lev Rokhlin was a politician of rare honesty and brevity, who refused to accept the Hero of Russia Gold Star from Pavel Grachev, then Minister of Defense, because he believed Grachev was corrupt. Being elected to the Duma he fought government corruption and advocated the resignation of Russian President Yeltsin, who fought back and managed to remove Rokhlin from the Defense Committee chairmanship. In 1998 Rokhlin started his own official Gore–Chernomyrdin deal investigation, requested all confidential government agreements and a list of high-ranked officials involved (including Chernomyrdin and Adamov — see file #4 for this one). Lev Maximov, the Nuclear Technologies Institute Director, who helped Rokhlin to obtain the documents, received death threats.

On July 3, 1998 Rokhlin was shot three times and killed in his house while he was sleeping. His wife, Tamara Rokhlina, was arrested and testified that she killed him "for reasons of personal enmity." She later recanted her testimony, saying she incriminated herself under threat. Rokhlin's bodyguard, who was there that night, testified that he heard no gunshots (the killers used a silencer). Within days three more dead bodies were found in the vicinity of the Rokhlin household and were cremated before they could be identified. In November 2000, Rokhlina was convicted of murder and sentenced to 8 years in prison, but the Supreme Court overturned the verdict and ordered a new trial.

On October 2, 1998 the US Congress, taking into account that Lev Rokhlin was a former Russian State Duma Defense Committee Chairman, asked President Clinton to "urge the Russia Government to promptly and thoroughly investigate" the case. Of course, Bill Clinton was smart enough not to dig his own grave, and just ignored this resolution.

3. Yuri Shchekotchikhin, a famous Russian reporter and corruption fighter, was elected to the Russian State Duma where he served as National Security Committee Deputy. After Rokhlin was murdered in 1998, Shchekotchikhin con-

tinued his Gore–Chernomyrdin investigation and concentrated his efforts in two directions: first, he tried to obtain the #1 Gore–Chernomyrdin Agreement (September 2, 1993), but President Yeltsin and, since 2000, President Putin denied the requests; second, he started a full-scale investigation into the Atomic Ministry corruption and — against Atomic Minister Adamov in person (again, see file 4). On June 16, 2003, he lost consciousness and was taken to the Central (Kremlin) Hospital. He was pronounced dead after lying still unconscious for 12 days. (The official diagnosis — a flu). All medical records are still classified, but experts insist he was poisoned by thallium or cadmium.

File 4. Who is Eugene Adamov?

Professor Eugene Adamov was in 1986-1998 a Director of the NIKIET (a secret Research and Development Institute of Power Engineering), one of the Russia's largest centers for nuclear reactors engineering for civil and military purposes. At the same time he was secretly involved in the Gore–Chernomyrdin deal as chief expert on the Russian side (even Russian Defense Minister Igor Rodionov knew nothing about it). On August 24, 1994 he opened the consulting and management company "Omeka, Ltd." registered in Pennsylvania (by the end of 1999 the company had assets valued of $5,080,000) by his wife. In 1996 he signed a forged contract between NIKIET and "Omeka," and opened other companies and banking accounts in Monaco, Switzerland and France to start money laundering the stolen funds the US Department of Energy provided Russia to improve safety at Russian nuclear facilities.

In 1998-2001 he was a Minister of Russia for Atomic Energy, then, in 2002-2004, adviser to the Chairman of Russian government, and finally, was back to NIKIET. On May 2, 2005 Adamov was arrested in Bern, Switzerland, and was charged with conspiracy to defraud the United States and to transfer stolen money and securities ($9 million), money laundering and tax evasion. US prosecutors demanded his extradition to the United States, but all of a sudden Russia did the same, asking to send Adamov back home where he would be faced a trial. Swiss authorities asked Adamov if he was willing to accept simplified extradition to the United States. He rejected that and Washington had to file a formal extradition request. The battle of titans began.

A regular crime with not too much money involved blew up into an international scandal. The American government's insistence looked strange until Bill Clinton appeared on the stage on October 5, 2005 to save Adamov from 60 years in jail. (Of course, he didn't show up himself. Adamov hired a lawyer — Lenny Breuer, a nice young fellow from the Washington, DC based "Covington & Burling." Breuer had worked as a special Counsel to President Clinton in 1997-1999 and represented him in the presidential impeachment hearings and trial.

Now, it became clear — this was not a battle between Russia and USA, it was not a problem of international diplomacy or American justice — it was a battle between the Republicans and Democrats for the Oval Office in 2008. Bill Clinton had to win this struggle no matter what — if Adamov was extradited to America, he would "sing" everything on that lovely Gore-Chernomyrdin business and share his federal cell with the most best-looking American President of the 20th century. Meanwhile President Bush, a Republican, needed victory to remove the Clintons from the political arena forever. Clinton won. On December 18, 2005 the Swiss Supreme Court overturned a previous ruling by the Justice Ministry, which had said that Adamov must first face the US courts. On December 30, 2005 Adamov was extradited from Switzerland to Russia, thus opening the door to the Big Presidential Game 2008 for Hillary Clinton.

What price will the Russians ask Hillary Clinton to pay for Adamov's silence, if she's elected?

Bonus file. I mentioned above that a list of dubious deaths have occurred in the wake of Bill Clinton since 1998. Here are some of them. If you ever wonder why a government official, reporter or other figure doesn't do what you'd expect him to do, you can wonder about what happens to those who act without due caution.

- Suzan Coleman, a student at the University of Arkansas, was 7 months pregnant at the time she was found dead of a gunshot wound to her head, ruled suicide. Reportedly had affair with Bill Clinton in 1977.
- Victor Raiser II, former National Finance Co-Chairman of "Clinton for President," died in a private plane crash (1992).
- Paul Tully, Democratic National Committee Political Director, was found dead from a "heart attack" in a Little Rock hotel room (1992)
- Paula Grover, Clinton's interpreter for the deaf in 1978-1992. Died in a one-car crash with no witnesses (1992).
- Brian Haney, Timothy Sabel, William Barkley, Scott Reynolds — all Marine Helicopter Squadron One members, died in a helicopter crash (1993).
- Jorrett Robertson, William Densberger, Robert Kelly, Gary Rhodes — Clinton's bodyguards, died in a helicopter crash in Germany same year (1993).
- Paul Wilcher, attorney investigating corruption. Investigated federal elections and delivered a report to Attorney General Janet Reno. His partially decomposed body was found in Washington, DC home (1993).
- Ed Willey, Clinton's fundraiser, found in the woods of Virginia with a gunshot wound to the head, ruled suicide. The same day, November 29, his wife met President Clinton and asked him to help the family out of financial problems (1993).
- Vincent Foster, White House counsel, very close friend of Clintons, found dead of a gunshot wound to the head, ruled suicide (1993).

- Jerry Parks, former Governor Clinton security team member (during 1992 presidential campaign), gunned down with ten bullets in Little Rock (1993).
- John Wilson, the Washington, DC Council Chairman, had ties to Whitewater scandal, died of hanging (suicide) (1993).
- Kathy Ferguson, former wife of Arkansas state trooper Danny Ferguson, the co-defendant with Clinton in Paula Jones lawsuit. Found dead in her living room of a gunshot wound to the head, ruled a suicide (1993). (Why Kathy, not her husband? Because she wanted to talk, not him.)
- Bill Shelton, Arkansas state trooper and Kathy Ferguson's boyfriend, allegedly committed suicide by shooting himself at her grave (1993).
- Hershell Friday, Arkansas lawyer and Clinton's fund-raiser, died in a private plane accident (1994).
- Dr. Donald Rogers, dentist, died in a plane crash on his way to an interview with reporter Ambrose Evans-Pritchard about Clinton (1994).
- Florence Martin, a former CIA employee, had information on the Barry Seal case, killed in her home by three gunshots to the head through a pillow. Barry Seal was international drug smuggling organization boss; while Attorney General of Arkansas Clinton signed a "get-out-of-jail" personal recognizance bond for Seal. (1994).
- Barbara Wise, Commerce Department secretary, worked with John Brown, found dead in her office on November 29, 1996. The death was attributed to natural causes.
- Mary Mohane, former White House intern, a Starbucks manager, killed in an armed "robbery" during which nothing was stolen. It was suspected she was about to testify about sexual harassment at the White House (1997).

Case 8. What about 9/11?

Any attack in which several commercial jets are hijacked and used to destroy major buildings would entail a complex, coordinated plan, that is, a conspiracy. When such an attack is allowed to play out despite advance warnings and despite announcements that the planes are off track also entails passive sabotage. And when buildings that were not hit by planes, that apparently had only small fires (none hot enough to break windows), like Building 7 at the World Trade Center, came down in what experts agree looked exactly like a standard controlled demolition, one can only conclude that the official story is far from complete and accurate. The 23rd floor of Building 7 housed the Emergency Command Center for then-Mayor Rudolf Giuliani, including sophisticated communications technology and bullet- and bomb-resistant windows. What kind of commands had the center been issuing?

When an event of this magnitude is investigated by a government-appointed committee (like the Warren Commission) and the conclusions presented are incompatible with the evidence, it is not because the Commission members are not clever. See that list of names above.

Is it conceivable that, through their patently inadequate report, the Commission on Terrorist Attacks Upon the United States (or The 9/11 Commission), finding themselves unable to state publicly what had actually happened, did what little they could by deliberately signaling that there is more here than meets the eye?

WHAT TO DO? A GLOBAL STRATEGY

"Terrorism is a tactic used by individuals to kill and destroy."

Wrong. Terrorism is a form of political struggle or political protest, either individual or organized. The 9/11 attack brought a clear message to the US President: stop supporting Israel and leave Saudi Arabia. A suicide bomber, for example, is not a terrorist, he is a tool of terror.

"Planning does make a difference, identifying where a little money might have a large effect."

Wrong. If you don't want to feed your army, you'll feed the enemy's. Clear.

"We should offer an example of moral leadership in the world."

Wrong. We have nothing to offer.

"America's strategy should be a coalition strategy, that includes Muslim nations as partners."

Wrong. We can have certain Muslim leaders as so-called partners, but not nations.

A DIFFERENT WAY OF ORGANIZING THE GOVERNMENT

"We recommend the establishment of a National Counterterrorism Center (NCTC), built on the foundation of the existing Terrorist Threat Integration Center (TTIC). NCTC should be a center for joint operational planning and joint intelligence, staffed by personnel from the various agencies."

Wrong. A regular bureaucratic trick when they re-name instead of re-forming a system or organization. Besides, there's a trick inside — "various agencies" never send their best officers to any other agency.

"The DCI now has at least three jobs. He is expected to manage the loose confederation agencies that is the intelligence community. He is expected to be the analyst in chief for the government, sifting evidence and directly briefing the President as his principal adviser.

No recent DCI has been able to do all three effectively.

Recommendation: the current position of Director of Central Intelligence should be replaced by a National Intelligence Director with two main areas of responsibility: (1) to oversee national intelligence centers on specific subjects of interest across the U. S. government and (2) to manage the national intelligence program and oversee the agencies that contribute to it."

Wrong. The DCI is not a presidential adviser, his job is to get and deliver raw information and keep his mouth shut in the Oval Office. His position is not political, it's technical, and that's why you don't have to replace him by any NID.

"Lead responsibility for directing and executing paramilitary operations, whether clandestine or covert, should shift to the Defense Department. There it should be consolidated with the capabilities for training, direction, and execution of such operations already being developed in the special operations command."

Right. This is the only professional idea I've heard from the government since 9/11.

"Congressional oversight for intelligence — and counterterrorism — is now dysfunctional. We have considered various alternatives..."

Wrong. Right now you have no alternatives. Sorry.

"A specialized and integrated national security workforce should be established at the FBI consisting of agents, analysts, linguists, and surveillance specialists who are recruited, trained, rewarded, and retained to ensure the development of an institutional culture combined with a deep expertise in intelligence and national security."

Wrong. America has no professionals with "deep expertise in intelligence and national security" as the 9/11 attack demonstrated.

At least you can read this book and get a head start.

About the Author

Mykhaylo Kryzhanovsky was born in 1958 in Ukraine. He graduated from Chernovtsy University (BS in languages) and received an extraordinary specialized education at Ivano-Frankovsk University of Social Studies, military college, the KGB counter-espionage school and the KGB Intelligence Institute.

He was involved in secret operations since 1978, and later served as a USSR intelligence officer, and a member of the KGB's "The Bell" top secret anti-terror group. He was a senior intelligence officer and top US government expert with the National Security Service of Ukraine (NSS). His outstanding record of producing up to 20 top-secret government intelligence reports (coded telegrams) a year made him the most productive spy in KGB history, and his unprecedented 30-year espionage career in Russia and the USA probably makes him the number one spy in the world.

In 1992 as NSS officer he managed an illegal espionage station in Moscow, Russia, and planned to substitute a stand-in or double for Russian President Boris Yeltsin, who was the biggest threat to Ukraine at the time. There was a leak, and Yeltsin pushed Ukrainian President Kravchuk to sign a secret agreement to end mutual espionage. Kryzhanovsky learned that a decision had been made to liquidate him and in 1995 he came to the United States. Another KGB officer, Vladimir Putin, a former FSB (Russian counter-espionage service) chief, used his plan and substituted a double for Yeltsin in 2000.